The Smart Estate: Collaborative Working with Digital Information Management

Jason Challender
University of Salford
United Kingdom

Akponanabofa Henry Oti
University of Bolton
United Kingdom

Registered Offices
John Wiley & Sons, Inc., 111 River Street, Hoboken, NJ 07030, USA
John Wiley & Sons Ltd, The Atrium, Southern Gate, Chichester, West Sussex, PO19 8SQ, UK

For details of our global editorial offices, customer services, and more information about Wiley products visit us at www.wiley.com.

Wiley also publishes its books in a variety of electronic formats and by print-on-demand. Some content that appears in standard print versions of this book may not be available in other formats.

Hardbook ISBN: 9781119911395

Library of Congress Cataloging-in-Publication Data

Names: Challender, Jason, author. | Oti, Akponanabofa Henry, author.
Title: The smart estate : collaborative working with digital information
    management / Jason Challender, Akponanabofa Henry Oti.
Description: Hoboken, NJ : WB-Wiley-Blackwell, 2024. | Includes
    bibliographical references and index.
Identifiers: LCCN 2023039055 (print) | LCCN 2023039056 (ebook) | ISBN
    9781119911395 (hardback) | ISBN 9781119911425 | ISBN 9781119911401
    (adobe pdf) | ISBN 9781119911418 (epub)
Subjects: LCSH: Construction industry—Technological innovations. |
    Building information modeling.
Classification: LCC HD9715.A2 C465 2024 (print) | LCC HD9715.A2 (ebook) |
    DDC 624.0285—dc23/eng/20231108
LC record available at https://lccn.loc.gov/2023039055
LC ebook record available at https://lccn.loc.gov/2023039056

Cover image: © abdulmoizjaangda/Adobe Stock Photos
Cover design by Wiley

Set in 9.5/12.5 pts, STIXTwoText by Lumina Datamatics, Inc.
Printed and bound by CPI Group (UK) Ltd, Croydon, CR0 4YY

C9781119911395_090224

Brief Contents

Contents

About the Authors

Dr Jason Challender, MSc, PhD, Eng. D.Hon, FRICS, FAPM, FAHE Dr Jason Challender has acquired thirty-four years 'client side' experience in the UK construction industry and procured numerous successful major construction programmes during this time. He is Director of Estates and Facilities at the University of Salford, member of its Senior Leadership Team, and responsible for overseeing a large department of approximately 350 estates and construction related staff. He is also a construction researcher with six books and twelve published academic journal and conference papers in recent years, all of which have been dedicated to his studies around construction and engineering management. Furthermore, he has previously participated as a book reviewer for Wiley. He has also attended many national and international construction and institutional conferences as a guest speaker over the years and is a Fellow and former Board Director of the Royal Institution of Chartered Surveyors and a current Board Member of the North West Construction Hub. He is also Chair of the Industry Advisory Board at the University of Bolton.

Akponanabofa Henry Oti, MSc, PhD, MIET, CEng, FHEA Akponanabofa Henry Oti is Senior Lecturer in the School of Engineering at the University of Bolton, UK. He is Academic Group Coordinator for Recruitment and Retention, and the Civil Engineering Degree Apprenticeship Lead. With several years of industry and teaching/research experience, Henry trained as a civil engineer and has expertise in extending building information modelling (BIM) concepts and applications to multidimensional subjects in the Built Environment. Some of his several published works include a proposed BIM-based integration of sustainability credentials into the early phases of structural design, using performance data from building management systems (BMS) simulated in a BIM environment to inform building design/operation and the integration of lessons learned knowledge in BIM.

Foreword

Inefficiency and poor predictability of delivery against success factors of time, cost, and quality within the built environment have led to an inability to produce successful outcomes and deliver to clients' requirements. The critical symptoms of failure and poor performance have been identified as lack of collaboration, partnering, and trust between contractual parties, coupled with a reluctance to embrace new digital technologies. As a consequence of these inherent difficulties, there is an absolute imperative for long-term transformational change, and I believe the UK construction industry is now at a critical juncture. The sector needs to be equipped with the tools to lead their project teams in a way more akin to achieving successful outcomes. For this reason, coupled with the aforementioned challenges and deficiencies, this book has been tailored to address these problems in a concerted attempt to increase collaborative working and at the same time engage with new digital technologies such as building information modelling (BIM). This requires a methodical and informed approach to roles and responsibilities and the impetus to explore and embrace digitalisation as a means to improve current practice. The methodology for doing this is supported and facilitated in this book through the creation of 'step-by-step' practical guidance in most cases. This represents a unique, inventive, and much-welcomed pragmatic approach to construction management, from the perspective of clients and their project teams.

The text admirably addresses the complexity of the subject area in a thoughtful way, using case studies and the insights of colleagues to give real-life examples and scenarios. I know Jason and Henry have written this book with the intention to incentivise improved ways of working. In this way, hopefully, it will inspire some of their readers to question their current practices, with the view that they would otherwise not have done, if they had not read of their experiences. It is a long journey ahead, so I believe that this book, which promotes better collaboration and digital advancement in the built environment, will prove a useful intervention for best practice. Accordingly, I hope this book inspires readers to take a different perspective on the procurement of construction services and will encourage real transformational change in practice.

Professor Peter Farrell, MSc, CEng, FRICS, FCIOB, FCABE, SFHEA

Acknowledgements

The authors would like to thank Alex Mbabu and Ben Iyere for their contributions to Chapters 10 and 13.

Service Works Global (SWG) provided a few of the case studies for which the authors are grateful.

The authors would like to thank their families for their support in writing the book including Margaret, Kristin, Bobby, Anthonia, Hannela, Glory, and Jemmy for their unequivocal support and encouragement throughout this journey.

1

The Smart Estate: Collaborative Working with Digital Information Management

Digital transformation is a fundamental reality for businesses today.
Warren Buffett, Chairman and CEO of Berkshire Hathaway

1.1 Introduction to the Book

With regard to Warren Buffett's quotation, organisations should realise that to postpone their digital transformation places them at risk of obsolescence. This is especially true in times of disruption. For instance, it has been reported that 97% of companies have advised that COVID-19 has sped up their digital transformation and 68% say the pandemic sped up their digital transformation significantly. Accordingly, it is up to a company's leadership team to commandeer this revolution while ensuring business continuity. With this in mind, the aim of this book is to explore how collaborative working and digital information management, including building information modelling (BIM) and digital twin technologies, can be aligned and integrated into modern estates management working practices. It responds to the increasing demand for practical, and industry-aligned, practice in estates and construction management. More specifically, the book addresses how digital information management can be pragmatically applied to current practice to increase collaborative working. To assist readers in this pursuit, case studies and example scenarios aligned to best practice methodologies are included. Practical advice is also provided to apply the theoretical principles of collaborative working and BIM and to introduce them within future estates management practices and projects.

The book explores the extent to which collaborative working in digital information management and BIM represents a viable tool in delivering improved estates management and construction outcomes and provides an important insight into the influence on the success of estates projects and programmes. In this regard, the book seeks to address the ongoing dilemma of improving collaborative working and act as a catalyst for improvements to professional and industry practices. It also encourages more organisations and individuals to embrace and embed collaboration and partnering within BIM digital platforms. This is a deliberate attempt to improve estates and construction practices in the UK, which have arguably not been delivering the impact and benefits that were intended in terms of successful outcomes.

The book focuses on:

- determining how collaborative working philosophies can be embedded and aligned in BIM technologies and practices to generate more successful project and estates management outcomes;
- developing a toolkit as a practical guide to assist companies in applying collaborative BIM strategies;
- identifying and detailing the steps required to enable digital information management, and specifically BIM, to benefit a building asset throughout its life cycle;
- building collaboration into FM delivery incorporating extended soft landings;
- case studies (featured in Chapters 8 and 9) detailing the successful and beneficial use of operational, maintenance, and facilities management software;
- the use, benefits, and value of digital twin technologies for collaborative information management;
- digital twin enablers for collaboration and the risks and barriers to adoption of digital twins; and
- Golden Thread initiatives and concepts around BIM.

The book is designed to assist students, academics, and practitioners in their awareness, understanding, and breadth of knowledge of the issues around collaboration philosophies and BIM digital platforms. These attributes will help to build trust and improved long-standing relationships between contracting parties on projects, with the overarching aim of delivering projects that are more successful. The overarching aim of this book is to create a practical guide for clients that can develop into a common client framework on how to initiate, procure, and manage collaborative BIM strategies. In this way it can offer clients turnkey solutions for defining, curating, coordinating, and maintaining the entire life cycle of digital building information.

The 'value proposition' of this book is that it will be read, understood, and accepted by readers as their main guidance and reference tool for improving best practices around the use of BIM and other digital portals. This is a book written for businesspeople by businesspeople based on sound theory (how to do it) and sound practice (lessons derived from case studies).

The book's objectives are:

- to be the standard reference for asset owners' understanding of the life cycle of their projects and therein reducing construction-based and operational-based risk;
- to identify a set of clear guidelines, national or international, to support the role of collaborative working in digital platforms such as BIM;
- to form the basis of a practical toolkit for guidance and teaching in the unique role that collaboration and BIM have for estates and project management practices;
- to look to future developments and identify the key role clients take in BIM, new developments in the RIBA Outline Plan Stage of Work, and other areas such as continuing project integration and collaborative working;
- to demonstrate the benefits of digital construction and information management in enabling a more efficient and effective estate; and
- to explore the role of digital twin technologies for the global built environment.

In previous studies into collaborative working, very little attention has been focused on the use of BIM technologies and methodologies for promoting improved estates outcomes. This book seeks to infill the literature and knowledge gaps through examination of mechanisms via the toolkit to encourage collaborative working within BIM strategies. It is also designed to address academic calls for greater insight into how collaboration can be created, mobilised, and developed using BIM as the catalyst.

Collaborative working is emerging as a 'hot' topic, considering the many cases over recent years when adversarial practices have emerged. Attempts by professional institutions to 'turn the tide' on this growing trend through codes of conduct have not always proved effective. Using BIM as a platform is hoped to address this growing concern. To address the deficiency of adversarial practices, this book is a practical 'how to do it' guide based on analysis of case studies and powerful practice examples for clients and professional practitioners to use in managing their estates and projects. Furthermore, the book does not just look at collaboration for project delivery, but it considers ongoing collaboration during the much lengthier operation and maintenance phase of a building. The book is a reflection on 'before digital' and 'after digital' and illustrates the benefits of the 'art of the possible' on an existing, complex university estate. It draws on case studies from the authors' experiences and interviews, as well as other widely known recent publications. The book also incorporates a toolkit as a practical guide to introducing interventions to embed collaborative working into BIM strategies and therein improve practices and behaviours, which the research has found to be particularly beneficial for generating more successful project outcomes.

The book is mainly intended for construction management practitioners but could suit a wide target audience, including under- and postgraduate students and academics. The research findings are presented to prioritise use by professional practitioners and therein provide a practical guide for adherence to collaborative working philosophies and BIM technologies, and as a toolkit for improvements in estates and construction project management. The book is not designed as a holistic course textbook, albeit it could be a worthy inclusion in a recommended reading list for courses related to estates management and construction procurement. As such, it is not intended solely as a practitioner guide. Rather, the book aims to cross this divide and provide useful insight to both academics and practitioners in developing their understanding of the topic area.

Although the research was undertaken in the UK, and all findings are likely to therefore have best fit with the UK construction industry, the overall knowledge and understanding provided by this book will have international relevance. Other countries seeking to develop strategies for improved ethical practices using similar approaches to the UK will be able to utilise the book, with consideration of how the findings fit with their own understanding in practice.

1.2 Context and Background to Collaborative Working in Estates and Construction

Partnering and collaboration have long been championed and heralded as the future of the UK construction industry. Latham (1994) sought to 'construct the team.' He was heavily critical of traditional procurement and contractual routes, largely due to the lack of coordination between construction and design. He suggested a change in culture and a move to partnering to increase fairness, encourage teamwork, and enhance performance through collaborative engagement of clients and design teams with contractors. This view was reinforced by Egan (1998) who saw early establishment of construction teams as an essential aspect of cooperative construction, with contractors able to contribute to management, buildability, health and safety, procurement, and supply chain management of projects. It was thought that such early collaboration reduced disputes and tender costs, and improved team working practices. More recently, the benefits of collaboration have been argued to include an increase in profits brought about by sharing expertise, knowledge, ideas, innovation, and best practice, and promoting efficiencies and improvements in decision-making (Hansen and Nohria, 2004). Collaborative working is also suggested to reduce the negative aspects of construction procurement by minimising conflicts and disputes through increased cooperation and developing relationships built on trust (Larson, 1997). Government support for partnering and collaborative thinking was championed by the Strategic Forum for Construction in the *Accelerating Change* report (Egan, 2002). Projects that had applied the principles of both Latham and Egan in the use of collaborative procurement methods were found to achieve significant improvements in client satisfaction, cost predictability, safety, and time predictability. Furthermore, there is an argument that when companies enter into highly complex, uncertain, and potentially risky projects as relative strangers, it is not surprising that frequent conflicts and disputes arise in traditional procurement systems (Chan *et al.*, 2004). Partnering and collaborative approaches seek to avoid conflicts and disputes by increasing levels of cooperation and developing organisational relationships built on trust (Larson 1997).

Notwithstanding the arguments in support of partnering and collaborative working, there is little evidence to suggest that such practices are becoming more widespread. Conversely, participation in these strategies is reducing in many cases. For instance, the RICS Contracts in Use Survey (RICS, 2012) found that partnering contracts during 2010 accounted for only 0.9% of all contracts by value, compared with 6.6% in 2004 and 15.6% in 2007. One possible explanation for this movement away from collaborative working could be reliance on the known and controllable which has previously been identified within the industry as a symptom of a 'negative culture' that is sceptical and suspicious of new initiatives. It has been argued that these old behavioural aspects, cultures, and attitudes are so deeply embedded in the construction sector that they are proving difficult to change (Thurairajah *et al.*, 2006). For collaborative working approaches to be more attractive to clients, they must seek to address problems of cultural indifference, old stereotypes, and the adversarial views of team members, alongside new ways of working being established (Liu *et al.*, 2004).

1.3 The Importance of Digital Information Management to Assist Collaborative Working

Estates strategies are embracing digital information systems for managing the life of buildings. This approach can create construction knowledge asset-based information platforms which can assist in developing more effective estates management practices

(Kiviniemi and Codinhoto, 2014). Notwithstanding this premise, there are sometimes many barriers and challenges to be overcome and these mainly revolve around cultural changes and interoperability issues. In the latter case, the ability of computer systems or software to exchange and make use of information has improved greatly in recent years. Technological advancements such as cloud-based applications have assisted in this regard and are continually being developed. Furthermore, governmental efforts to develop such initiatives as the building information modelling (BIM) development communities are about to be addressed in future years (Nica and Wodyński, 2016). Since 85% of life-cycle costs are spent in facilities management (FM) (Lewis *et al.*, 2010), the implementation of BIM in FM and maintenance, alongside the use of cloud-based applications, is seen to be essential. Wherever possible, such systems should avoid operational complexities and employ simplified user interfaces, allowing the systems to bridge more easily between existing FM workflows to model-based workflows. However, these transitions are significant and complex and help to explain why so few owners are adopting BIM (Cavka *et al.*, 2015).

The use of BIM can provide turnkey solutions for defining, curating, coordinating, and maintaining the entire life cycle of digital building information and should accordingly increase collaborative working in estates strategies. Furthermore, collaborative working has been associated with generating more beneficial outcomes for BIM technologies. This prognosis would suggest that there is a positive relationship between collaboration and BIM, with both supporting the development of the other. Later chapters of the book will explore how collaborative working and BIM can be aligned and integrated into modern working practices in construction and estates management.

The common data environment (CDE) has long been a mainstay of the topography of digital information management and BIM, but the evolving nature of the digital technologies, which may not be capable of addressing certain issues relating to FM, means that more comprehensive, user-friendly systems are required. Some software companies are already rising to this challenge with the development of their information management platforms (IMP). Such platforms are designed to support procuring, managing, and maintaining of interoperable data, to realise the full benefits of data management across an asset life cycle, from inception through to decommissioning.

1.4 Structure of the Book

The book has been structured into 13 chapters and covers the subject of the smart estate and specifically collaborative working aligned to digital information management. It approaches this subject from many different angles and perspectives but particularly in the context of the built environment. A brief outline of the themes of each chapter are detailed below.

Chapter 1: The Smart Estate: Collaborative Working with Digital Information Management

This chapter provides readers with an introduction to the book and the justification for choosing the subject area as its focus. There is an articulation and explanation of the aims and objectives, and an identification of the potential readership of the book. This is followed by a brief description of the areas covered and the overall structure of the book.

Chapter 2: Introduction and Background to Collaborative Working and Partnering

An introduction to the concept of collaborative working and partnering is provided in this chapter, together with a description and explanation of what they are. An articulation of the different types and variations of collaborative working, as applied to the built environment, is also covered.

This chapter provides an overall context for collaborative working and partnering in terms of how they can be embedded into organisational cultures, policies, and procedures and the potential benefits they can generate for the built environment. Furthermore, it analyses how collaborative working and partnering can generate improved project outcomes.

The chapter starts by providing context for the discussions that follow around collaborative working and partnering. Accordingly, it provides background to the concepts of collaborative working and partnering. The choice of procurement strategies on projects is analysed with specific reference to the many different government reports which have been published. Thereafter, the overarching reasons for using collaborative working and partnering, as opposed to traditional procurement strategies, are discussed and the many benefits articulated. The different definitions of collaborative working and partnering are then presented to provide readers with a clear perspective of what they constitute. In addition, the different types of partnering are examined with reference to alliancing.

The chapter then covers the adversarial nature of the construction industry and some of the many problems that traditional forms of contracting procurement can create for projects and the built environment generally. Modern working practices are discussed in the context of collaborative working and partnering. A link is forged between collaboration, the use of building information modelling (BIM), and the introduction of innovative initiatives.

In summary the main areas covered in the chapter include the following:

- context of collaboration within the estates and construction sectors
- construction contracts that have embedded collaborative philosophies
- importance of trust within the context of collaboration
- trust as a collaborative necessity
- alternative definitions and meanings of trust
- different perspectives of collaboration and trust
- exemplar models of collaborative working around 'perfection through partnering' concepts
- philosophy and benefits of teamwork and integration of the whole supply chain
- different types of trust are identified alongside the 'propensity to trust' theory

Chapter 3: The Importance of Trust, Collaboration, and Partnering for the Built Environment

This chapter starts by articulating the problems around general traditional procurement in the built environment, as context for the discussion on partnering as a potential worthy alternative to past practices. For this reason, it describes the traditional adversarial nature of the construction industry and past problems with the procurement processes for building projects. This description encapsulates discussions around some of these problems including the appointment of consultants, main contractors, subcontractors, and suppliers on the basis of lowest price tenders. The chapter concludes by discussing some of the implications around competing commercial interests associated with traditional procurement practices.

In summary the main areas covered in the chapter include the following:

- lack of trust leading to a reluctance to collaborate
- differing contexts to the problem of trust and collaboration
- in-depth analysis of why collaboration and partnering is important for estates management and the construction industry
- recent government reports (Construction 2025) focusing on the need to improve delivery by collaborative means and the introduction of NEC3 forms of contract to enable this
- explanation of the importance and benefits of collaborative working from a dependency and interdependency perspective

Chapter 4: Analysis for the Lack of Collaborative Working and Partnering in the Built Environment

This chapter of the book is largely based on the research study by Challender *et al.* (2014) which focused on collaborative construction procurement strategies. It concentrates on the lack of collaborative working and partnering in the built environment and specifically around the wide-ranging consensus that potential barriers in the construction industry could have hindered their success. For this reason, these barriers in are examined and they include fear of the unknown, perceived loss of control, uncertainty, and the lack of understanding of how to change the way one works. The chapter then discusses the downward trend in the popularity and participation of collaborative working practices, once heralded as a breakthrough in construction management, but now making a return to traditional procurement based on lowest cost tenders. Following on from this it attempts to reconcile this downward trend by presenting evidence of low levels of client satisfaction, owing mostly to poor cost and time predictability, which have in turn been attributed to a low level of trust in practice. Furthermore, it examines reports that clients may be feeling the only way to assure themselves that they are not paying too much is to market test their projects in a highly competitive environment.

In summary, the main areas covered in the chapter include the following:

- risks associated with unethical practices under partnering arrangements
- abuse of power by clients towards main contractors, or main contractors towards their supply chains
- inequitable working arrangements – the disparity of power between clients and other organisations
- an examination of how partnering and collaborative working have been influenced in the past by austerity and economic uncertainty
- why collaborative procurement may be perceived as a risky alternative to traditional competitive tendering
- measures that could be introduced for partnering to succeed in the future, including BIM

Chapter 5: Potential Risks, Problems, and Barriers for Collaborative Working in Estates and the Built Environment

This chapter outlines some of the most common adversarial practices, relationships, and behaviours that exist in estates and construction as context to the challenges posed for these sectors. It explains the possible reasons for such predicaments by reference to the 'one-off' project nature of construction contracting and the resistance against changing old familiar traditional working practices. It then develops the discussions further by offering potential ways and means to address the risks, problems, and barriers brought about by these dilemmas, while contemplating the commercial, economic, and contractual pressures in the sector.

In summary the main areas covered in the chapter include the following:

- influence of legislative and governance measures alongside organisational barriers
- various incentives, problem-solving, and dispute resolution procedures as a means to address risks, problems, and barriers
- potential risks, problems, and barriers for collaborative working in estates and the built environment
- the fractious nature of the UK construction industry, based largely on 'one-off' projects
- potential barriers, systemic problems, and challenges to collaborative working and partnering
- propensity for contracting partners to trust one another in a commercially sensitive industry with large amounts of money at stake
- the short-term nature of construction projects and the imbalance and abuse of power between contracting parties
- partnering and collaborative working in times of economic uncertainty
- strategic partnering as a means to achieve greater opportunities for successful outcomes
- factors which could inhibit trust in partnering
- constructs, attributes, and factors which could influence trust in the context of partnering practices

Chapter 6: Collaborative Working with Digital Information Management in Estates and Construction

This chapter examines the emerging digital technology innovations in digital information management in engineering and construction. It covers the following areas:

- definition and scope of digital information management in construction
- the origin and development of digital information management
- aspects of digital information management and its requirements
- trends and innovations in digital information management

Chapter 7: Technologies for Collaborative Digital Information Management in Estates and Construction

Following on from the Chapter 6 covering emerging digital technology innovations in digital information management, this chapter considers those innovations which are applicable in estates operations. It focuses on the wide-ranging variations in the way applications are implemented, owing to the peculiar nature of estates operations being different from other sectors in the built environment. Furthermore, it considers the nature of estates operations which adds some additional complexities and challenges regarding uptake and diffusion of innovations. For these reasons this chapter covers the intricacies in the digital transformation of estates by reference to the following sections:

- 7.2 Technologies Featuring in Digital Transformation of Estates
- 7.3 The Uptake of Digital Technologies in Estates
- 7.4 Factors Affecting Adoption of Digital Technology Applications in Estates

Chapter 8: Infrastructures for Collaborative Digital Information Management for Estates

In this chapter, the enabling infrastructures for digital transformation are examined focusing on key features characterising the pillars of socialism, mobility, analytics, and clouds driving progress. Further, key processes in the estates industry are delineated to expose specific areas of application. The discussions are covered under the following section headings:

- 8.2 Elements of Digital Transformation Infrastructure
- 8.3 Digital Transformation Processes in Estates
- 8.4 Aspects and Tools of Data Acquisition Aiding Digital Transformation
- 8.5 Digital Information Management Cases in Healthcare Facilities

Chapter 9: Actors in Digital Information Management for Estates

The role of actors in driving the information management process is covered in this chapter. The chapter establishes that while advances are made in the digital transformation journey, new roles emerge and training needs evolve. What these new roles are in the contemporary estates and associated markets are examined under the following headings:

- key actors in digital information management and transformation
- actors and professional institutions in estates digital information management
- emerging roles in estates digital information management

This chapter concludes with further case studies of digital technology application in estates.

Chapter 10: The Role of Digital Technology in Healthcare Facilities Management

The chapter is based on the MSc research of Ben Lyre, University of Bolton, and looks specifically at the role of digital technology in healthcare facilities management. Accordingly, while the chapter articulates and discusses the role of digital technology in the built environment, it is geared specifically to case studies around the healthcare sector. The use of digital twins for the built environment is just beginning, and yet to catch up with healthcare, which was the motivation for choosing this sector as a model of good practice for the future.

The chapter starts by considering the importance of facilities management (FM) in the healthcare sector and examining the different digital technologies that can be used to streamline estates services. For this reason, it considers such digital technologies as the enablers to overcoming problems, creating efficiencies, and generating other benefits for managing large complex healthcare estates. It introduces the concept of artificial intelligence (AI) in estates management and the crucial role that this can play. In addition, it discusses the knowledge management technologies required to effectively manage healthcare facilities with an emphasis on achieving organisational objectives. In this sense, it articulates the benefits that knowledge management can provide identifying knowledge and skill gaps. It then explains build competencies for developing human resource professionals and establishing a knowledge-driven culture to facilitate the success of the innovation framework or process. Accordingly, this chapter investigates the knowledge management technologies required to effectively manage healthcare facilities with an emphasis on achieving organisational objectives. This is to provide an overview of the significant research efforts in digital technology that apply to improving the FM processes for the management of infrastructural assets and to present a road map for future research on digital FM applications.

In addition, the chapter explains the various digital technologies, systems, and software currently being used within healthcare FM. These include the following:

- geographic information systems (GIS)
- Internet of things (IoT)
- mobile-first
- machine learning and predictive analytics
- building information modelling (BIM)

Finally, the chapter provides some conclusions based around the future of digital technologies and a brief overview on the aspects covered.

Chapter 11: An Introduction to Smart Estates and Digital Information Management for Collaboration in the Built Environment Using Case Studies

This chapter of the book discusses the immense potential of digital twins for the urban built environment in solving some of the current urbanisation-led challenges. The research further recommends strategies on how best to derive the value of a digital twin to improve the future state of the urban built environment, such as target value design, knowledge sensitisation, continuous upskilling, collaboration, secure and safe data, infrastructure, and the need for standardisation.

The chapter uses case studies carried out in Singapore and the town of Herrenberg in Germany, which are two examples of where digital twins, albeit on different scales, have proved very influential in promoting such technology globally. It starts by giving context to the digital transformation in the built environment. In this regard it discusses how digital technologies have allowed the construction and engineering industries to develop what could not be created before, to construct new forms of building, and therein transform cities. It then explains the work of the Centre for Digital Built Britain (CDBB) that provided the framework for information management to enable stable, resilient data sharing between digital twins. Furthermore, it refers to the work of the UK Government's Digital Framework Task Group (DFTG) which has devised a set of principles to promote the creation of a UK network of the digital twin.

The chapter then provides a background and context to digital twins and describe what they are, with alternative definitions given. It explains the three virtual models that make up digital twins and their key characteristics as a context for what they represent. An articulation is also made of the six recognisable elements that form part of the digital twins' maturity spectrum. The original concept, history, and evolution of digital twins are then discussed with reference to certain similar technologies dating back to the Apollo missions of 1968–1972. The chapter then proceeds to explain and discuss the importance of digital twins on the built environment and urbanisation on a global scale. The need for urban built environments to pave the way for continuous evolution, integrating emerging technologies for more effective global sustainability, is then discussed.

The ways and means by which digital twins have been regarded by many as a natural evolution of BIM is discussed and evaluated. Following on from this, the challenges around the built environment, particularly focused on fragmentation and low, underachieving productivity levels, are covered. To address these challenges, the use of digital twins in the built environment as a collaborative tool for creating smart cities in terms of urban modelling and planning is analysed. In this sense, the chapter explains how digital twins allow a high-degree simulation of urban plans, real-time monitoring and control of urban transport infrastructure, future mobility, and improved sustainability, with reference to the Singapore case study. Finally, the other benefits to digital twin technologies is described relating to efficiency and streamlined information workflows in capital delivery, health and well-being, security, building automation, and predictive maintenance.

Chapter 12: The Benefits and Value of Digital Twin Technologies for Collaborative Information Management

The chapter will discuss the full value and benefits of digital twins especially linked to collaboration and information management, using Singapore and Herrenberg, Germany as case studies. With reference to these case studies, the chapter articulates how Herrenberg established an 'Integrated Mobility Plan' and formed a digital twin pilot to reduce its high levels of traffic, while improving its environmental sustainability through reduced carbon and noise emissions. Conversely, it explains how Singapore, developed 'Virtual Singapore', a city-state digital twin and collaborative data platform designed to allow users from government and different industries to create and test new technologies, applications, and services.

The chapter discusses collaborative insights for the built environment by enhancing live real-time capabilities and data capture. It then explains how digital twin-related technologies are maturing to deliver intelligent solutions for urban planning and city science. Virtual technologies to help us manage demands on transport infrastructure, emissions, increasing energy use, and other challenges in urban areas more effectively are discussed. In addition, the chapter explores the means to address the ever-growing challenges around environmental sustainability through digital technologies. It then assesses the ability for digital twins to monitor and control real-time asset outputs and how this technology can boost any number of adaptable services. The chapter then covers scenario planning and risk assessments and the notion of 'digital siblings' to understand the 'what if' scenarios, where things go wrong, and systems and assets fail. Predictive analytics and scheduling are discussed and also how a digital twin can act as a validation model framework with data from the real world. It then examines how this technology can provide a more effective and informed support system for decision-making, with the aim of transforming decision-making and investment.

Better synergies in intra- and inter-team collaboration are then explored. From this angle the chapter explains how digital twins allow information and data flow to enhance collaboration across the supply chain, reduce silos, and increase the understanding of existing built asset projects. This is followed by an insight into the optimisation of asset performance and sustainability. This covers the measures to improve the performance of future buildings through sensor networks linked to building elements and components. A case study in this context is discussed – namely the Energy House research by the University of Salford in the UK.

In addition to the above, greater efficiency in safety from digital technologies is examined, whereby individuals can get real-time monitoring and warnings, including updates of dangers and guidance for responding to emergencies. Finally, the ecosystem of connected networks, portfolios, and sectors is discussed. This includes examples whereby sensors, using IoT technologies linked to physical assets, can be utilised to evaluate their performance, condition, and status in real time.

Chapter 13: Digital Twin Enablers for Collaboration and the Risks and Barriers to Adoption of Digital Twins

This chapter of the book looks at enabling technologies for urban digital twins. It explains the role and importance of the following aspects:

- building information modelling (BIM)
- Internet of things (IoT)
- big data
- cloud computing and data analytics
- 3D and 5G modelling and high definition simulations
- artificial intelligence (AI)
- digital twin ecosystems
- smart buildings
- smart cities

In addition to the above, the chapter covers the current state of adoption and development of digital twins across the world. The digital twin market and uptake outlook and the importance of this to global economies are then analysed. Also, some emerging market case studies are used to demonstrate the successful outcomes that these have generated, and the challenging plans for future expansion and development. Following on from this, the digital twin information framework is discussed, includingthe Digital Twin Hub launched by the Centre for Digital Built Britain (CDBB) as a platform for organisations and researchers who wish to improve governance around digital technology for the built environment.

The chapter then introduces the various issues that need to be considered for the adoption of digital twins, with reference to the complexity of the technology that is involved in their composition. In this regard, the technological challenges associated with addressing some of these issues are articulated including the following:

- spatial–temporal sensor data resolution
- connectivity latency
- broad data volumes
- high data generation rate
- wide data variety
- high data veracity
- fast archival retrieval and online data processing

Following this, the chapter then looks at the specific risks and barriers to development and implementation including:

- insufficient business case and evidence-based case studies
- complexity in data
- slow industry uptake in BIM
- multidimension fragmentation
- incompatibility in data language
- incompatibility in modelling social, economic, and environmental data sets
- data ownership, privacy, and security

Finally, conclusions and recommendations are identified and discussed, which includes the best ways to introduce digital twins for the urban built environment. These cover the potential of smart cities, which could herald the adoption of city-scale digital twins to solve current global urbanisation challenges.

Chapter 14: Reflections, Overview, and Implications for Future Practice and Closing Remarks

This final chapter summarises each chapter of the book and extrapolate the key findings and issues raised. Following on from what has been articulated and discussed, it presents some reflections and recommendations for the future of collaborative working and digital information management in the built environment, taking account of the inherent dilemmas and challenges that are faced.

1.5 Summary

There are many different aspects and themes relating to smart estates, especially within the context of collaborative working with digital information management. For this reason, the book's focus has become an increasingly 'hot topic' over recent years, predominantly to address some of the challenges in the sector on a national and international level. Such challenges have revolved around not only the lack of collaborative working and partnering but also the quality and availability of useful digitally enhanced information and technologies. Accordingly, *The Smart Estate: Collaborative Working with Digital Information Management* is concerned with how we make improvements and positively contribute to the estates and facilities, construction, and engineering sectors and adopt different innovative initiatives and measures in addressing some of these challenges. For this reason, the book covers collaboration and partnering philosophies working alongside digital technologies, such as building information modelling (BIM) and digital twins, for procuring more successful project outcomes. In recent years, companies have realised that they need to focus on non-financial strategies linked to these aspects alongside their economic goals. This involves investing jointly in their staff and their systems which can bolster their reputations and in turn increase their success in the marketplace. In addition, commitment to collaborative partnering and investments in digital technologies can have a positive relationship with the job satisfaction and career success of employees and provide a safe and caring environment for them to prosper. As a result, companies that have embraced these areas have found that this raised the motivation levels of employees and increased the productivity and retention of the workforce. Accordingly, the evidence would therefore suggest that collaborative working linked to investment in digital technological advancements could have far-reaching positive effects on organisational success. Notwithstanding this assertion, such positive measures are not always easy to integrate into the built environment, which is predominantly associated with fragmented, complex, and potentially confrontational practices. This can create a dilemma for the sector and is evidenced in reported case studies referenced throughout the book. The book responds to this dilemma and addresses how standards can be pragmatically applied to professional practice and provides case studies and example scenarios aligned to modern-day requirements.

The book's toolkit includes the use of case studies to look at how successes, failures and key risks can be influenced by collaboration policies working with digital technologies. Other sections identify how policies and strategies,that can support t smart estates, including BIM and digital twins, that can assist businesses in the built environment achieve more successful outcomes. These tools are intended to assist academics, construction-related practitioners, and clients in their awareness, breadth of knowledge, and comprehension of the issues around collaborative working with digital information management. This can then be linked to development of their smart estates with the overarching aim of delivering more successful project outcomes.

Although the research was mostly undertaken in the UK, the book utilises international case studies including those from Germany and Singapore. Accordingly, the findings are likely to have best fit with the UK construction industry, albeit the overall knowledge and understanding provided by this book will have international relevance.

References

Cavka, H.B., Staub-French, S. and Pottinger, R. (2015). Evaluating the alignment of organizational and project contexts for BIM adoption: a case study of a large owner organization. *Buildings* 5(4), 1265–1300.

Chan A.C., Chan D.W.M., Chiang Y., Tang B., Chan E.H.W. and Ho K.S.K. (2004). Exploring critical success factors for partnering in construction projects. *Journal of Construction Engineering and Management* 130(2), 188–189.

Egan, J. (1998). *Rethinking Construction*. The Report of the Construction Task Force. London: DETR.TSO.

Egan, J. (2002). *Accelerating Change*. London: Rethinking Construction.

Hansen, M.T. and Nohria, N. (2004). How to build collaborative advantage. *MIT Sloan Management Review* 46(1): 22–30.

Kiviniemi, A. and Codinhoto, R. (2014). Challenges in the implementation of BIM for FM —Case Manchester Town Hall complex. *Computing in Civil and Building Engineering* (2014), 665–672.

Larson, E. (1997). Partnering on construction projects: A study of the relationship between partnering activities and project success. *IEEE Transactions on Engineering Management* 44(2): 188–195.

Latham, M. (1994). *Constructing the Team*. London: The Stationery Office.

Lewis, A., Riley, D. and Elmualim, A. (2010). Defining high performance buildings for operations and maintenance. *International Journal of Facility Management* 1(2): 1–16.

Liu, A., Fellows, R. and Ng, J. (2004). Surveyors' perspectives on ethics in organisational culture. *Engineering, Construction and Architectural Management* 11(6): 438–449.

Nica, A.K. and Wodyński, W. (2016). Enhancing facility management through BIM 6D. *Procedia Engineering.* 164: 299–306.

RICS (2012). *Contracts in Use: A Survey of Building Contracts in Use During 2010*. London: Royal Institution of Chartered Surveyors Publications.

Thurairajah, N, Haigh, R and Amaratunga, R.D.G. (2006). Cultural transformation in construction partnering projects. *Proceedings of the Annual Research Conference of the Royal Institution of Chartered Surveyors 7–8 September*. University College London.

2

Introduction and Background to Collaborative Working and Partnering

Success is best when it is shared.
Howard Schultz, former Chairman and CEO, Starbucks, 1986–2000

2.1 Introduction

The chapter starts by providing context for the discussions that follow around collaborative working and partnering. Accordingly, it provides background to the concepts of collaborative working and partnering. The choice of procurement strategies on projects is analysed with specific reference to the many different government reports which have been published. Thereafter, the overarching reasons for using collaborative working and partnering as opposed to traditional procurement strategies are discussed and the many benefits articulated. The different definitions of collaborative working and partnering are then presented to provide readers with a clear perspective of what they constitute. In addition, the different types of partnering are examined with reference to alliancing.

The chapter then covers the adversarial nature of the construction industry and some of the many problems that traditional forms of contracting procurement can have for projects and the built environment generally. Modern working practices are discussed in the context of collaborative working and partnering. A link is forged between collaboration, the use of building information modelling (BIM), and the introduction of innovative initiatives.

The overall context of collaboration within the estates and construction sectors is discussed and data related to the proportion of overall construction contracts that have embedded collaborative philosophies is given. Thereafter, the importance of trust within the context of collaboration is looked at in detail. In this regard, trust as a collaborative necessity is analysed against many different literature sources. Trust itself is scrutinised by giving alternative definitions and meanings. Following on from this, the reasons why trust is important for collaboration and partnering is articulated from many different perspectives. Finally, the different types of trust are identified alongside the 'propensity to trust' theory.

The Smart Estate, First Edition. Edited by Jason Challender/Henry Oti.
© 2024 John Wiley & Sons, Ltd. Published 2024 by John Wiley & Sons, Ltd.

2.2 Background to the Concept of Collaborative Working and Partnering

The choice of procurement strategies on projects has long been a contentious issue within the construction industry. Emerson (1962) and Banwell (1964) outlined deficiencies within traditional procurement methods and made recommendations for change and improvement, which included bridging the gap between design and construction and encouraging early contractor involvement in such areas as value management and buildability. Perhaps the most prominent report which made recommendations on procurement is *Constructing the Team* by Sir Michael Latham (Latham, 1994) which was critical of traditional procurement and contractual routes, owing largely to a lack of coordination between designers and constructors, and recommended an integrated project team approach.

There has been a general consensus of opinion that a change of culture towards partnering is required to increase fairness and buildability, encourage teamwork, and enhance performance through more collaborative engagement of contractors with clients and design teams (Latham, 1994; Larson, 1997; Egan, 1998). Furthermore, it was thought that such early collaboration minimised disputes and facilitated significant improvements in client satisfaction, cost predictability, safety, and time predictability. More recently, the suggested benefits of collaboration include an increase in profits brought about by sharing expertise, knowledge, ideas, innovation, and best practice, and promoting efficiencies and improvements in decision-making (Hansen and Nohria, 2004). Such benefits could be facilitated by cultural and behavioural reform, fostering more trusting relationships, and improving communication and dialogue (Lann *et al.*, 2011). This, they explain, can reduce potential project risks by possible remedies being identified early and thereby allowing projects to be more effectively managed. Traditional procurement methods may be less suitable on complex and challenging projects which are reliant on greater contractor cooperation and interface, especially at the design stages. In such cases, more collaborative procurement routes could have a positive impact on project success (Eriksson and Westerberg, 2011).

2.3 What is Partnering, Collaborative Working, and Alliancing?

Although there are many different definitions of partnering (National Audit Office, 2001), it could be defined as 'business relationships designed to achieve mutual objectives and benefits between contracting organisations' (Wong and Cheung, 2004) or alternatively as 'a structured management process to focus the attention of all parties on problem resolution' (Larson, 1997). Academic literature commonly refers to (Abdul Nifa and Ahmed, 2010) who define partnering as 'a set of strategic actions which embody the mutual objectives of a number of firms, which are achieved by cooperative decision-making aimed at using feedback to continuously improve joint performance'. Partnering arrangements can vary and include both one-off projects on a relatively short-term basis (project partnering) and multiple projects between two or more organisations as part of a long-term strategic commitment, otherwise known as strategic partnering (Constructing Excellence, 2004).

The terms 'partnering' and 'collaborative working' are used interchangeably in this book, referencing a wider philosophy of trust, fairness, and equity, rather than specific details of practice. Although the concept of these terms is widely used, there appears to be a distinct lack of understanding of what it means to collaborate and the ways and means to improve and support its successful practice (Patel *et al.*, 2012). To respond to this, the Construction Industry Council defines partnering as 'a structured management approach to facilitate team working across contractual boundaries'. Partnering and alliancing are two forms of collaborative working or 'relationship contracting' at a high level (Wu and Udeaja, 2008) although they are terms that are again frequently used interchangeably (Ingirige and Sexton, 2006). The important difference between alliances and partnering is that aims, objectives, escalation plans, and dispute resolution provision are agreed with partnering, but partners maintain their independence and may individually gain or suffer in the relationship. Project performance in partnering relies mostly on non-legal measures such as integrity and trust (Manley, 2002). However, in alliances the parties share a contractual and commercial framework, in which they work as a single integrated team, sharing risks and rewards, to deliver project objectives (Gunn, 2002; Yeung *et al.*, 2007). Furthermore, 'strategic' alliances, unlike alliances and partnering, are arrangements designed to achieve the strategic objectives of the allied organisations and could include joint ventures, joint research and development, minor equity, and co-production (Das and Teng, 1998)

The mechanisms for partnering can be facilitated through binding contracts or non-binding alliance or partnership provisions (Oyegoke *et al.*, 2009). The RICS (2009) definition explained that contracts to incorporate collaborative working are differentiated by clauses relating to measurement of performance, payment, allocation of risk, and the obligations of the parties, and the range of contracts includes the JCT Constructing Excellence Contract, NEC3 Engineering and Construction Contract, and the Project Partnering Contract PPC 2000.

2.4 The Traditional Adversarial Nature of the Construction Industry

Over recent years, many arguments have presented traditional procurement strategies as achieving low client satisfaction levels, and poor cost predictability and time certainty, largely attributable to coordination difficulties associated with separation of design and construction and the greater need for teamwork (Latham, 1994, Egan, 1998, Egan, 2002). Collaborative working at an early stage between contractors and design teams has been, post-Latham, regarded as a means to bridge the gap between design and construction to improve project outcomes. Accordingly, many have identified collaborative procurement routes, such as partnering, as a critical success factor on construction projects (Vaaland, 2004).

The UK Government's Construction 2025 report identified that fractious qualities are embedded in the UK construction industry, emanating from low vertical integration and poor levels of design and management interface in the supply chain. This is limiting the scope for knowledge-sharing across projects, hampering familiarisation and learning from experiences, and reducing innovation and investment within the sector. Furthermore, it reinforced a view that increased collaboration within project teams is a crucial factor to deliver successful construction projects but explained that funding opportunities in the present climate may prohibit this integrated approach. Findings from the Construction Products Association (HM Government, 2010) confirm a growing need for increased collaboration and integration across the industry, especially between the supply chain and clients, to make greater contributions to the pursuit of efficiencies. In this regard, cross-institutional collaboration through advisory panels could promote modern working practices, the use of building information modelling (BIM) and the introduction of innovative initiatives to promote lean production, including off-site prefabrication.

2.5 Perfection through Procurement

Partnering and collaboration have long been championed as the future of the UK construction industry. Latham (1994) sought to 'construct the team' and was heavily critical of traditional procurement and contractual routes, largely due to the lack of collaboration and integration of construction and design stages. He suggested a change in culture and a move to partnering to increase fairness, encourage teamwork, and enhance performance through collaborative engagement of clients and design teams with contractors (ibid 1994:50). Furthermore, Egan (1998) saw early establishment of construction teams as an essential aspect of cooperative construction, with contractors able to contribute to management, buildability, health and safety, procurement, and supply chain management of projects. It was thought that such early collaboration would reduce disputes and tender costs and improve team working practices (ibid 1998). The benefits of collaboration have been argued to include an increase in profits brought about by sharing expertise, knowledge, ideas, innovation, and best practice, and promoting efficiencies and improvements in decision-making (Hansen and Nohria, 2004). It is also suggested that collaborative working would reduce the negative aspects of construction procurement by minimising conflicts and disputes through increased cooperation, and developing relationships built on trust (Larson, 1997).

Government support for partnering and collaborative thinking was championed by the Strategic Forum for Construction in the *Accelerating Change* report (Egan, 2002). Projects that had applied the principles of both Latham and Egan in the use of collaborative procurement methods were found to achieve significant improvements in client satisfaction, cost predictability, safety, and time predictability.

2.6 Different Types and Variations of Collaborative Working

Many authoritative sources are calling for collaborative and integrated working to be used as a vehicle to obtain better value, quality, and service delivery. However, clients in the past, especially during times of uncertainty brought about by recessions and the global COVID-19 pandemic, may have felt vulnerable about entering into arrangements built upon collaborative working practices, which could have been deemed as taking unnecessary risk.

Notwithstanding the perceived benefits that increased partnering and collaborative working practices could bring to the UK construction industry, these alternative procurement methods are still relatively rare. This is supported by findings in the RICS Contracts in Use Survey (RICS, 2012) that partnering contracts during 2010 accounted for only 0.9% of all contracts by value, compared with 6.6% in 2004 and 15.7% in 2007. This could possibly emanate from client perceptions that open and competitive procurement systems, that truly market test prices, are the only way to assure stakeholders of the lowest possible initial capital cost (Ross, 2011). Accordingly, in this economic context it could be argued that 'partnering has simply not lived up to expectations' (Gadde and Dubois, 2010).

This study seeks to explore the concept of trust during austerity in collaborative working and partnering arrangements. Trust is considered in the literature to be an essential element in successful partnering (Kaluarachchi and Jones, 2007). The terms 'partnering' and 'collaborative working' are used interchangeably within this paper, referencing a wider philosophy of trust, fairness, and equity, rather than specific details of practice.

2.7   The Importance of Trust within the Context of Collaboration

2.7.1   Trust as a Collaborative Necessity

Much has been written on trust as a collaborative necessity (Larson, 1997; Chan *et al.*, 2004, Walker, 2009; Morrell, 2011) and this has largely focused on the advantages and merits of collaborative working and practice. The 'Intelligent Client' (HM Government, 2012) recommends a model of procurement through which relationship management between the client and the supply chain creates a work environment in which collaboration and trust flourish. This generates a framework at the outset from which stems a much more sophisticated approach.

There is an argument that when companies enter into highly complex, uncertain, and potentially risky projects as relative strangers, it is not surprising that frequent conflicts and disputes arise in traditional procurement systems (Chan *et al.*, 2004). Partnering and collaborative approaches seek to avoid conflicts and disputes by increasing levels of cooperation and developing organisational relationships built on trust (Larson, 1997). It is, however, recognised that such approaches do not provide guaranteed mechanisms for the development of trust (Bresnen and Marshall, 2000), and the complexities of developing trust in a single combined operational entity through collaboration are vast. In adopting these approaches, it is important for project teams to communicate well and operate within an environment leading to 'an upward cycle of trust' (Cheung *et al.*, 2003). Accordingly, a shared ethos based on equity and fairness between partners is essential for collaborative success, and all these philosophies should be embedded in aligned organisational strategies (Adams, 1963; Thurairajah *et al.*, 2006; Morrell, 2011). Wong *et al.* (2008) concurred that the level of trust can grow if it is reciprocated. Furthermore, trust is likely to be dependent on a number of factors, including social interaction, power, identities and expectations, and project team individuals may inherently have varying propensities to trust and be trusted (Marshall and Bresnen, 2000; Walker, 2009; Chow *et al.*, 2012). Fawcett *et al.* (2012) present a 'trust maturity framework' as a model of its development giving a hierarchy of stages with collaborative trust at the highest level. They explain that progressing through the stages is not without its risks and potential costs can render construction organisations exposed in some cases.

The degree of trust between key members of teams has been identified as a critical factor in shaping relationships between all project team participants, as well as a key influence in project outcomes (Walker, 2009). Gadde and Dubois (2010) referred to the concept of 'the relationship atmosphere', which is determined by the 'balance of collaboration' that encompasses both constructive elements, such as commitment and trust, and negative elements, such as power and conflict. Kaluarachchi and Jones (2007) also found that communication, trust, change in mindset, and commitment of participants were all major factors in developing successful and innovative partnering agreements.

Morrell (2011) argued that greater coordination is needed in the preparation of project documentation to encourage partnering, buildability, standardisation, prefabrication, and collaborative working in the pursuit of value for money. Yet in order to enable the communication and sharing of knowledge necessary for fully integrated practice, trust between supply chain members, from clients to the smallest SMEs, is a fundamental requirement. Through development of their propensity to trust theory, Briscoe and Dainty (2005) identified a potential lack of desire amongst specialist supply chain partners to trust their more powerful main contractor partners. They reported that specialists had negative experiences in sharing information and prompt payment initiatives, leading to organisational mistrust. The placing of risk where it can be controlled best has emerged as a key contributor to collaboration. Black *et al.* (2000) and Strahorn *et al.* (2014) considered shared risk as a major generator of trust. They concurred that risks should be identified by all parties and that those organisations and individuals best placed to manage them and take responsibility for them should be agreed upon. They justified this approach on the basis that one cannot simply transfer risk without someone else ultimately paying for it. Risk workshops could also overcome any perceptions that risks may have become unfairly allocated, which Walker (2009) regarded as a major barrier for trust development.

The quality of collaboration can be reinforced or weakened, depending on the behaviour, approaches, and attitudes of both organisations and individual participants (Coulson-Thomas, 2005). There is heavy reliance on relationships within teams, but in practice the time needed to nurture these relationships is often lacking in construction management procurement systems (Walker 2009). For this reason, trust is a vital factor in the development of successful partnering and collaborative working practices. Furthermore, according to Ceric (2014), the issue of trust in the quest for greater commitment to partnering, needs to be fully addressed to facilitate better working relationships. Mistrust and scepticism towards partnering practices could, however, be the result of a general lack of understanding of partnering philosophies and the wider benefits of collaborative working (Dainty *et al.*, 2001). To address these issues, a greater awareness of the underlying problems of trust relating to adversarial behaviours is required. Furthermore, there is an argument that the formation stages of partnering arrangements are particularly challenging when negotiations are progressing and interactions between the parties are complex.

2.7.2 What Do We Mean by Trust in the Context of Collaboration and Partnering?

Although there is a general lack of consensus as to the meaning of trust (Bigley and Pearce, 1998) it could be defined as 'the willingness to become vulnerable to another whose behaviour is beyond his control' (Chow *et al.*, 2012). A similar definition of trust could be 'a psychological state comprising the intention to accept vulnerability based upon positive expectations of the behaviour of another' (Rousseau *et al.*, 1998). Bigley and Pearce (1998) explained that such vulnerability, referred to in both these definitions, is a prerequisite for trust where at least one of the partners has something important at stake and where there is potential for betrayal and opportunistic behaviour. An alternative definition could be a 'willingness to rely on an exchange partner in whom one has confidence' (Huang and Wilkinson, 2013). Trust has also been defined as an 'expectancy held by an individual that the word, promise, oral or written statement of another individual or group can be relied upon' or conversely as a 'belief in a person's competency' (Rotter, 1980). The Oxford Current English Dictionary (1990) offered a further definition as 'confidence in or reliance on some quality; attribute of a person and thing; or the truth of a statement'. Conversely, others have regarded trust as 'an expression of confidence that cannot be compromised by the actions of another party' (Jones and George, 1998) or 'one party's optimistic expectation of the behaviour of another, when the party must make a decision about how to act under conditions of vulnerability and dependence' (Hosmer, 1995). Perhaps the most prolific definition in recent times comes from Mayer *et al.* (1995) who described it as 'the willingness of a party to be vulnerable to the actions of another party based on the expectation that the other party will perform a particular action important to the trustor, irrespective of the ability to monitor or control that other party'.

Korczynski (2000) explained the importance of trust from economic and sociological perspectives: the former relating to mutual objectives not to exploit each other and the latter linked to motivations not to damage personal relationships and friendships. Trust constitutes a construct which is multidimensional with different conditions in which it may develop, and it incorporates emotional, cognitive, and moral components and qualities (Jones and George, 1998). In such cases, levels of trust can grow if acts of trust can be reciprocated (Wong *et al.*, 2008), but the risks of non-reciprocation can be high, especially at the early stages of a new relationship (Blau, 1964). This concept could be applied to construction partnering, in which all parties should be conscious of the virtues of instigating acts of trust, such as sharing sensitive information, and the need for reciprocating their partners trusting behaviours (Chow *et al.*, 2012).

Expectations of trust, when broken, can have emotional consequences with parties feeling violated and can signal that relationships have become damaged. Furthermore, this can change the dynamics of trust between parties and, in extreme cases, can lead to its complete collapse. In less severe cases, however, specific behaviours may need to be changed to repair and prevent further damage to relationships (Jones and George 1998). In practice, perhaps this justifies the claim that more is required to train project teams to deal with situations as they arise. This can be corroborated by recent findings from Strahorn *et al.* (2014) who report that in UK construction management 'trust repair skills appear to be rare', especially following disputes.

Academics have long considered the origins and make up of trust in an attempt to understand its meaning. From a social sciences perspective, its origins may emerge from a series of beneficial exchanges between two parties, where relationships are built up on cooperation and collaboration. In such exchanges, one party could create an obligation to the other to reciprocate by providing a benefit to them (Blau, 1964). Types could include interpersonal, firm-based, and supply chain trust and these have been traditionally regarded as consisting of two main components: benevolence and capacity (Fawcett *et al.*, 2012).

Alternatively, it can be categorised into 'cognition-based' and 'affect-based' trust where the former is based on competence and the latter on personal relationships (Parayitam and Dooley, 2009). Wong *et al.*, (2008) reinforced these two categories alongside 'system-based' trust which is related to formal, procedural, and contractual arrangements, and policy that shapes and develops organisational relationships. Furthermore, trust can be categorised and operated on an interpersonal, intergroup, and interorganisational basis (Chow *et al.*, 2012).

Trust is considered to be a 'bonding agent' between collaborating partners and as an 'essential foundation for creating relational exchange' (Silva *et al.*, 2012). It has been identified as a critical factor in shaping relationships between all project team participants, as well as a key influence in project outcomes (Kaluarachchi and Jones 2007; Walker 2009; Ibrahim *et al.*, 2013). Fawcett *et al.* (2012) present a more extreme perspective in this regard and concur that 'without trust collaborative alliances cannot be created or maintained'. They suggest that the lack of understanding around trust is the core reason why organisations have failed to develop in the same way as their more successful competitors in enhancing collaborative capacity and opportunities. Perhaps this explains why trust appears to be a stranger in construction contracting where confrontation remains the prevalent environment (Wong *et al.*, 2008; Chow *et al.*, 2012). One contributory factor for such lack of understanding may emanate from trust receiving only limited attention in construction project management (Maurer, 2010).

Notwithstanding the above premise, the creation of trust between partnering organisations has not always been forthcoming. In addition, the project-based nature of much construction work can be seen as a fundamental barrier to the development of trust in practice, where relationships are often perceived to be short-term and true collaborative working practices struggle to emerge (Walker, 2009). Perhaps then the quality of collaboration can be reinforced or weakened, depending on the behaviour, approaches, and attitudes of organisations and individual participants. However, in practice, the time that is needed to nurture key relationships is often lacking in construction management procurement systems (Walker, 2009). Reliance on the known and controllable has previously been identified within the UK construction industry as a symptom of a lack of trust and 'negative culture', sceptical and suspicious of new initiatives. It has been argued that these old behavioural aspects, cultures, and attitudes are so deeply embedded in the construction sector that they are proving difficult to change (Thurairajah *et al.*, 2006). Accordingly, for partnering approaches to be more attractive to clients, they must seek to address problems of trust, cultural indifference, old stereotypes, and adversarial views of team members alongside establishing new ways of working (Liu *et al.*, 2004).

In previous studies of collaborative working, very little attention has been focused on the trust-building process (Harris and Lyon, 2013). Support for this argument comes from Thorgren *et al.* (2011) who concurred that 'scant attention has been paid to the role and development of trust in partner alliances'. While findings from such studies have indicated that greater levels of collaborative working can increase the successful performance of projects (Wong *et al.*, 2008; Pinto *et al.*, 2009), there is still limited research into the specific impact of trust within partnering practices (Wu and Udeaja, 2008). To address this deficiency, trust-building initiatives can be designed and implemented in developing a framework for improving public sector procurement strategies. The flowchart in Figure 2.1 illustrates the variables (independent and dependent) and the relationships between trust, collaboration, and performance in securing more successful project outcomes.

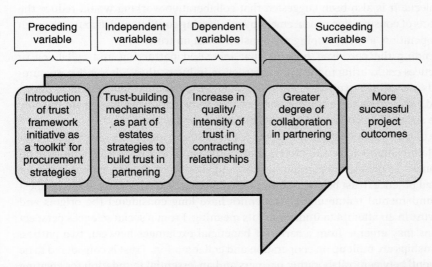

Figure 2.1 Flowchart to illustrate the influence of trust on improved project performance (adapted from Wong *et al.*, 2008, Pinto *et al.*, 2009; and Wu and Udeaja, 2008).

2.8 Summary

The choice of procurement strategies on projects has long been a contentious issue within the construction industry. Government reports of the past have identified deficiencies with traditional procurement strategies, predicated on commercially orientated contracts. Such approaches have had a negative effect on project outcomes, in a lot of cases brought about by adversarial relationships and disputes.

Although there are many different definitions of partnering, it could be defined as a business relationship designed to achieve mutual objectives and benefits between contracting organisations. The definitions of partnering and collaborative working have been articulated in the chapter alongside an understanding of what it means to collaborate and the ways and means to improve and support its successful practice. Early collaboration, under partnering-type contracts, minimises disputes and facilitates significant improvements in client satisfaction, cost predictability, safety, and time predictability. The benefits of collaboration have been argued to include an increase in profits brought about by sharing expertise, knowledge, ideas, innovation, and best practice, and promoting efficiencies and improvements in decision-making.

Traditional procurement strategies have achieved low client satisfaction levels, poor cost predictability, and time certainty, largely attributable to coordination difficulties associated with separation of design and construction and the greater need for teamwork. Collaborative working and partnering were introduced as a way to 'turn the tide' on procurement in the built environment. In this sense, collaborative working at an early stage between contractors and design teams has been, post-Latham, regarded as bridging the gap between design and construction to improve project outcomes. Accordingly, many have identified collaborative procurement routes, such as partnering, as a critical success factor on construction projects. It is also been suggested that collaborative working would reduce the negative aspects of construction procurement by minimising conflicts and disputes through increased cooperation, and developing relationships built on trust.

Notwithstanding the perceived benefits that increased partnering and collaborative working practices could bring to the UK construction industry, these alternative procurement methods are still relatively rare. This could possibly emanate from client perceptions that open and competitive procurement systems, that truly market test prices, are the only way to assure stakeholders of the lowest possible initial capital cost.

The degree of trust between key members of teams has been identified as a critical factor in shaping relationships between all project team participants, as well as a key influence on project outcomes. To enable the communication and sharing of knowledge necessary for fully integrated practice, trust between supply chain members, from clients to the smallest SMEs, is a fundamental requirement. Academics have long considered the origins and make up of trust in an attempt to understand its meaning. From a social sciences perspective, its origins may emerge from a series of beneficial exchanges between two parties, where relationships are built up on cooperation and collaboration. Trust is considered to be a 'bonding agent' between collaborating partners and an 'essential foundation for creating relational exchange'. In addition, levels of trust can grow if acts of trust can be reciprocated but the risks of non-reciprocation can be high, especially at the early stages of a new relationship. Furthermore, expectations of trust, when broken, can have emotional consequences with parties feeling violated and can signal that relationships have become damaged. In such cases, this can change the dynamics of trust between parties and, in extreme cases, can lead to its complete collapse.

The project-based nature of much construction work can be seen as a fundamental barrier to the development of trust in practice, where relationships are often perceived to be short-term, and true collaborative working practices struggle to emerge. Finally, the quality of collaboration can be reinforced or weakened, depending on the behaviour, approaches, and attitudes of organisations and individual participants.

References

Abdul Nifa, F.A. and Ahmed, V. (2010). The role of organisational culture in construction partnering to produce innovation. In: *Proceedings of the 26th Annual ARCOM Conference*, (ed. C. Egbu), 6–8 September 2010, Leeds, UK, Association of Researchers in Construction Management, pp. 725–734.

Adams, J.S. (1963). Toward an understanding of inequity. *Journal of Abnormal and Social Psychology* 67(5): 422–436.

Banwell, H. (1964). *The Placing and Management of Contracts for Building and Civil Engineering Work*. London: HMSO.

Bigley, G.A. and Pearce, J.L. (1998). Straining for shared meaning in organization science: Problems of trust and distrust. *The Academy of Management Review* 23(3): 405–421.

Black, C., Akintoye, A. and Fitzgerald, E. (2000). An analysis of success factors and benefits of partnering in construction. *International Journal of Project Management*, 18(2000): 423–434.

Blau, P.M. (1964). *Exchange and Power in Social Life*. New York: Wiley.

Bresnen, M. and Marshall, N. (2000). Partnering in construction: A critical review of issues, problems and dilemmas. *Construction Management and Economics*. 18(2): 229–237.

Briscoe, G. and Dainty, A. (2005). Construction supply chain integration: An elusive goal? *Supply Chain Management: An International Journal*, 10(4): 319–326.

Ceric, A. (2014). Communication risk and trust in construction projects: A framework for interdisciplinary research. In: *Proceedings of the 30th Annual ARCOM Conference*, (eds A.B. Raiden and E. Aboagye-Nimo), 1–3 September 2014, Portsmouth, UK, Association of Researchers in Construction Management, pp. 835–844.

Chan A.P.C., Chan D.W.M., Chiang Y., *et al.* (2004). Exploring critical success factors for partnering in construction projects. *Journal of Construction Engineering and Management* 130(2): 188–189.

Cheung S.O., Thomas, S.T., Wong S.P. and Suen, C.H. (2003). Behavioral aspects in construction partnering. *International Journal of Project Management* 21(5): 333–343.

Chow P.T., Cheung S.O. and Chan K.Y. (2012). Trust-building in construction contracting: Mechanism and expectation. *International Journal of Project Management* 30(8): 927–937.

Constructing Excellence (2004). Partnering 31/3/04: Innovation, Best Practice and Productivity. London: Constructing Excellence. **https://constructingexcellence.org.uk/ wp-content/uploads/2015/03/partnering.pdf** (accessed 22 November 2023).

Coulson-Thomas, C. (2005). Encouraging partnering and collaboration. *Industrial and Commercial Training*. 37(4): 179–184.

Dainty, A., Briscoe, G. and Millet, J. (2001). Subcontractor perspectives on supply chain alliances. *Construction Management and Economics* 19(2): 841–848.

Das, T.K. and Teng B.S. (1998). Between Trust and control: Developing confidence in partner cooperation in alliances. *The Academy of Management Review* 23(3): 491–512.

Egan, J. (1998). *Rethinking Construction*. The Report of the Construction Task Force. London: DETR. TSO.

Egan, J. (2002). *Accelerating Change*. London: Rethinking Construction.

Emerson, R.M. (1962). Power-dependence relations. *American Sociological Review* 27(1): 31–41.

Eriksson, P.E. and Westerberg, M. (2011) Effects of cooperative procurement procedures on construction project performance: A conceptual framework. *International Journal of Project Management* 29(2): 197–208.

Fawcett, S.E., Jones, S.L. and Fawcett, A.M. (2012). Supply chain trust: The catalyst for collaboration. *Business Horizons* 55(2): 163–178.

Gadde, L.E. and Dubois, A. (2010). Partnering in the construction industry: Problems and opportunities. *Journal of Purchasing and Supply Management* 16(4): 254–263.

Gunn, J. (2002). *The Effective Use of Partnering and Alliancing*. Sydney: Minter Ellison.

Hansen, M.T. and Nohria, N. (2004). How to build collaborative advantage. *MIT Sloan Management Review* 46(1): 22–30.

Harris, F. and Lyon, F. (2013).Transdisciplinary environmental research: Building trust across professional cultures. *Environmental Science & Policy*. 31(2013): 109–119.

HM Government (2010). Low Carbon Construction Final Report (November 2010). London: HM Government. pp. 52–62, 196–199.

HM Government (2012). Government Construction Strategy. London: HM Government. https://assets.publishing.service.gov.uk/media/5a75bbc2ed915d506ee8115e/GCS-One-Year-On-Report-and-Action-Plan-Update-FINAL_0.pdf (accessed 28 November 2023).

Hosmer, L.T. (1995). Trust: The connecting link between organisational theory and philosophical ethics. *The Academy of Management Review* 20(2): 379–403.

Huang Y. and Wilkinson, I.F. (2013). The dynamics and evolution of trust in business relationships. *Industrial Marketing Management* 42(3): 455–465.

Ibrahim, C.K.L., Costello, S.B. and Wilkinson, S. (2013). Overview of key indicators of team integration in construction projects: New Zealand practitioners' point of view. *Proceedings of the CIB World Building Congress Construction and Society*, 5–9 May 2013, Brisbane, Australia.

Ingirige, B. and Sexton, M. (2006). Alliances in construction: Investigating initiatives and barriers for long-term collaboration. Engineering, Construction and Architectural Management 13(5): 521–535.

Jones, G.R. and George, J.M. (1998). The experience and evaluation of trust: Implications for cooperation and teamwork. *The Academy of Management Review* 23(3): 531–546.

Kaluarachchi, D.Y. and Jones, K. (2007). Monitoring of a strategic partnering process: The Amphion experience. *Construction Management and Economics* 25(10): 1053–1061.

Korczynski, M. (2000). The political economy of trust. *Journal of Management Studies* 37(1): 1–21.

Lann, A., Voordijk, J. and Dewulf, G. (2011). Reducing opportunistic behaviour through a project alliance. *International Journal of Managing Projects in Business* 8(4): 660–679.

Larson, E. (1997). Partnering on construction projects: A study of the relationship between partnering activities and project success. *IEEE Transactions on Engineering Management* 44(2): 188–195.

Latham, M. (1994). *Constructing the Team*. London: The Stationery Office.

Liu, A., Fellows, R. and Ng, J. (2004). Surveyors' perspectives on ethics in organisational culture. *Engineering, Construction and Architectural Management* 11(6): 438–449.

Manley, K. (2002). Partnering and alliancing on road projects in Australia and internationally. *Road and Transport Research* 11(3): 46–60.

Marshall, N. and Bresnen, M. (2000). Partnering in construction: A critical review of issues, problems and dilemmas. *Construction Management and Economics* 18(2): 229–237.

Maurer, I. (2010). How to build trust in inter-organizational projects: The impact of project staffing and project rewards on the formation of trust, knowledge acquisition and product innovation. *International Journal of Project Management* 28(7): 629–637.

Mayer, R.C., Davis, J.H. and Schoorman, F.D. (1995). An integrative model of organisational trust. *The Academy of Management Review* 20(3): 709–734.

Morrell, S. (2011). Major strategic priorities and opportunities for construction. *Build Offsite*.

National Audit Office (2001). Modernising Construction. *Report by the Controller and Auditor General HC 87 Session 2000–2001*. London: The Stationary Office.

Oxford Current English Dictionary (1990). Oxford University Press.

Oyegoke, A.S., Dickinson, M., Malik, M.A., *et al.* (2009). Construction project procurement routes: An in-depth critique. *International Journal of Managing Projects in Business* 2(3): 338–354.

Parayitam, S. and Dooley, R.S. (2009). The interplay between cognitive and affective conflict and cognition- and affect-based trust in influencing decision outcomes. *Journal of Business Research* 62(8): 789–796.

Patel, H., Pettitt, M. and Wilson, J.R. (2012). Factors of collaborative working: A framework for a collaboration model. *Applied Ergonomics* 43(1): 1–26.

Pinto, J.K., Slevin, D.P. and English, B. (2009). Trust in projects: An empirical assessment of owner/contractor relationships. *International Journal of Project Management* 27(6): 638–648.

RICS (2009) *Proceedings of the Construction and Building Conference of the Royal Institution of Chartered Surveyors*. 10–11 September, University of Cape Town.

RICS (2012) *Contracts in Use. A Survey of Building Contracts in Use during 2010*. London: Royal Institution of Chartered Surveyors Publications.

Ross, A. (2011). Supply chain management in an uncertain economic climate: A UK perspective. *Construction Innovation* 11(1): 5–13.

Rotter, J. (1980). Interpersonal trust, trustworthiness and gullibility. *American Psychologist* 35(1): 1–7.

Rousseau, D., Sitkin, S., Burt, R. and Camerer, C. (1998). Not so different after all: A cross-discipline view of trust. *The Academy of Management Review* 23(3): 393–404.

Silva, S.C., Bradley, F. and Sousa, C.M.P. (2012). Empirical test of the trust performance link in an international alliances context. *International Business Review*, 21(2012): 293–306.

Strahorn, S., Gajendran, T. and Brewer, G. (2014). Experiences of trust in construction project management: The influence of procurement mechanisms In: *Proceedings of the 30th Annual ARCOM Conference*, (eds A.B. Raiden and E. Aboagye-Nimo), 1–3 September 2014, Portsmouth, UK, Association of Researchers in Construction Management, pp. 463–472.

Thorgren, S., Wincent, J. and Eriksson, J. (2011). Too small or too large to trust your partners in multipartner alliances? The role of effort in initiating generalized exchanges. *Scandinavian Journal of Management* 27(1): 99–112.

Thurairajah, N., Haigh, R. and Amaratunga, R.D.G. (2006). Cultural transformation in construction partnering projects. *Proceedings of the Annual Research Conference of the Royal Institution of Chartered Surveyors*, 7–8 September, University College London.

Vaaland, T.I. (2004). Improving project collaboration: Start with the conflicts. *International Journal of Project Management* 22(6): 447–454.

Walker, A. (2009). *Project Management in Construction*. 5e. Oxford: Blackwell Publishing Ltd. pp. 150–158.

Wong S.P. and Cheung S.O. (2004). Trust in construction partnering: Views from parties of the partnering dance. *International Journal of Project Management* 22: 437–446.

Wong W.K., Cheung S.O., Yiu T.W. and Pang H.Y. (2008). A framework for trust in construction contracting. *International Journal of Project Management* 26(8): 821–829.

Wu S. and Udeaja, C. (2008). Developing a framework for measuring collaborative working and project performance. In: *Proceedings of the 24th Annual ARCOM Conference*, (ed. A. Dainty), 1–3 September 2008, Cardiff, UK, Association of Researchers in Construction Management, pp. 983–992.

Yeung J.F.Y., Chan A.P.C. and Chan D.W.M. (2007). The definition of alliancing in construction as a Wittgenstein family-resemblance concept. *International Journal of Project Management* 25(3): 291–231.

3

The Importance of Trust, Collaboration, and Partnering for the Built Environment

The most expensive thing in the world is trust. It can take years to earn and just a matter of seconds to lose.

3.1 Introduction

This chapter of the book is largely based on the research study by Challender (2017) which was focused on trust in collaborative construction procurement strategies. It starts by examining the potential benefits and incentives to trust and the positive influences on job performance. Citing many different literature sources, it offers context on how these benefits can lead to successful project outcomes and develop good working relationships between contracting parties. This articulates how trust can allow vital risk taking, where there are no other safeguards to protect partners. Notwithstanding these benefits, it explains why trust appears to be a stranger in construction contracting where confrontation remains the prevalent environment.

The chapter then considers the factors that can encourage trust, and, from the research by Challender (2017), explain why there are many wide-ranging sources or attributes of trust. It explains how factors such as confidence, teamwork, and the personalities of individual team members were all found to affect trust positively or negatively between organisations. In addition, there is an analysis of how trust originating from previous positive relationships and dealings between individuals at senior levels can be critical in the cascading of trust throughout partnering organisations.

The chapter then looks at the successful outcomes brought about by partnering and collaborative working. Construction cost predictability, value for money, and client risk are discussed and the ways and means that partnering and collaborative working can benefit these aspects. It then considers how partnering strategy can more readily facilitate the early integration of main contractors and subcontractors into the wider project team than traditional procurement strategies. The benefits that this early integration can have are identified for projects, as well as how the expertise and familiarisation of the supply chain can be embedded at earlier stages of the design development. Some of the advantages that this brings for projects are then discussed. Programme timescales and quality control benefits by partnering are also explored. This involves an explanation of how specialist input and value-engineered solutions at preliminary design stages, possibly brought on board by early integration of contractors, can shorten pre-tender periods while enhancing quality control and greater client satisfaction.

The chapter then considers the suitability of partnering and collaborative working to different types of building project, including complexity and specialism. Following on from this, the importance of the contractor selection process and appointing a 'trustworthy partner' is covered. This includes an articulation of why having the right contractor on board is more crucial in partnering arrangements, owing to teamwork and shared philosophies, than in more traditional procurement routes. The chapter then highlights the barriers to successful implementation of partnering, including factors related to fairness, cooperation, and sharing information. Finally, it explains why building information modelling (BIM) as a management tool in encouraging greater collaboration can assist in changing the culture of the UK construction industry and facilitate integration across the whole supply chain to address perceived deficiencies.

3.2 Potential Benefits and Incentives to Trust

The construction industry has in the past been characterised by complex processes and exchanges of information, and some believe that they can lead to the emergence of opportunistic behaviours. To address these issues, research has focused on theories relating to the creation and development of trust as a potential means to reduce opportunism (Chow *et al.*, 2012). For example, the existence of trust has been an important counterweight when business environments and organisational relationships have been prone to hidden agendas and conflicting objectives (Silva *et al.*, 2012). Other theories, conversely, have advocated that trust within relationships can safeguard against excessive formal contractual relationships developing between partnering organisations (Pinto *et al.*, 2009). This is supported by the perspective that it is not practical to include contractual provisions for every possible occurrence on projects, and that too many provisions could be misinterpreted as signs of mistrust (Li, 2008). The same argument is supported by Colquitt *et al.* (2007) who found that the potential benefits of developing and nurturing trust in the workplace can have positive influences on job performance while allowing vital risk taking, where there are no other safeguards to protect partners. The emergence of these views would appear to justify claims that financial benefits can emanate from trusting relationships. Ceric (2014) certainly supported this argument and advocated that 'trust reduces agency costs both before and after the contract is signed between the principal and the agent'. Conversely, and perhaps unsurprisingly, the opposite effect is evidenced for mistrust in the same study with additional agency costs being generated.

Another interesting perspective comes from Korczynski (2000) who opined that the benefits of trust within a capitalist economy should allow for greater cooperation without exertion of power and, from a transaction cost economics perspective, reduce opportunism. This perspective has become more profound in developing economies where there have been economic shifts from large independent competing firms to smaller interdependent firms who cooperate which each other more readily (Korczynski 1996). The perceived benefits of trust have, however, attracted their critics in some instances. Some have debated whether such reliance on trust is appropriate where large sums of money are involved and opportunism could emerge (Lann *et al.*, 2011). This is clearly at odds with the aforementioned views of Silva *et al.* (2012). The other contentious factor is whether the fractious nature of the UK construction industry, based largely on 'one-off' projects, facilitates the right environment and conditions for trust to prosper (Fawcett *et al.*, 2012).

3.3 Trust as a Collaborative Necessity in Benefitting Construction Partnering

Despite trust being regarded as a positive force for the built environment, it appears to be a stranger in construction contracting where confrontation remains the prevalent environment (Wong *et al.*, 2008). One contributory factor for such lack of understanding may emanate from trust receiving only limited attention in construction project management (Maurer, 2010). Observations support the case that trust among construction project teams needs to be significantly increased (Dainty *et al.*, 2007), especially since it is 'central to every transaction that demands contributions from the parties involved' (Cheung *et al.*, 2011). Despite this there has been much debate in academia as to how to achieve trust in practice. Cheung *et al.*, (2003), in this regard, stressed the importance for project teams to communicate well and operate within an environment leading to 'an upward cycle of trust'. Conversely, some academics have argued that it is the creation of a shared ethos, based on equity and fairness and embedded in aligned organisational strategies, that best promotes trust between partners (Thurairajah *et al.*, 2006). Notwithstanding these views, there has been little written on trust-building measures and mechanisms for construction relationships, and even less for construction partnering.

3.4 The Importance of Trust in Partnering and Collaborative Working

Increased trust in partnering can encourage greater scope for cooperation, teamwork, and collaboration, and it can lessen the need for excessive monitoring and formal control mechanisms through reduced risk of opportunism. Notwithstanding this premise, Chow *et al.* (2012) and Silva *et al.* (2012) opined that robust contractual provisions must remain in place despite the presence of a trusting relationship. This is to lessen the risk of potential exploitation where one party may be disadvantaged by the other. From research undertaken by Challender (2017), trust may be more important for strategic partnering and less so for project partnering based on 'one-off' projects. This is justified on the basis of greater scope and motivation for building relationships and learning from experiences in strategic partnering, where repeat business from one project to another is facilitated. In this way, strategic partnering it would address the fundamental problem outlined by Walker (2009) and Fawcett *et al.* (2012) concerning the short-term nature of the construction industry. Notwithstanding the support for trust in collaboration and partnering, some professional practitioners still remain suspicious of the realisable benefits. This has emanated from past experiences where traditional commercial positions have re-emerged, through claims and disputes, causing parties to retreat back to adversarial contractual positions.

3.5 Providing the Right Environment for Trust in Partnering; Possible Trust-building Mechanisms

In consideration of what can encourage trust, research by Challender (2017) found that there are many wide-ranging sources or attributes of trust. Either positively or negatively, confidence, teamwork, and the personalities of individual team members were all found to be important trust-building attributes in partnering within this research study. Notwithstanding this, findings indicated that the strength of trust generated is more dependent on individual personal relationships, developed from mutual respect, rather than simply 'good' working relationships. Trust originating from previous positive relationships and dealings between individuals at senior levels is regarded as critical in the cascading of trust throughout partnering organisations. The influence of senior-level trust supports findings in Thurairajah *et al.* (2006) where one participant referred to them as 'aligned synergies'. Not surprisingly, at an operational level, 'human' attributes, such as integrity, honesty, consistency, reliability, and competency, are regarded as essential facilitating factors in building trust and gaining good collaborative working relationships. These attributes are supported by other qualities, including commitment, communication, initiative, and conscientiousness, to provide the required degree of integration within teams. Such 'soft' factors and skills, as depicted by Cheung *et al.* (2011), were confirmed by Challender (2017) to be vital for the greater integration and cohesion of project teams. Yet, hard factors are also put forward by those interviewed as crucial in the partnering process: experience, technical ability, education and competence of individuals, management systems, and the resources of the partnering organisations. Furthermore, when appointing a partner, the robustness of the partner selection processes has been found to be important in evaluating the preferred and most compatible partner.

In the research study undertaken by Challender (2017), the professional practitioners who were interviewed outlined their opinions on many different trust-building mechanisms to increase trust in partnering arrangements. These included measures to increase the fairness of contract terms, the existence of a dispute resolution process which could address the abuse of power (National Audit Office, 2001), and deployment of market leverage (RICS, 2005) scenarios. Other measures were to encourage informal and open communications and willingness to share sensitive information. Workshops were also suggested as the means to facilitate continuing professional development (CPD) and networking events to promote open informal communications and engagement on other trust-building initiatives. The participants opined that these could encourage dialogue and teamwork to provide the right conditions for embedding those partnering philosophies, as advocated by HM Government (2013). In this regard one interviewee, referring to previous projects, suggested that a partnering charter to encompass such measures had been successful in the past. A potential counter argument also emerged, however, in that even when there are great intentions to commit to such measures and undertakings some partners simply lack the practical experience, knowledge, and resources to embed and develop trust within interorganisational relationships. The research participants (Challender, 2017) were also asked for their opinions on a whole host of qualitative themes around trust, partnering, and collaborative working and these are listed in Table 3.1.

Table 3.1

Qualitative themes	Literature source	Observation, proposition, or explanation	Data inconsistencies	Data similarities
Factors that instil trust in partnering arrangements Trust-building mechanisms	Cheung et al. (2003) Briscoe and Dainty (2005) Thurairajah et al. (2006) Wong et al. (2008)	Shared ethos based on trust, equity, and fairness between partners is essential Levels of trust could grow if trust reciprocated between partners Social interaction, power, identities, and expectations influence the degree and quality of trust	Trust generated from previous relationships, especially at senior levels Lack of knowledge and commitment to initiatives in some cases	Equitable working relationships coupled with dispute resolution process Importance of communications and commitment Sharing of information Use of workshops for facilitating teamwork
Importance of and reliance on trust in partnering arrangements	Kaluarachchi and Jones (2007) Walker (2009) Lann et al. (2011) Silva et al. (2012)	More trusting relationships facilitate increased collaboration Trust considered to represent 'bonding agent' between collaborating partners Degree of trust shapes relationships of project teams and influences project outcomes	Trust only felt desirable to project partnering while essential to strategic partnering Trust appears to be a stranger in construction contracting	Loss of trust can result in untenable working relationships Trust enhances collaboration and bonds teams together. Closer working relationships can provide right context for trust
Perceived benefits of trust in partnering arrangements	Larson (1997) Colquitt et al. (2007) Silva et al. (2012) Li (2008) RICS (2005)	Increased collaboration is a crucial factor in delivering successful construction projects Trust can safeguard against excessive contractual provisions and/or risk-averse practices Can reduce opportunism	Suspicion of realisable benefits and negative past experiences Risk of exploitation Perception of too 'cosy' business relationships Can increase opportunism	Less antagonistic and stressful environment, improved teamwork, cooperation, and collaboration Risks, especially on complex projects, can be identified earlier and managed more effectively
Potential barriers to trust in partnering arrangements Potential origins of lack of trust/mistrust		Use of market leverage and lack to trust in more powerful partners Fragmentation and short-term nature of industry Negative, adversarial behaviours and attitudes	Lack of professional development, education, and training felt to be most important factors Conflict can be a positive factor	Insecurity, uncertainty, and scepticism of trusting relationships

Qualitative themes and data analysis

3.6 Successful Outcomes Brought about by Partnering and Collaborative Working

3.6.1 Construction Cost Predictability, Value for Money, and Client Risk

Most of the practitioners in the research by Challender (2017) supported some of the findings of Egan (1998) and Latham (1994) on improved cost predictability in partnering practices, which may partly stem from establishing clients' requirements more comprehensively, especially at tender stage. They believed that early design intervention, introducing innovation, and considering alternative design options at the outset could potentially give rise to considerable cost savings in some cases, but not all. Certainly, on smaller scale projects of less than £5 million they felt that potential reports of significant cost savings had become exaggerated over time. However, practitioners did concede that there is greater scope for value engineering on larger and more complex projects where, for example, specialist supply chain advice on sophisticated and specialist mechanical and electrical installations or working within live environments is required at an early stage. Another example was given by one of the project managers who referred to a new cladding system being introduced on a large high-rise office project where potentially high costs, associated with increased health and safety risks, were prevalent. Recommendations provided by the specialist subcontractor on this project brought buildability benefits and associated cost savings.

There was a belief from those interviewed as part of the Challender (2017) research study that collaborative processes in partnering arrangements can potentially provide more effective open book mechanisms for developing final contract sums with contractors, ensuring that tendering processes are fully transparent, fair, and appropriate, in most cases. They outlined that there are still too many instances of contractors, in traditional contracts, inflating the value of claims for variations. For this reason, collaborative working under partnering may offer an alternative procurement route in managing such claims, thereby lessening the risks of overspend and potential contractual disputes. In this way, commercial issues could be identified earlier and addressed accordingly, consequently avoiding potential delays and protracted disputes through early dialogue and communication

3.6.2 Early Integration of Main Contractors and Subcontractors into the Project Team

It is generally accepted in the construction and engineering industries that partnering and collaborative working can facilitate the early integration of main contractors and subcontractors into the wider project team. This can bring many benefits for projects in having their expertise and familiarisation embedded at earlier stages of the design development. Some of the advantages that this brings for projects are illustrated in Figure 3.1.

3.6.3 Programme Timescales and Quality Control

Specialist input and value-engineered solutions at preliminary design stages, possibly enabled by early integration of contractors, could shorten pre-tender periods while enhancing quality control and giving greater client satisfaction. The research of Challender (2017) concurred with Walker (2009) and Eriksson and Westerberg, (2011) that procurement

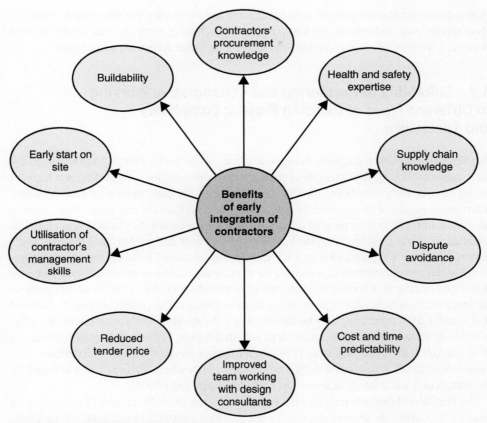

Figure 3.1 Benefits of early integration of contractors
(adapted from the findings of Latham, 1994; Egan, 1998; and Egan, 2002).

routes should be tailored to the nature of projects, especially with the growing trend for more demanding deadlines and project outcomes in recent years – scenarios in which traditional procurement routes may be less effective and/or unsuitable. In the same research, views were also presented that partnering could be more successful than traditional procurement routes where health and safety issues on projects represent greater risks to programme and quality. This was explained by the intervention of contractors at preliminary design stages bringing the associated benefits of early dialogue to address and overcome such issues.

Partnering on longer projects, which potentially involve sophisticated and challenging phasing and programming to best suit a specific employer's requirements, could offer more scope than traditional procurement routes in reducing overall project durations. This is possibly a consequence of enhanced teamwork and contractors working alongside clients with common objectives to achieve phased handover dates. This is especially the case when working within live building environments, where disruption to the overall end-users' operations is a key issue. In this way, construction programme timescales could be improved at the early design stages by clients working with contractors to specify the most suitable and conducive materials and construction techniques to suit the nature of projects.

Furthermore, through improved team integration partnering has the potential to raise levels of quality and performance by reducing conflict, allowing more efficient deployment of resources, increasing job satisfaction, and facilitating fewer defects on completion.

3.7 Suitability of Partnering and Collaborative Working to Different Types of Building Project; Complexity and Specialism

Partnering is generally regarded as being best suited to large or complex projects where, in the early stages especially, the expertise of contractors in value engineering and project logistics would be extremely beneficial. As an example, one of the construction project managers interviewed as part of the research by Challender (2017) referred to a refurbishment scheme on a museum which incorporated a sophisticated and complex mechanical and electrical installation. It was explained that the building services were designed around the specialist's requirements for a sophisticated and technologically advanced building management system. For this reason, partnering presented the most appropriate and suitable option to ensure that initial interfaces of specialists' expertise were introduced early in the life of that particular project. Conversely, where projects are less complicated the project managers deduced that benefits from partnering may be significantly reduced, since early contractors' specialist advice may represent desirable rather than essential inputs. This tends to confirm findings from Hackett *et al.* (2007) and Egan (1998) that for some simpler projects, collaborative procurement routes may not be a suitable option, particularly where the expertise and inputs of the contractors and subcontractors in the early design are less critical.

The duration of projects may also have some influence over the success of partnering in practice. For instance, shorter projects do not facilitate enough time to build strong working relationships and for partners to become familiar with each other's ways of working. Furthermore, more controlled financial management on projects through partnering and collaborative working could be achieved on projects with longer contract durations. It is generally accepted that longer projects give rise to more variations as clients' requirements change over time and partnering can facilitate more cost-effective solutions than under traditionally procured contracts. In addition, longer projects provide more time for reflection on alternative building systems and ways of working which could provide the most suitable context for value engineering. It was also felt that when managing clusters of many projects of short duration strategic partnering may be more desirable than project partnering, as trust can be generated within encouraging contexts where the developmental nature of this collaborative process aligns with the long-term vision of integrated teams.

3.8 The Importance of the Contractor Selection Process and Appointing a Trustworthy Partner

A surprising outcome of the research by Challender (2017) is the suggestion that the choice of contractors and the individuals deployed on projects was felt by construction project managers to be more important than the choice of procurement route. This outcome clearly needs more testing and validation since it seems to contradict certain aspects of Egan

(1998) and Latham (1994). It can perhaps be explained by the sense that teamwork can be maximised by having the right team members appointed on projects and that benefits emanate from this. The project managers also reiterated that traditionally procured projects have had extremely successful results from teamwork, even though contractors may have had little influence on the design processes. For this reason, trust between the team members was regarded by the practitioners as a key factor irrespective of the nature and particulars of projects and procurement routes. Notwithstanding this, the study suggests that having the right contractor on board is more crucial in partnering arrangements, owing to teamwork and shared philosophies, than in more traditional procurement routes. Perhaps this indicates that the quality of collaboration can be reinforced or weakened, depending on the behaviour, approaches, and attitudes of organisations and individual participants. Clearly the contractor selection process is important in terms of evaluating these criteria, alongside expertise, experience, and specialism, in choosing the right partner. The study by Challender (2017) also found that the selection process should incorporate robust selection criteria, interviewing, shortlisting, and quality assurance measures to ensure that the resources and specialisms of contractors are suitable for the project. Research participants on the study concurred that having the wrong contractors on board, especially at early design stages, could severely jeopardise the success of projects. One practitioner felt that, in partnering, having 'aligned cultural synergies' was one of the most important criteria to evaluate and concurred that 'if organisations and individuals working within partnering agreements are not working as one collective project team or committed to the same beliefs, values and objectives then such projects will be severely compromised from the start'. This again demonstrates the importance of, and reliance on, the choice of suitable contractors for the benefits of partnering to be fully realised.

The research participants all agreed that a 'culture' of trust allows projects to move forward effectively and creates an environment where problems can be shared and therefore solved more easily. In this regard, they believe that trust is not something that can be engineered through contractual conditions or procurement routes alone, but needs to be developed, built up, and earned over time. Notwithstanding this, they concurred that where trust is compromised, it could lead to a downward cycle of trust where working relationships may become untenable. The study also highlighted the belief of those interviewed that the perceived return to short-term contracts and the constant quest for the lowest initial bid price could be jeopardising the development of trust between organisations. However, where long-term organisational collaboration is a potential future work-stream, the development of trust within such relationships may become 'incentivised' and consequently active in practice.

There is an consensus of opinion in the research study by Challender (2017) that partnering can bring about improved cost certainty, reduced project durations, improvements in quality of build, and benefits to project management and construction innovation in some contexts, but not all. The research participants strongly felt that assessing the suitability of projects to partnering is critical to realising the potential benefits in practice. Certainly, on very complex projects, it was generally accepted that the early intervention of contractors, subcontractors, and suppliers through partnering was essential in ensuring project success, where more traditional forms of contract, based on separation of design and construction, may be unsuitable. Other less tangible and softer outcomes can be used as key performance indicators to measure the success of a given project through partnering arrangements. These include motivation, team building, trust, and respect and are more likely to be generated through partnering and, in doing so, create the right environment for successful projects. Perhaps the most surprising outcome from this study is that the practitioners regarded the individuals deployed on projects as having more influence on success than the choices of partnering per se. They believe that both traditional and collaborative procurement can both produce successful outcomes provided that the right individuals are employed, with suitable experience, expertise, motivation, and proactive attitudes to team working.

The study clearly highlights barriers to successful implementation of partnering including factors related to fairness, cooperation, and sharing information. Perhaps building information modelling (BIM) as a management tool, in encouraging greater collaboration, could assist in changing the culture of the UK construction industry and facilitate integration across the whole supply chain to address perceived deficiencies. In addition, certain elements of best practices for partnering have been highlighted in this study. These include ensuring that the nature of the project and partnering are appropriately matched and choosing the most suitable contractors through a robust selection process. Ideally, this will ensure the right choice of partners who are committed to 'the spirit of partnering' and not just those individuals and organisations that 'pay lip service' to its philosophies and values. Without this commitment partners will feel propelled to 'collaborate' by the terms of the contract only, which could risk reversion back to traditional adversarial behaviours.

One of the limitations of the research study by Challender (2017) is that it was based on a very small sample of interviewees. This reduced the reliability and validity of the study and the findings are accordingly not representative of the population at large. It is intended that further qualitative work, with a larger sample and broader range of experienced construction professionals, may need to be undertaken to interpret existing data more effectively.

3.9 Summary

This chapter of the book is largely based on the research study by Challender (2017) which focused on trust in collaborative construction procurement strategies.

The construction industry has in the past been characterised by complex processes and exchanges of information, and some believe that they can lead to the emergence of opportunistic behaviours. The benefits of trust within a capitalist economy should allow for greater cooperation without exertion of power and from a transaction cost economics perspective, reduce opportunism. The development of trust in the built environment could be a potential means of reducing opportunism, while encouraging greater cooperation to improve project outcomes. The perceived benefits of trust have, however, attracted their critics in some instances. Notwithstanding this premise, some have debated whether such reliance on trust is appropriate where large sums of money are involved, and opportunism could emerge.

To encourage trust-building, it is important for project teams to communicate well and operate within an environment leading to 'an upward cycle of trust'. Increased trust in partnering can encourage greater scope for cooperation, teamwork, and collaboration, and it can lessen the need for excessive monitoring and formal control mechanisms.

Notwithstanding the support for trust in collaboration and partnering, some professional practitioners still remain suspicious of the realisable benefits. This has emanated from past experiences where traditional commercial positions have re-emerged, through claims and disputes, causing parties to retreat back to adversarial contractual positions. Possibly,this could explain why trust appears to be a stranger in construction contracting where confrontation remains the prevalent environment. One contributory factor for such lack of understanding may come from trust receiving only limited attention in construction project management.

In consideration of what can encourage trust, research by Challender (2017) found that there are many wide-ranging sources or attributes of trust. Either positively or negatively, confidence, teamwork, and the personalities of individual team members were all found to be important trust-building attributes in partnering. In the research study, professional practitioners outlined their opinions on many different trust-building mechanisms to increase trust in partnering arrangements. These included measures to increase fairness of contract terms, the existence of a dispute resolution process which could address the abuse of power, and deployment of market leverage scenarios.

It is generally accepted in the construction and engineering industries that partnering and collaborative working can facilitate the early integration of main contractors and subcontractors into the wider project team. This can bring many benefits for projects by having their expertise and familiarisation embedded at earlier stages of the design development. Furthermore, collaborative processes in partnering arrangements can potentially provide more effective open book mechanisms for developing final contract sums with contractors, ensuring that tendering processes are fully transparent, fair, and appropriate, in most cases. Specialist input and value-engineered solutions at preliminary design stages, possibly enabled by early integration of contractors, could shorten pre-tender periods while enhancing quality control and giving greater client satisfaction. In addition, partnering could be more successful than traditional procurement routes, where health and safety issues on projects represent greater risks to programme and quality.

The suitability of partnering and collaborative working may be affected by the different types of building project, especially in terms of complexity and specialism. Partnering is generally regarded as being best suited to large or complex projects where, in the early stages especially, the expertise of contractors in value engineering and project logistics would be extremely beneficial. The duration of projects may also have some influence over the success of partnering in practice. For instance, shorter projects do not facilitate enough time to build strong working relationships and for partners to become familiar with each other's ways of working.

The research study by Challender (2017) suggested that having the right contractor on board is more crucial in partnering arrangements than in traditional procurement. A possible reason for this may be the greater sense of teamwork and shared philosophies required in partnering. In more traditional procurement routes, the contractor selection process is still important in terms of evaluating expertise, experience, and specialism.

A 'culture' of trust allows projects to move forward effectively and creates an environment where problems can be shared and therefore solved more easily. Trust generated from previous relationships and dealings between individuals at senior levels is regarded as critical in the cascading of trust throughout organisations, and between those currently operating partnering arrangements. Not surprisingly at an operational level, 'human' attributes such as integrity, honesty, consistency, reliability, and competency are regarded as important in facilitating trust and good collaborative working. The research study by Challender (2017) clearly highlights barriers to successful implementation of partnering including factors related to fairness, cooperation, and sharing information. Perhaps building information modelling (BIM) as a management tool, in encouraging greater collaboration, could assist in changing the culture of the UK construction industry and facilitate integration across the whole supply chain to address perceived deficiencies.

References

Ceric, A. (2014). Communication risk and trust in construction projects: A framework for interdisciplinary research. In: *Proceedings of the 30th Annual ARCOM Conference*, (eds A.B. Raiden and E. Aboagye-Nimo), 1–3 September 2014, Portsmouth, UK, Association of Researchers in Construction Management, pp. 835–844.

Challender, J. (2017). Trust in collaborative construction procurement strategies. *Management, Procurement and Law Proceedings of the Institution of Civil Engineers* 170(3): 115–124.

Cheung S.O., Thomas, S.T., Wong S.P. and Suen, CH (2003) Behavioural aspects in construction partnering. *International Journal of Project Management* 21(5): 333–343.

Cheung S.O., Wong W.K., Yiu T.W. and Pang H.Y.(2011). Developing a trust inventory for construction contracting. *International Journal of Project Management* 29(2): 184–196.

Chow P.T., Cheung S.O. and Chan K.Y. (2012). Trust-building in construction contracting: Mechanism and expectation. *International Journal of Project Management* 30(8): 927–937.

Colquitt, J.A., Scott, B.A. and LePine, J.A. (2007). Trust, trustworthiness, and trust propensity: A meta-analytic test of their unique relationships with risk taking and job performance. *Journal of Applied Psychology* 92(4): 909–927.

Coulson-Thomas, C. (2005) Encouraging partnering and collaboration. *Industrial and Commercial Training* 37(4): 179–184.

Dainty, A., Green, S. and Bagihole, B. (2007). *People and Culture in Construction*. New York: Taylor and Francis.

Egan, J. (1998). *Rethinking Construction*. The Report of the Construction Task Force. London: DETR. TSO.

Egan, J. (2002). *Accelerating Change*. London: Rethinking Construction.

Eriksson, P.E. and Westerberg, M. (2011). Effects of cooperative procurement procedures on construction project performance: A conceptual framework. *International Journal of Project Management* 29(2): 197–208.

Fawcett, S.E., Jones, S.L. and Fawcett, A.M. (2012). Supply chain trust: The catalyst for collaboration. *Business Horizons* 55(2): 163–178.

Hackett, M., Robinson, I. and Statham, G. (2007). *The Aqua Group Guide to Procurement, Tendering and Contract Administration*. London: Blackwell Publishing. pp. 116–117.

HM Government (2013). *Construction 2025. Industry Strategy: Government and Industry in Partnership*. London: HM Government. pp. 23–25, 61–71.

Korczynski, M. (1996). The low-trust route to economic development: Inter-firm relations in the UK construction industry in the 1980s and 1990s. *Journal of Management Studies* 33(6): 787–808.

Korczynski, M. (2000). The political economy of trust. *Journal of Management Studies* 37(1): 1–21.

Lann, A., Voordijk, J. and Dewulf, G. (2011). Reducing opportunistic behaviour through a project alliance. *International Journal of Managing Projects in Business* 8(4): 660–679.

Latham, M. (1994). *Constructing the Team.* London: The Stationery Office.

Li P.P. (2008). Toward a geocentric framework of trust: An application to organisational trust. *Management and Organisation Review* 4(3): 413–439.

Maurer, I. (2010). How to build trust in inter-organizational projects: The impact of project staffing and project rewards on the formation of trust, knowledge acquisition and product innovation. *International Journal of Project Management* 28(7): 629–637.

National Audit Office (2001). Modernising Construction. *Report by the Controller and Auditor General HC 87 Session 2000–2001.* London: The Stationery Office. pp. 5–6

Pinto, J.K., Slevin, D.P. and English, B. (2009). Trust in projects: An empirical assessment of owner/contractor relationships. *International Journal of Project Management* 27(6): 638–648.

RICS (2005). An exploration of partnering practice in the relationships between clients and main contractors. *Findings in Built and Rural Environments.* London: RICS Research. pp. 2–3.

Silva, S.C., Bradley, F. and Sousa, C.M.P. (2012). Empirical test of the trust performance link in an international alliances context. *International Business Review* 21(2): 293–306.

Thurairajah, N., Haigh, R. and Amaratunga, R.D.G. (2006). Cultural transformation in construction partnering projects. *Proceedings of the Annual Research Conference of the Royal Institution of Chartered Surveyors,* 7–8 September, University College London.

Walker, A. (2009). *Project Management in Construction.* 5e. Oxford: Blackwell Publishing Ltd. pp. 150–158.

Wong W.K., Cheung S.O., Yiu T.W. and Pang H.Y. (2008). A framework for trust in construction contracting. *International Journal of Project Management* 26(8): 821–829.

4

Analysis for the Lack of Collaborative Working and Partnering in the Built Environment

Collaboration allows us to know more than we are capable of knowing by ourselves.

4.1 Introduction

This chapter of the book is largely based on the research study by Challender *et al.* (2014) which focused on collaborative construction procurement strategies. It focuses on the lack of collaborative working and partnering in the built environment and specifically around the wide-ranging consensus that potential barriers in the construction industry could have hindered the success of companies in that industry. For this reason, these barriers are examined; they include fear of the unknown, perceived loss of control, uncertainty, and the lack of understanding of how to change the way one works. The chapter then discusses the downward trend in the popularity of and participation in collaborative working practices, a development that was heralded as a breakthrough in construction management, and a return to traditional procurement based on lowest cost tenders. Following on from this, it attempts to highlight the consequences ofthis downward trend by presenting evidence of low levels of client satisfaction, owing mostly to poor cost and time predictability, which have in turn been attributed to a low level of trust between clients and practitioners. Furthermore, it examines reports that clients may be feeling the only way to assure themselves that they are not paying too much is to market test their projects in a highly competitive environment.

The chapter then moves on to identify risks associated with unethical practices under partnering arrangements, and occasions where there is an abuse of power by clients toward main contractors, or main contractors toward their supply chain. Such cases of inequitable working arrangements, which give little or no benefit to partnered organisations, are discussed alongside why, in some cases, organisations have suffered financially. In this sense, the disparity of power between clients and other organisations is analysed, as well as how some clients have used the power derived from scarcity of work in times of economic uncertainty. This includes how some employers can use a 'take it or leave it' approach to bully contractors into accepting unfair contract terms. Such exploitation through partnering frameworks is discussed and how this may present an unwelcome risk for this

The Smart Estate, First Edition. Edited by Jason Challender/Henry Oti.
© 2024 John Wiley & Sons, Ltd. Published 2024 by John Wiley & Sons, Ltd.

partnering procurement option, reducing its attractiveness and contributing to a reduction in willing partners.

The chapter examines how partnering and collaborative working have been influenced in the past by austerity and economic uncertainty, which was certainly the case during the recession in the UK during 2008–2012 and the COVID-19 pandemic between 2021 and 2022. Thereafter, it considers why there is sometimes suspicion and scepticism of realisable benefits from partnering and collaborative working, with reference to case studies. Cases are discussed where partnering projects were open to abuse owing to the scale of the commercial interests involved, and did not gain successful outcomes, leaving clients feeling that they paid too much for their products. For these reasons, the chapter articulates why collaborative procurement may be perceived as a risky alternative to traditional competitive tendering and, logically, unlikely to be launched by clients as a new initiative in austere times or where there is economic uncertainty. Finally, it discusses the measures that can be introduced for partnering to succeed in the future. These include narrative around the development of trust, which could be considered as crucial in this regard, and initiatives, such as building information modelling (BIM), which could 'keep the collaborative procurement flag flying'.

4.2 Context for the Lack of Collaborative Working and Partnering

Despite the arguments in support of collaborative procurement strategies, as referred to in previous chapters of the book, such approaches have attracted their critics. There are, for instance, views that partnering practices within the UK construction industry have failed to realise the full extent of benefits and positive effects that they have experienced in other sectors, such as manufacturing (Miller *et al.*, 2002; Morgan, 2009; Bygballe *et al.*, 2010). This position was reiterated by Gadde and Dubois (2010) who stated simply that 'partnering has not lived up to expectations'. Perhaps this could partly explain the reported downward trend in the popularity of, and participation in, what was heralded as a major breakthrough in construction management and a return to traditional procurement based on lowest cost tenders (RICS, 2012).

There is a wide-ranging consensus that potential barriers in the construction industry could have hindered successful partnering. These barriers include fear of the unknown, perceived loss of control, uncertainty, and the lack of understanding of how to change the way one works (Thurairajah *et al.*, 2006). Within the context of these potential barriers, some advocates of partnering may be displaying acted behaviours to collaborative working but ultimately behaving consistently with their true beliefs. Accordingly, they may be only 'paying lip service to the principles of partnering' (Gadde and Dubois, 2010). Certainly, Boes and Doree (2013) corroborated this view, and their findings indicate that partnering can frequently be classified as superficial and be used to disguise traditional adversarial power relationships and attitudes. There is, however, a careful balance required in and around these arguments, rather like competitiveness versus cooperation, with respect to how construction-related organisations behave and this balance is linked very much to predictability and confidence in the other party brought about by trust (Cheung *et al.*,

2001). Perhaps the aforementioned attitudes and behaviours demonstrate that partnering principles and philosophies are still not being fully embraced by the built environment in the UK.

Over recent years, organisations have largely focused on increasing partnering strategies for collaborative procurement of major capital projects. Such initiatives are often heralded as vehicles to obtain best value, improve levels of quality, and optimise service delivery. Yet there is still evidence of low levels of client satisfaction, owing mostly to poor cost and time predictability, which have in turn been attributed to a low level of trust in practice (Kumaraswamy and Mathews, 2000; Kumaraswamy et al., 2005; Chow et al., 2012). This potential lack of trust in collaborative working practices, alongside the general recent 'tightening' of the market, could explain the downward trend in favour of more market-based approaches to construction procurement (Ross, 2011).

The UK Government's Construction 2025 report (HM Government, 2013) and the Construction Products Association (HM Government, 2010) both highlighted a growing need for increased collaboration, integration, and trust across the industry in order to pursue greater efficiencies. Notwithstanding these measures and the perceived benefits for construction clients, consultants, and contractors, partnering and other collaborative strategies have not always achieved their expected outcomes. This may have resulted from poor stakeholder commitment to partnering arrangements grounded in a lack of trust which damages the interests of the whole supply chain (Challender et al., 2014). This lack of trust, according to Larson (1997), has emerged from the highly competitive nature of the UK construction industry where commercial considerations and opportunities have prevailed over partnering philosophies. Examples include clients adopting strategies of bullying contractors to gain lowest price tenders and main contractors deliberately slowing construction progress to force clients into instructing costly acceleration programmes (Korczynski, 1996). This has led, in some cases, to deep-seated adversarial practices and behaviours. Wong et al. (2008) supported this argument and articulated that 'trust appears to be a stranger in construction contracting where confrontation remains the prevalent environment'. Such lack of trust could therefore explain the downward trend in collaborative working practices in recent years as identified by the RICS (2012), in favour of more market-based approaches to contractor procurement. Initiatives designed to encourage partnering have also suffered from 'collaborative inertia' due to lack of trust, guidance, support, and understanding (Challender et al., 2014).

4.3 Possible Move from Partnering Philosophies Back to Traditional Procurement Practices

Collaborative working through partnering arrangements has been spearheading the introduction of such efficiencies on capital projects to lower costs, achieve earlier completion dates, and increase quality. Other benefits for clients, contractors, and consultants include greater innovation and cooperation brought about through the integration of design and construction. Despite authoritative calls for such partnering practices there has been a growing trend over recent years for organisations to move back to traditional procurement routes. There have been reports that clients may be feeling the only way to assure themselves that they are not paying too much is to market test their projects in a highly competitive environment. Organisations have been feeling vulnerable to partnering and have been reluctant to take unnecessary perceived risks. The main barriers and challenges for partnering have emerged from a general lack of trust between partners. These have been reportedly brought about through cases of inequitable working relationships, opportunism, lack of commitment, and adversarial behaviours. In recent years, there have also been reports of scepticism by some practitioners within the construction industry about the realisable benefits of partnering arrangements. Furthermore, the 'one-off' and short-term, project-based nature of the construction industry has hindered the development of trust through good working relationships and repeat business.

Despite the perceived advantages, collaborative working practices within the construction industry are still relatively rare (RICS, 2007) and appear to have become more so during times of austerity. The RICS Contracts in Use Survey (RICS, 2012) found that partnering contracts during 2010 accounted for only 0.9% of all contracts by value, compared with 6.6% in 2004 and 15.6% in 2007, a trend which could be attributed to the recent UK economic crisis. It is perceived by some clients that open and competitive procurement systems, that truly market test prices, are the only way to assure stakeholders of the lowest possible initial capital cost (Ross, 2011); and in this economic context 'partnering has not lived up to expectations' (Gadde and Dubois 2010).

4.4 Opportunities for Unethical Practices under Partnering Arrangements

When partnering is used, there may on occasion be an abuse of power by clients towards main contractors, or main contractors toward their supply chain – that abuse is to 'squeeze too hard' (National Audit Office, 2001). In times of austerity and during the COVID-19 pandemic the desire to squeeze became a necessity, challenging the benefits of the partnering relationship. Indeed, one of the most prolific barriers to increased collaboration could be psychological, whereby clients seek to prolong strategies associated with market leverage and power to disadvantage their 'partners' (RICS, 2005). This view could also apply to the relationships between main contractors and subcontractors, where 'buyers' dictate to 'sellers' the terms of their employment and what is required of them (Mathews *et al.*, 2003). Partnering, at times, could also become superficial where organisations and individuals 'pay lip service' to its values and principles and frequently use it to disguise traditional adversarial power relationships and attitudes (Boes and Doree, 2013).

The concept of integrated teams and partnering has been tainted in the past by inequitable working arrangements. This can result in giving little or no benefit to partnered organisations and, in some cases, anecdotal evidence has been presented of organisations that suffered financially (Challender *et al.*, 2014). Such 'ghost stories' could reinforce fears and anxieties over risks within the industry and promote a reluctance to move away from traditional working methods. Arguably, the disparity of power between clients and other organisations may have allowed the former to use the power, derived from scarcity of work elsewhere in the economy, to adopt a 'take it or leave it approach' to 'bully' contractors into accepting unfair contract terms under the banner of a collaborative arrangement. The temptation to abuse power to secure gains at the expense of others has become too much to resist. Such a shift in philosophy during operational partnering frameworks, can render organisations highly vulnerable to exploitation as they are virtually held to ransom; they may be forced to accept revised or reduced terms, or be cast back into 'the other' competitive cut-throat marketplace. Such exploitation through partnering frameworks may increase the risk of this procurement option, reducing its attractiveness and contributing to a reduction in willing partners.

4.5   The Influence of Economic Uncertainty on Partnering and Collaborative Working

There is a concern that sharing of knowledge results in loss of knowledge, adding to general uncertainty (Thurairajah *et al.*, 2006; Challender *et al.*, 2013). Such managerial uncertainty is unlikely to encourage new collaborative working arrangements, especially during a time of economic doubt and austerity, which could signal a return to familiar traditional procurement systems. It is unlikely that any economic downturn could provide a suitable context for such paradigm shifts toward relatively untested practice (Beach *et al.*, 2005; RICS, 2012). Conversely, there is an argument that during times of uncertainty, when there are increased time, competition, and cost pressures, organisations working closer together can benefit from shared knowledge and achieve higher performance levels (Wu and Udeaja, 2008). Furthermore, it is widely accepted that the benefits of partnering become apparent in long-term and multiple projects. Notwithstanding this, the constraints and challenges for many clients to provide a continuous supply of work during times of economic uncertainty could make partnering a problematic aspiration, as clients are forced to limit themselves to mere single-project awards (Mason, 2006).

When the economic climate puts financial strain on many construction organisations the management of cash flow and financial accounting becomes ever more focused, and short-term commercial interests override the principles and perceived benefits of partnering (Morgan, 2009; RICS 2012). A continued reliance on experience and the familiar provides comfort for some clients, where competitive tendering and traditional procurement based on lowest costs has been the norm for many years (Mason, 2006). Clearly, this could result in false economies for clients as the supply side will be looking for claims and variations to make up for what was not in the tender (Wolstenholme, 2009).

Austerity, as experienced in the UK during the last recession between 2009–2013, has stymied resources within some organisations and investment in continuing professional development (CPD), training programmes, and systems designed for integration with other partnering organisations has significantly reduced, restricting the development of collaborative processes (Dainty *et al.*, 2001; Challender *et al.*, 2013). This was felt most in the context of building information modelling (BIM), which requires investment in technology and participation in new systems to support collaborative project teams. For collaborative practices to succeed, a cultural shift is required, and BIM has been put forward as the necessary catalyst (Challender *et al.*, 2013). The advent of digital technologies, including BIM, for assisting collaborative working strategies will be discussed in later chapters of this book. Furthermore, during the last recession in the UK, austerity influenced personal relationships, as individuals focused on their own situations, rather than wider organisational concerns, reflecting growing uncertainty (Thurairajah *et al.*, 2006).

4.6 Suspicion and Scepticism of Realisable Benefits from Partnering and Collaborative Working

Notwithstanding the advantages of partnering and collaborative working as articulated in earlier chapters, collaborative procurement has also attracted its critics. In this regard, the RICS reported that successful experiences in collaborative procurement 'are largely anecdotal and focus on the experiences of exemplar organisations'. They argued that the focus on success rather than failure had posed an unbalanced view and false impression in terms of the contribution that partnering and collaborative procurement has had within the construction industry, and therefore raised questions around the reliability of reported experiences (RICS, 2005). A similar argument was presented by Morgan (2009), formerly procurement director at BAA, who concluded that, with major capital projects, procurement routes that promote alliances and partnerships are not always appropriate. Morgan found that partnering projects are often open to abuse owing to the scale of the commercial interests involved, do not guarantee success, and clients may be paying far too much for their products. Perhaps a more controversial augment is presented by Alderman and Ivory (2007) who describe partnering at its worst as 'a disruptive smokescreen behind which to conceal business as usual while at the same time motivating suppliers and contractors to go the extra mile.'

Although partnering potentially creates a less antagonistic and stressful working environment, facilitating better individual performance, and arguably better team and project performance, according to the review of literature, it has sometimes been met with scepticism from construction professionals. Suspicion of realisable benefits has emerged from previous research (Challender *et al.*, 2014). For example, cost savings for clients from collaborative working are perceived by some of those interviewed as being exaggerated over time. While shared ethos built upon trust between partners is supported theoretically, some practitioners have raised concerns that it is rarely, in their experiences, realised in practice. Furthermore, the research study by Challender *et al.* (2014) revealed negative experiences in sharing information and prompt payment initiatives, leading to organisational mistrust.

The perceived lack of financial benefits or incentives to move toward integrated teams and collaborative practices appears to have grown in influence, especially during the COVID-19 pandemic. A short-term focus remained for those not tempted by partnering strategies during this period of economic uncertainty, or has returned to those who embarked on collaborative strategies. In some cases, this led to parties favouring contract awards through the lowest bid price, rather than exploring other criteria which may enable the development of long-term collaborative relationships.

A 'culture' of trust allows projects to move forward effectively and creates an environment where problems can be shared and therefore solved more easily. Notwithstanding this, where trust is lost, working relationships can become untenable. However, trust is not something that can be engineered through contractual conditions, or procurement routes alone, but needs to be developed, built up, and earned over time. The return to short-term contracts and the constant quest for lowest initial bid price perhaps inhibits the development of trust between organisations. However, where long-term organisational collaboration is a potential future work-stream, the development of trust within such relationships may become 'incentivised' and consequently active in practice. Strategic, rather than project, partnering may be more desirable, especially on a cluster of many projects of short duration. It is therefore suggested that trust can be generated within encouraging contexts, where the developmental nature of this collaborative process aligns with the long-term vision of integrated teams. Potential long-term work in times of austerity needs to promote the development of personal relationships and integrated teams to support collaborative working.

The importance of trust was also found to be influenced by organisational position within the wider project team, and design team–client relationships were considered to be potentially more important than client–contractor relationships. Abuse of trust, depending on position within the project hierarchy, can lead to abuse of practice, with reports that client and design team changes are expected to be absorbed within budgets in 'the spirit of collaborative arrangements'. This is another perspective to be considered in the challenges of partnering and collaborative working.

Some have been critical of the development and employment of trust within the wider organisational context. Either positively or negatively, communications, commitment, confidence, teamwork, and the personalities of individual team members have been found to be important elements in the building of trust in organisational operations, as suggested by Walker (2009).

4.7 The Effects of a Downturn in the Economic Climate on Partnering and Collaborative Working

In times of austerity, such as experienced in the UK during the recession of 2008–2013 or economic uncertainty brought about by the COVID-19 pandemic, there is much insecurity and individuals and organisations may feel it is not the right time to be engaging in new practices that are, relatively speaking, still not properly tested. In these instances, there is a fear of the unknown and individuals and organisations may not be prepared to take the associated risks. Job security and 'playing safe' may therefore override the adoption of collaborative working practices. Findings from the research study by Challender *et al.* (2014) confirmed the importance of trust, especially within the context of austerity, may also be affecting institutions as well as companies and individuals within the construction sector. One example of this could be that professional bodies may feel threatened if they engage with initiatives designed to enhance integration across professional boundaries. Possible motives for this reluctance to collaborate could emanate from a perceived threat that competitive advantage for their members could be diluted.

The research findings from Challender *et al.* (2014) supported the academic view (adopted from Beach *et al.*, 2005; Oyegoke *et al.*, 2009; Wolstenholme, 2009; Challender *et al.*, 2013) that professional development, education and training, operational and cultural change, and commitment are vital for future continual improvement in partnering practices. Notwithstanding this, the financial strain could in practice affect the affordability of such initiatives and consequently the deployment of the necessary resources. This is consistent with the findings of Dainty *et al.*, (2001) which suggested that there is sometimes reluctance from organisations and individuals to expend time and resources in developing collaborative relationships, especially when affordability is an issue.

Any downturn in the economic climate of a country could affect the trust element in collaborative procurement, potentially undermining collaboration from several positions. From the perspective of individuals, job security could become paramount, influencing choices made within work practices and leading to possible reluctance to take risks. From an organisational perspective, collaborative working may become a less attractive prospect in uncertain economic times. Long-stated, sceptical arguments against partnering could, in such an economic climate, gain credibility as tales may emerge of abuse in organisational relationships and the trust on which they are based. A return to traditional competitive practices in such cases could be driven by perceptions that partnering is expensive; there is a need to assure the lowest possible price at bid stage.

In times of austerity, there is a perception that the economic climate could incentivise some to deploy market leverage to achieve lowest price tenders and that, accordingly, long-term best value may have become less important. If this perception is correct, it not only hinders but also potentially abuses the development of collaborative working. Clients in this climate may try to 'squeeze' contractors, and, in response, contractors may seek profit through commercial claims and variations in the supply chain. A possible return to traditional practices may offer psychological security and could focus on what arguably matters most in austere times–money. Yet this is a very short-term perspective, and a lack of investment in collaborative training and innovations, such as building information modelling (BIM), could result in missing a major technological shift in practice.

Collaborative procurement may be perceived as a risky alternative to traditional competitive tendering and, logically, unlikely to be launched by clients as a new initiative in austere times or where there is economic uncertainty. Many clients who have previously practised collaboration may consider reverting to market testing through open and competitive traditional bidding, such as was the case in the UK during the COVID-19 pandemic. Accordingly, it is possible that the market share of collaborative procurement systems, based on trust, could fall further into decline. For partnering to succeed it certainly needs all the help it can get, and the development of trust could be considered crucial in this regard. However, BIM may be the initiative that 'keeps the collaborative procurement flag flying'. Other ways forward for industry to develop trust and break down traditional adversarial barriers are: (i) informal networking and social events: (ii) in-house, project-based continuing professional development (CPD); (iii) informal team workshops; (iv) improved understanding at board level of the value of collaborative trust in partnering; and (v) organisational and interorganisational restructuring to improve communication and cooperation.

4.8 Summary

Over recent years, organisations have largely focused on increasing partnering strategies for collaborative procurement of major capital projects. Such initiatives have often been heralded as vehicles to obtain best value, improve levels of quality, and optimise service delivery, as has been articulated in earlier chapters of this book. Notwithstanding this premise, such approaches have attracted their critics. There remains evidence of low levels of client satisfaction, owing mostly to poor cost and time predictability, which have in turn been attributed to a low level of trust in practice. Views have been presented in this chapter that partnering practices within the UK construction industry have failed to realise the full extent of benefits and positive effects that have been experienced in other sectors, such as manufacturing. In addition, there is a wide-ranging consensus that potential barriers in the construction industry could have hindered successful partnering: these barriers include fear of the unknown, perceived loss of control, uncertainty, and the lack of understanding of how to change the way one works. Within the context of these potential barriers, there have been reports that some advocates of partnering may be displaying acted behaviours to collaborative working but ultimately behaving consistently with their true beliefs, which only 'pay lip service' to partnering.

A lack of trust has emerged from the highly competitive nature of the UK construction industry, where commercial considerations and opportunities have prevailed over partnering philosophies. Despite authoritative calls for such partnering practices there has been a growing trend over recent years for organisations to move back to traditional procurement routes. There have been reports that clients may be feeling the only way to assure themselves that they are not paying too much is to market test their projects in a highly competitive environment. Organisations have been feeling vulnerable to partnering and reluctant to take unnecessary perceived risks. Furthermore, the 'one-off' and short-term, project-based nature of the construction industry has hindered the development of trust through good working relationships and repeat business.

When partnering is used, there may on occasion be an abuse of power by clients toward main contractors, or main contractors toward their supply chain–that is to 'squeeze too hard'. In times of austerity and during the COVID-19 pandemic, the desire to squeeze became a necessity, challenging the benefits of the partnering relationship. Indeed, one of the most prolific barriers to increased collaboration could be psychological, whereby clients seek to prolong strategies associated with market leverage and power to disadvantage their 'partners'. The concept of integrated teams and partnering has been tainted in the past by inequitable working arrangements. This can result in giving little or no benefit to partnered organisations and, in some cases, anecdotal evidence has been presented of organisations that have suffered financially. In addition, any exploitation through partnering frameworks may increase the risk of this procurement option, reducing its attractiveness and contributing to a reduction in willing partners.

When the economic climate puts financial strain on many construction organisations, the management of cash flow and financial accounting becomes ever more focused, and short-term commercial interests override the principles and perceived benefits of partnering. Suspicion of realisable benefits has emerged from previous research (Challender *et al.*, 2014). For example, cost savings for clients from collaborative working are perceived by some as being exaggerated over time. Other reports have revealed negative experiences in sharing information and prompt payment initiatives, leading to organisational mistrust.

In times of austerity, such as experienced in the UK during the recession of 2008–2012 or the economic uncertainty brought about by the COVID-19 pandemic, job security and 'playing safe' may therefore override the adoption of collaborative working practices. Furthermore, there is sometimes reluctance from organisations and individuals to expend time and resources in developing collaborative relationships, especially when affordability is an issue. Finally, to overcome some of these issues, professional development, education and training, operational and cultural change, and commitment are considered vital for future continual improvement in partnering practices.

References

Alderman, N. and Ivory, C. (2007). Partnering in major contracts: Paradox and metaphor. *International Journal of Project Management* 25(4): 386–393.

Beach, R., Webster, M. and Campbell, K.M. (2005). An evaluation of partnership development in the construction industry. *International Journal of Project Management* 23(8): 611–621.

Boes, H. and Doree, A. (2013). Public procurement at local level in the Netherlands: Towards a better client–contractor cooperation in a competitive environment. In: *Proceedings of the 29th Annual ARCOM Conference*, (eds S.D. Smith and D.D. Ahiaga-Dagbui), 2–4 September 2013, Reading, UK, Association of Researchers in Construction Management, pp. 717–727.

Bygballe, L.E., Jahre, M. and Sward, A. (2010). Partnering relationships in construction: A literature review. *Journal of Purchasing and Supply Management* 16(4): 239–253.

Challender, J., Farrell, P. and Sherratt, F. (2013). Collaborative procurement: An exploration of practice and trust in times of austerity. In: *Proceedings of the 29th Annual ARCOM Conference*, (eds S.D. Smith and D.D. Ahiaga-Dagbui), 2–4 September 2013, Reading, UK, Association of Researchers in Construction Management, pp. 827–836.

Challender, J., Farrell, P. and Sherratt, F. (2014). Partnering in practice: An analysis of collaboration and trust. *Proceedings of the Institution of Civil Engineers: Management, Procurement and Law* 167(6): 255–264.

Cheung S.O., Lam T.I., Leung M.Y. and Wan Y.W. (2001) An analytical hierarchy process based procurement selection method. *Construction Management and Economics* 19(4): 427–437.

Chow P.T., Cheung S.O. and Chan K.Y. (2012). Trust-building in construction contracting: Mechanism and expectation. *International Journal of Project Management* 30(8): 927–937.

Dainty, A., Briscoe, G. and Millet, J. (2001). Subcontractor perspectives on supply chain alliances. *Construction Management and Economics* 19(2): 841–848.

Gadde, L.E. and Dubois, A. (2010). Partnering in the construction industry: Problems and opportunities. *Journal of Purchasing and Supply Management* 16(4): 254–263.

HM Government (2010). Low Carbon Construction Final Report (November 2010). London: HM Government. pp. 52–62, 196–199.

HM Government (2013). *Construction 2025. Industry Strategy: Government and Industry in Partnership*. London: HM Government. pp. 23–25, 61–71.

Korcynski, M. (1996). The low-trust route to economic development: Inter-firm relations in the UK construction industry in the 1980s and 1990s. *Journal of Management Studies* 33(6): 787–808.

Kumaraswamy, M.M. and Mathews, J.D. (2000). Improved subcontractor selection employing partnering practices. *Journal of Management in Engineering* 16(3): 47–57.

Kumaraswamy, M.M., Yean F.Y.L., Rahman, M.M. and Phng S.T. (2005). Constructing relationally integrated teams. *Journal of Construction Engineering and Management* 131(10): 1076–1084.

Larson, E. (1997). Partnering on construction projects: A study of the relationship between partnering activities and project success. *IEEE Transactions on Engineering Management* 44(2): 188–195.

Mason, J. (2006). The views and experiences of specialist contractors on partnering. *Proceedings of the Annual Research Conference of the Royal Institution of Chartered Surveyors*, 7–8 September, University College London.

Mathews, J., Kumaraswamy, M. and Humphreys, P. (2003). Pre-construction project partnering: From adversarial to collaborative relationships. *Supply Chain Management* 8(2): 166–178.

Miller, C., Packham, G. and Thomas, B. (2002). Harmonization between main contractors and subcontractors: A prerequisite for lean construction. *Journal of Construction Research* 3(1): 67–82.

Morgan, S. (2009). The right kind of bribe. *Building Magazine* 9th October 2009, pp. 8–9.

National Audit Office (2001). Modernising Construction. *Report by the Controller and Auditor General HC 87 Session 2000–2001*. London: The Stationery Office. pp. 5–6

Oyegoke, A.S., Dickinson, M., Malik, M.A., McDermott, P. and Rowlinson, S. (2009). Managing projects in construction project procurement routes: An in-depth critique. *International Journal of Business* 2(3): 338–354.

RICS (2005). An exploration of partnering practice in the relationships between clients and main contractors. *Findings in Built and Rural Environments*. London: RICS Research. pp. 2–3.

RICS (2007). *An Exploration of Partnering Practice in the Relationships Between Clients and Main Contractors*. London: Royal Institution of Chartered Surveyors Publications. pp. 26–27.

RICS (2009). *Proceedings of the Construction and Building Conference of the Royal Institution of Chartered Surveyors*. 10–11 September, University of Cape Town.

RICS (2012). *Contracts in Use. A Survey of Building Contracts in Use during 2010*. London: Royal Institution of Chartered Surveyors Publications.

Ross, A. (2011). Supply chain management in an uncertain economic climate: A UK perspective. *Construction Innovation* 11(1): 5–13.

Thurairajah, N., Haigh, R. and Amaratunga, R.D.G. (2006). Cultural transformation in construction partnering projects. *Proceedings of the Annual Research Conference of the Royal Institution of Chartered Surveyors*, 7–8 September. University College London.

Walker, A. (2009). *Project Management in Construction*. 5e. Oxford: Blackwell Publishing Ltd. pp. 150–158.

Wolstenholme, A. (2009.) *Never Waste a Good Crisis: A Review of Progress since Rethinking Construction and Thought for our Future*. London: Constructing Excellence in the Built Environment.

Wong W.K., Cheung S.O., Yiu T.W. and Pang H.Y. (2008). A framework for trust in construction contracting. *International Journal of Project Management* 26(8): 821–829.

Wu S. and Udeaja, C (2008). Developing a framework for measuring collaborative working and project performance. In: Dainty, A (Ed) *Proceedings of the 24th Annual ARCOM Conference*, (ed. A. Dainty), 1–3 September 2008, Cardiff, UK, Association of Researchers in Construction Management, pp. 983–992.

5

Potential Risks, Problems, and Barriers for Collaborative Working in Estates and the Built Environment

Effectively, change is almost impossible without industry-wide collaboration, cooperation and consensus.

5.1 Introduction

This chapter of the book focuses on identifying and discussing many potential risks, problems, and barriers for collaborative working in estates and the built environment. It looks at the fractious nature of the UK construction industry, based largely on 'one-off' projects and debates whether partnering and collaborative working facilitates the right environment and conditions for trust to prosper.

The potential barriers to collaborative working and partnering are examined alongside the systemic problems and challenges associated with the construction industry. These include the propensity for contracting partners to trust one another in a commercially sensitive industry with large amounts of money at stake. This is especially poignant given the short-term nature of construction projects and the imbalance and abuse of power that frequently exists between clients and their design teams and main contractors. Following on from Chapter 4 there is a reiteration of the specific challenges for partnering and collaborative working in times of economic uncertainty. In such cases, clients as paymasters might not be able to resist the temptation to renegotiate contract terms with their supply chains to their commercial advantage. This type of adversarial behaviour when 'times are tough' is also analysed.

There is a debate on whether strategic partnering, predicated on a programme of redevelopment, rather than project partnering, based on a single project, offers a greater opportunity for successful outcomes. Furthermore, some of the culture and old stereotypes in the built environment are put under the microscope to offer solutions to long-standingl dilemmas in the industry. Finally, the factors which could inhibit trust in partnering are considered and the need to focus 'upstream' on constructs, attributes, and factors which could influence trust in the context of partnering practices.

The Smart Estate, First Edition. Edited by Jason Challender/Henry Oti.
© 2024 John Wiley & Sons, Ltd. Published 2024 by John Wiley & Sons, Ltd.

5.2 Challenges for Developing Trust in Construction Partnering

While the potential benefits of partnering practices have been widely articulated in earlier chapters of this book, ccollaborative working practices have attracted criticism and there is evidence to suggest that there can be barriers to the adoption of partnering. Egan (1998) was among the first to raise issues about partnering. He referred to these potential difficulties in recognising that collaborative procurement is fast becoming a challenging option for contractors, subcontractors, and suppliers and stated that:

> There is already some evidence that it is more demanding than conventional tendering, requiring recognition of interdependence between clients and constructors, open relationships, effective measurement of performance and an ongoing commitment to improvement.

This assertion can be corroborated by the RICS (2005) who outlined that collaborative working practices and partnering 'may be difficult to integrate within a traditionally adversarial environment owing to its reliance on trust' with economic and cultural factors becoming the main barriers to greater participation. Furthermore, some have debated whether such reliance on trust is appropriate where large sums of money are involved and opportunism could emerge (Lann *et al.*, 2011). The other contentious factor is whether the fractious nature of the UK construction industry, based largely on 'one-off' projects, facilitates the right environment and conditions for trust to prosper (Fawcett *et al.*, 2012). This may explain why the UK construction industry has been slow to take on board the concept of trusting behaviours in supply chain management when compared to other sectors such as manufacturing (Akintoye *et al.*, 2000).

The quality of collaboration can be reinforced or weakened, depending on the behaviour, approaches, and attitudes of organisations and individual participants (Kaluarachchi and Jones, 2007), which presents another challenge. In practice, the time that is needed to nurture key relationships is often lacking in construction management procurement systems (Walker, 2009). In addition, the project-based nature of much construction work can be seen as a fundamental barrier to the development of trust in practice, where relationships are often perceived to be short-term, and true collaborative working practices struggle to emerge (Walker, 2009).

Other problems for partnering have emerged on occasions where a perceived abuse of power has occurred (National Audit Office, 2001), as referred to in Chapter 4 of this book, or there has been deployment of market leverage to disadvantage 'partners' (RICS, 2005). Briscoe and Dainty (2005) supported this perspective through development of their 'propensity to trust' theory and in practice this could manifest itself as 'buyers' dictating to 'sellers' the terms of their employment and what is required of them (Mathews *et al.*, 2003). Korczynski (1994) referred to this type of practice, and other forms of opportunism, as the main source of mistrust in the UK construction industry.

5.3   Potential Barriers to Collaborative Working and Partnering

According to Hansen and Nohria (2004) potential barriers to collaboration could result from a variety of factors and some examples of these are shown in Figure 5.1.

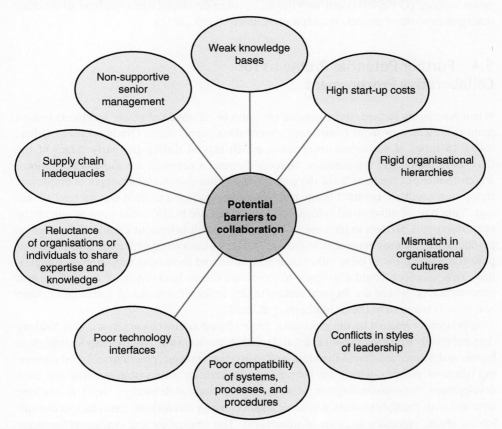

Figure 5.1   Potential barriers to collaboration (adapted from Hansen and Nohria, 2004).

There are clearly problems and challenges for construction partnering, owing to the perceived lack of trust between 'partners' and potential barriers that exist within the construction industry. There are conflicting views on whether trust is appropriate, beneficial, or detrimental and the arguments presented around opportunism highlight the alternative debates that currently exist. In some cases, where trust becomes an issue for project teams, or where they believe there is an imbalance of power, parties may feel that there is a 'loss of control' which can act as a barrier to collaborative working. In such cases, there is a concern that sharing of knowledge results in loss of knowledge, adding to a more general uncertainty

(Thurairajah *et al.* 2006). Such managerial uncertainty is unlikely to encourage new collaborative working arrangements, especially during periods of economic uncertainty where there may be a tendency for parties to return to familiar and trusted traditional procurement systems. Perhaps these concerns over control would not have emerged if trust had been more prevalent. This view is justified on the premise that trust is 'the most important risk-minimisation strategy' (Ceric, 2014) and 'very fragile, but once developed it can outshine all the other strategies in terms of project controls and contracts' (Ceric, 2012).

5.4 Further Potential Problems for Collaborative Procurement

When partnering is used, there may on occasion be an abuse of power by clients toward main contractors, or main contractors toward their supply chain (National Audit Office, 2001). In times of economic uncertainty, which existed during the early stages of the COVID-19 pandemic, the desire to 'squeeze' became a necessity for some organisations, which challenged the benefits of the partnering relationship. Cases emerged of employers trying to renegotiate contract terms with their supply chains to their commercial advantage. This type of adversarial behaviour when 'times are tough' could present one of the most important barriers to increased collaboration. Such behaviour could be classified as psychological, where clients seek to prolong strategies associated with market leverage and power, achieving lowest price rather than best value, and increasing supply chain competition. This approach could also apply to the relationships between main contractors and subcontractors, where the 'buyers' dictate to the 'sellers' the terms of their employment and what is required of them (Mathews *et al.* 2003).

As previously referred to, the short-term, project-based nature of the construction industry does not readily lend itself to partnering and collaborative working. This is clearly an important barrier and companies should therefore look to progress strategic 'programme'-based partnering wherever possible, which has been proven to facilitate relationship building and trust development. Notwithstanding this premise, the sense that collaboration is ideally for the long term and over multiple projects, economic conditions may dictate that clients cannot commit too far ahead, especially in times of uncertainty. The constraints and challenges for many clients make partnering a problematic aspiration, and they are forced to limit themselves to mere single-project awards (Mason 2006).

Reliance on the known and controllable has previously been identified within industry as a symptom of a 'negative culture', one that is sceptical and suspicious of new initiatives. It has been argued that these old behavioural aspects, cultures, and attitudes are so deeply embedded in the construction sector that they are proving difficult to change (Thurairajah *et al.*, 2006). For partnering approaches to be more attractive to clients, they must seek to address problems of cultural indifference, old stereotypes, and the adversarial views of team members, alongside establishing new ways of working (Liu *et al.*, 2004). Yet it is unlikely that any economic uncertainty will provide a suitable context for such paradigm shifts in practice. Indeed, the RICS (2012) have suggested that partnering is not compatible with an economic climate of recession; the most competitive capital cost becomes politically more important than long-term best-value measures.

Research studies have found that some clients commonly fixate on obtaining the most competitive bid price rather than best value (Beach *et al.*, 2005). This may become more profound, especially where a 'bullish' private sector employer may wish to take advantage of the depressed economy to achieve cheaper construction costs, often at the expense of the supply chain. Some would argue that such a practice serves to bully and intimidate contractors into accepting unfair returns under the banner of collaboration (Challender *et al.*, 2013).

5.5 Factors Which Could Inhibit Trust in Partnering

Despite a prolonged government push, via framework initiatives and other interventions designed to raise participation in partnering practices, there still remains little appreciation of the difficulties inherent in the reliance on trust in working collaboratively. Long-stated, sceptical, theoretical arguments against partnering may have gained credibility from what happens in practice, as tales of abuse in organisational relationships and a lack of the trust that should underpin them have been told. The absence of trust certainly appears to be a major obstacle for realising the potential benefits from partnering strategies. In addressing this challenging dilemma, a greater understanding of those trust-building mechanisms that are effective in 'turning the tide' and embedding more trust in partnering is required.

Further research to focus 'upstream' on those constructs, attributes, and factors which could influence trust in the context of partnering practices is therefore recommended. This could identify and evaluate trust 'generators' and 'inhibitors', with the aim of understanding how trust-building initiatives can be designed and implemented to improve public sector procurement strategies.

5.6 Challenging the Philosophy of Collaboration

Collaboration is based on trust, equity, and fairness. A shared ethos between partners is essential for collaborative success, and all these philosophies should be embedded in aligned organisational strategies (Bresnen and Marshall, 2000; Thurairajah *et al.*, 2006). However, while supported theoretically, rarely is there realisation in practice. Some industry practitioners have reported that partnering has been tainted by inequitable working arrangements, which give little or no benefit to partnered organisations.

The disparity of power between clients and other organisations may have allowed the former to take advantage of collaborative arrangements to serve their own organisational needs; arrangements for sharing knowledge, expertise, and information have become significantly one-sided. Some organisations take advantage of austerity to bully partners further down the supply chain; they use the power derived from the scarcity of work elsewhere in the economy to employ a 'take it or leave it' approach. The abuse of power to secure organisational gains at the expense of others has become too much to resist. A shift in philosophy during an operational partnering framework renders organisations highly vulnerable to exploitation as they are virtually held to ransom: they either have to accept revised or reduced terms or be cast back into a cut-throat marketplace. Such exploitation through partnering frameworks increases the risk of this procurement option, reducing its attractiveness and contributing to a reduction in willing partners.

5.7 Collaboration in Practice

Although collaborative working can provide a less antagonistic and stressful working environment, facilitating better individual performance and subsequently better team and project performance, it is still met with scepticism by some practitioners. Suspicion of realisable benefits has emerged in some circles; for example, cost savings for clients from collaborative working are perceived to have become exaggerated over time. Further, partners lower down the supply chain have provided anecdotal evidence of having suffered financially. Such 'ghost stories' reinforce fears and anxieties over risks within the industry and promote a reluctance to move away from traditional working methods.

Indeed, a continued reliance on experience and the familiar can, for some, provide the right environment or 'comfort zone', especially where competitive tendering and traditional procurement have been the norm for many years (Mason, 2006). In periods of insecurity and uncertainty, it may simply not be the right time to implement untested new practices. This fear of the unknown can also relate to the personal uncertainty felt by construction professionals, who are unwilling to take risks. Job security and 'playing safe' in times of austerity may influence procurement practices.

The perceived lack of financial benefits or incentives to move toward collaborative practices appears to have grown in influence over the years. A short-term focus either remains for those not tempted by partnering strategies or has returned to those who embarked on collaborative strategies, favouring contract awards through the lowest bid price, rather than exploring other criteria which may enable the development of long-term collaborative relationships. Initial capital tender costs are seen by some clients as most important, irrespective of the fact that there are many authoritative claims that low bid costs lead to higher final accounts and poor life cycle value. Indeed, as suggested by the RICS (2012) and Morgan (2009), short-term commercial interests override the principles and perceived benefits of partnering. As the economic climate puts financial strain on many construction organisations, the management of cash flow and financial accounting becomes ever more focused.

Other work practices have also been affected by uncertainty in the economy, especially as experienced in the UK between 2020–2023 where inflation and interest rate rises have become a concern for many organisations. The potential for clients to provide a continuous supply of work in difficult times may become more problematic, minimising the implementation of partnering in practice. Resources within organisations could become stymied; investment in continuing professional development (CPD), training programmes, and systems designed for integration with other partnering organisations may significantly reduce, restricting developments toward more collaborative processes. The effects of this may be felt most in the context of building information modelling (BIM), which requires investment in technology and participation in new systems to support collaborative project teams.

For collaborative practices to succeed a cultural shift is required (Thurairajah *et al.*, 2006), and BIM has been put forward as the necessary catalyst. Yet embracing cultural change and engaging in further training, investment, and CPD is presently not high on the agenda. Organisations, and the individuals who work within them, are facing an uncertain future. Industry may not feel the time is right to embark on new initiatives and methods of working practice while insecurity looms large.

5.8 Summary

Despite the benefits of collaborative working practices, identified in the earlier chapters of the book, these practices have attracted criticism. There is evidence to suggest that there can be barriers to the adoption of partnering and that the practices may be difficult to integrate within a traditionally adversarial environment. Another contentious factor is whether the fractious nature of the UK construction industry, based largely on 'one-off' projects, facilitates the right environment and conditions for trust to prosper.

The quality of collaboration can be reinforced or weakened depending on behaviour, where relationships are perceived to be short term and true collaborative working practices struggle to emerge. Other problems for partnering could occur on occasions where an abuse of power has occurred, with 'buyers' dictating to 'sellers' the terms of their employment and what is required of them. In fact, there are many potential adversities for partnering and collaborative working, including:

- poor compatibility of systems, processes, and procedures;
- poor technology interfaces;
- reluctance of organisations or individuals to share expertise and knowledge;
- supply chain inadequacies;
- non-supportive senior management;
- weak knowledge bases;
- high start-up costs;
- rigid organisational hierarchies;
- mismatch in organisational cultures; and
- conflicts in styles of leadership.

Where trust becomes an issue for project teams, or where they believe there is an imbalance of power, some parties may feel that there is a loss of control which can act as a barrier to collaborative working. In such cases, there is a concern that sharing of knowledge results in loss of knowledge, adding to a more general uncertainty. In times of economic uncertainty, which existed during the early stages of the COVID-19 pandemic, the desire to 'squeeze' became a necessity for some organisations which challenged the benefits of the partnering relationship. Cases emerged of employers trying to renegotiate contract terms with their supply chains to their commercial advantage.

For the above reasons, there is evidence that partnering and collaborative working is met with scepticism by some practitioners. Suspicion of realisable benefits has emerged in some circles; for example, cost savings for clients from collaborative working are perceived to have become exaggerated over time. The perceived lack of financial benefits or incentives to move toward collaborative practices has grown in influence over the years.

For collaborative practices to succeed, a cultural shift is required and building information modelling (BIM) has been put forward as the necessary catalyst.

References

Akintoye, A., McIntosh, G. and Fitzgerald, E.(2000). A survey of supply chain collaboration and management in the UK construction industry. *European Journal of Purchasing & Supply Management*, 6(3–4): 159–168.

Beach, R., Webster, M. and Campbell, K.M. (2005). An evaluation of partnership development in the construction industry. *International Journal of Project Management* 23(8): 611–621.

Bresnen, M. and Marshall, N. (2000). Partnering in construction: A critical review of issues, problems and dilemmas. *Construction Management and Economics* 18(2): 229–237.

Briscoe, G. and Dainty, A. (2005). Construction supply chain integration: An elusive goal? *Supply Chain Management: An International Journal* 10(4): 319–326

Ceric, A (2012) Strategies for minimising information asymmetries in construction projects: project managers' perceptions. *Journal of Business Economics and Management*, 13(2): 23–33.

Ceric, A. (2014). Communication risk and trust in construction projects: A framework for interdisciplinary research. In: Raiden, A B and Aboagye-Nimo, E (Eds) *Proceedings of the 30th Annual ARCOM Conference*, (eds A.B. Raiden and E. Aboagye-Nimo), 1–3 September 2014, Portsmouth, UK, Association of Researchers in Construction Management, pp. 835–844.

Challender, J., Farrell, P. and Sherratt, F. (2013). Collaborative procurement: An exploration of practice and trust in times of austerity. In: *Proceedings of the 29th Annual ARCOM Conference*, (eds S.D. Smith and D.D. Ahiaga-Dagbui), 2–4 September 2013, Reading, UK, Association of Researchers in Construction Management, pp. 827–836.

Egan, J. (1998). *Rethinking Construction*. The Report of the Construction Task Force. London: DETR. TSO, pp. 18–20.

Fawcett, S.E., Jones, S.L. and Fawcett, A.M. (2012). Supply chain trust: The catalyst for collaboration. *Business Horizons* 55(2): 163–178.

Hansen, M.T. and Nohria, N. (2004). How to build collaborative advantage, *MIT Sloan Management Review*, 46(1): 22–30.

Kaluarachchi, D.Y. and Jones, K. (2007). Monitoring of a strategic partnering process: The Amphion experience. *Construction Management and Economics* 25(10): 1053–1061.

Korczynski, M. (1994). Low trust and opportunism in action: Evidence on inter-firm relations from the British Engineering Construction Industry. *Journal of Industry Studies* 1(2): 43–64.

Lann, A., Voordijk, J. and Dewulf, G. (2011). Reducing opportunistic behaviour through a project alliance. *International Journal of Managing Projects in Business* 8(4): 660–679.

Liu, A., Fellows, R. and Ng, J. (2004). Surveyors' perspectives on ethics in organisational culture. *Engineering, Construction and Architectural Management* 11(6): 438–449.

Mason, J. (2006). The views and experiences of specialist contractors on partnering. *Proceedings of the Annual Research Conference of the Royal Institution of Chartered Surveyors*, 7–8 September, University College London.

Mathews, J., Kumaraswamy, M. and Humphreys, P. (2003). Pre-construction project partnering: From adversarial to collaborative relationships. *Supply Chain Management* 8(2): 166–178.

Morgan, S. (2009). The right kind of bribe. *Building Magazine 9th October 2009*, pp. 8–9.

National Audit Office (2001). Modernising Construction. *Report by the Controller and Auditor General HC 87 Session 2000–2001*. London: The Stationery Office. pp. 5–6.

RICS (2005). An exploration of partnering practice in the relationships between client and main contractors. *Findings in Built and Rural Environments*. London: RICS Research. pp. 2–3

RICS (2012). *Contracts in Use. A Survey of Building Contracts in Use during 2010*. London: Royal Institution of Chartered Surveyors Publications.

Thurairajah, N., Haigh, R. and Amaratunga, R.D.G. (2006). Cultural transformation in construction partnering projects. *Proceedings of the Annual Research Conference of the Royal Institution of Chartered Surveyors*, 7–8 September. University College London. pp. 5–8.

Walker, A. (2009). *Project Management in Construction*. 5e. Oxford: Blackwell Publishing Ltd.

6

Collaborative Working with Digital Information Management in Estates and Construction

Advances in digital technologies and data are transforming how our economy functions and the way we live our lives.

KPMG, 2021

6.1 Introduction

Collaboration remains a key success factor on projects in the built environment. How collaboration may be achieved varies from one project to another depending on the way the teams in question apply themselves toward mutual goals. The digital tools used by various parties can enhance the levels of collaboration attainable at any time or on any activity in a project. Such collaboration can be horizontal across team members working together at a certain level or it can be vertical along the supply chain network. Whichever is the case, it is important that digital systems used to enhance the discharge of tasks, and as such collaboration, are interoperable and able to seamlessly exchange information. This is particularly important if professional platforms are using proprietary software packages by different vendors. As it is not possible to guarantee seamlessly interoperable systems in all cases among all members of a team, software packages are equipped with features that can allow interaction with open file formats to overcome such bottlenecks. One of the open file formats that has proved beneficial to the built environment is the Industry Foundation Classes (IFC). Such advancements have been achieved due to the need for improvements in digital information management in the built environment.

The subject of digital information management is vast and cuts across different economic and industrial sectors. It is therefore important to adopt an acceptable definition from the perspective of the built environment sector. To provide a background on which the definition can be based, the historical dimension of digital information management is examined in this chapter. The consensus that there is no universally accepted definition is highlighted with emphasis on ensuring the acquisition, processing, and exploitation of valuable information to its maximum potential. The connections of the origin of information management to early IT hardware, such as giant calculators, and progressing to the creation of the World Wide Web is established in the historical account covered. History paved the way for examining standard digital information requirements in connection to the built

The Smart Estate, First Edition. Edited by Jason Challender/Akponanabofa Henry Oti.
© 2024 John Wiley & Sons, Ltd. Published 2024 by John Wiley & Sons, Ltd.

environment, which links up nicely to drill down into trends in the innovations of digital information management. Finally, leading innovations on common data environment (CDE) are identified and discussed.

6.2 Definition and Scope of Digital Information Management in Construction

Before defining digital information management, it is important to understand the term 'information management'. Researchers have argued that the word 'information' has no universally accepted definition other than a consensus suggestion that it is a set of evaluated, validated, or useful data (Meadow *et al.*, 2000; Mitchell, 2000), where data refers to a series of strings in the form of elementary symbols, digits, or letters. Information is not static and changes over time through the processes of accumulation, refinement, total overhauling, or replacement. The efficient and effective management of such a dynamic resource therefore appears daunting, yet key to human development. The built environment is no exception as information management has been pivotal to the stages of development that the construction industry has undergone. As Hicks (2007) suggests, management of information is critical to the efficient and effective development of knowledge-dependent organisations. The built environment and the construction industry are conglomerates of knowledge-dependent organisations that have been operating through time. Like many other industry sectors, information management in the built environment/construction industry helps ensure valuable information is acquired, processed, and exploited to its maximum potential. The scope of information management activity can vary but generally covers the following nine aspects (Hicks, 2007):

- creation
- representation
- organisation
- maintenance
- visualisation
- reuse
- sharing
- communication
- disposal.

A typical information management set up can include all or some of the nine aspects depending on the associated goals or functions of a particular establishment. For example, many establishments, such as schools, construction firms, estate agents, and hospitals, are involved in creating information from their primary functions of dealing with people, improving existing systems, or embarking on various projects. Managing created information may involve aspects of sighting (visualisation) evidence, making hard copies, recording in dedicated mediums, sharing with others within agreed remits, and storing digitally or on shelves. Aspects of disposal within such organisations may involve shredding of hard copy documents to protect personal information and adhering to other legal information privacy requirements. Disposal of information is a lot more technically demanding for digitised (electronic) data contained in hardware, such as computers, which usually require upgrades or replacements due to technology advancements. Disposal may require the support of specialist firms whose main function is destroying (including formatting and complete erasing) all electronic records contained in hardware in the safest way possible. Complete erasing of electronic data is an important aspect of protecting vital information in digital infrastructure and preventing security breaches, especially if hardware is going to be recycled or reused elsewhere (Bergren and Murphy, 2005). Activities within each of these aspects also vary according to tasks and mediums of information dissemination or sharing. For instance, an environmentally friendly way of disposing of information on sheets of paper, widely used even before the advent of computers, is by means of shredding. However, information on digital media (e.g. pen drives or hard drives) can easily be disposed of via 'complete' deletion or by the formatting of the media in question. Clearly, there have been changes in how information is managed over the different eras of human development, influenced by the tools available for processing information. The understanding that the tools used to process information influence how information is managed is crucial to examining the roots of digital information management. In this book, in line with the report by KPMG (2021) commissioned by the Centre for Digital Built Britain (CDBB), we define digital information management as: 'the process by which an organisation collects, structures, stores, uses and shares its data to perform its core business across asset lifecycle activities'.

6.3 The Origin and Development of Digital Information Management

The development of digital information management is closely tied to progress in information technology (IT). Approaching the origins of IT from the aspect of contributions made to technological growth, we examine inventions that have aided the amount of digital data created, shared, and consumed. Giant calculators were among the first tools used to digitally process and manipulate data in the form of numbers, which then extended to airline reservations (Press, 2013). In the history of IT, Press (2013) suggests three interesting events are at the top. The first is John von Neumann's publishing of the First Draft of the EDVAC (Electronic Discrete Variable Automatic Computer) Report in 1945 on the stored programme concept and the blueprint for computer architecture that has shaped today's world. EDVAC, one of the earliest electronic computers, was built by the Moore School of Electrical Engineering, University of Pennsylvania. Bob Metcalfe's invention of the Ethernet at the Xerox Palo Alto Research Center (PARC) in 1973 is the second. The third occurred in 1989 when Tim Berners-Lee proposed the hypertext system creating a foundation for the World Wide Web.

Although there may be a few more milestones in the digital information journey, the focus of activities in the 1980s was on interactions between a person and a computer, clouding the function of the first personal computers (PC) built. From home-related productivity applications, a quantum leap was achieved when work PCs connected via local area networks (LAN) and then later with wide area networks (WAN) for long distance connections. PCs made production, including proliferation and effecting of corrections and distribution of memos, easier than its predecessor, the typewriter. The considerable improvement in data processes and consumption changed the landscape in information management with networking and distributed systems, enterprise applications, and data mining quests. The 1990s saw a big stride in IT applications with the likes of Apple developing complete PCs, Microsoft focusing on operating systems, Intel on processors, Oracle on database management systems, and Cisco on networking (Press, 2013). The invention of the World Wide Web, and it taking root in the 1990s, caused the information management landscape to change, extending information exchange beyond enterprise networks to connecting people in all corners of the globe. The development created demand for new ways to manage and analyse data generated from interactions on the Web. The growth in demand for better information management has continued to drive the information management landscape, giving rise to cloud computing to cope with the volumes, velocity (speed), and variety of data (big data) now generated across the globe. Thus, the information management strides that mark 2010s and beyond are big data management and the Internet of things (IoT), linking huge numbers of monitoring/measurement devices generating digital information.

6.4 Digital Information Management Requirements

The availability and use of quality data, raw or processed, is a precursor for an efficient information management process. Processes of information management are also expected to operate at high standards to avail quality information as intended outputs for organisations to use in drawing insights and achieving value (KPMG, 2021). Effective information management is a function of six factors: accuracy, completeness, validity, timeliness, uniqueness, and consistency (Institute of Asset Management, 2015). Data should be: accurate in all details and be a true record; have the complete attribute values necessary for its intended purpose: valid in conforming to all expected standards; timely in accessibility and up-to-date; unique in identity; and consistent representation across different repositories. These factors are closely related to general requirements in the implementation of information technology (IT) systems. The quality of IT systems is a measure of the extent to which the requirements are satisfied. This makes requirement engineering and analysis an important activity in digital systems development, including aspects of information management.

By definition, systems requirement engineering is the process of discovering the intended purpose (Nuseibeh and Easterbrook, 2000). Generally, it should be: purposeful, with clear objectives to fulfil; appropriate in expression of representations; and truthful in terms of expressing representations (Aouad and Arayici, 2010). Oti and Tizani (2015) suggested six elements as requirements to meet in the implementation of an emerging building information modelling (BIM)-based system (Figure 6.1).

Requirements for system implementation vary from one business process to another. For many systems, requirements can be derived from existing knowledge which needs to be organised for the purpose of clear and adequate description (Robillard *et al.*, 2002). Stakeholders' needs, application domain, and the vision/goal of the system need to be well understood for a good requirement development. Essentially, as depicted in Figure 6.1,

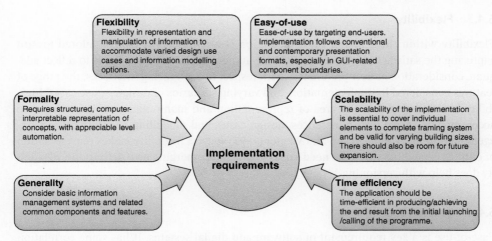

Figure 6.1   Systems implementation requirements (modified after Oti and Tizani, 2015).

fit-for-purpose solutions should be easy-to-use and represent domain concepts appropriately in a generic, formal, and flexible way. The system should also exhibit a good degree of scalability, to an adequate extent, and generate expected results in optimum time. The aspect of generality is associated with representation, reasoning, and versatility in considering task-specific needs. These requirements are considered in more detail in the following sections.

6.4.1   Generality

Generality, in terms of representation, reasoning, and management of information and approaches, is a key requirement to address (Haymaker *et al.*, 2004). The target is that developed systems should be simple enough to understand, as well as being versatile enough when considering task-specific needs. This can relate to the applicability of the system to different situations (Li, 2009).

6.4.2   Formality

It is important that representation of features, processes, information, and concepts observes a formal structure interpretable by computer. The representation should include attributes and functions that allow for a good degree of automation, as necessary. With the emergence of BIM, the extent of formality should support and be able to interact with BIM representation and future extensions/expansions. BIM is based on object-oriented programming principles governed by attributes and rules. Adherence to widely used formal structures of organising data is essential. For example, systems can adopt: object-oriented principles of encapsulation; structured interfaces; and small, simple, and stable interfaces. Minimal programming alterations/additions are essential in minimising the cost of maintenance of a software system (Graham, 1998).

6.4.3 Flexibility

Flexibility within the scope of implementation is a requirement that is tailored toward capturing the satisfaction of a relatively wide audience. This attribute tends to reflect adequate consideration of user preferences with respect to configuring interfaces, the range of features considered in implementation, and varying scenarios of design or use cases. Flexibility is also required in the area of representation and manipulation of information to accommodate varied user preferences, design cases, and modelling or information management options. Van Leeuwen and Wagter (1997) suggest flexibility makes representation of entities extendible when the need arises to integrate emerging new definitions. Flexibility does help with versioning.

6.4.4 Ease-of-Use

Ease-of-use is a key requirement of software and digital systems. It has some correlation with user satisfaction. The implementation of systems may follow conventional and contemporary presentation formats, especially in response to graphical user interface (GUI) and component boundaries. Users should be able to follow the system process through with minimal guidance or reference to manuals. The system should be explicit enough for domain practitioners to understand the logical flow of the system's presentation structure. Ease-of-use is about users being able to understand and be comfortable enough to operate systems without being software programmers or the need to know underlying concepts (Nepal, 2011).

6.4.5 Scalability

The length of time a system stays relevant is a function of its scalability. Scalability in system architectures encourages prolonged usage in design systems (Fahdah, 2008). How much data can a system handle in terms of storage and processing? Is it possible to expand or extend the limits of components or the systems as whole? A scalable system takes these questions into consideration, and it is able to respond positively in demonstrating the required versatility regarding expansion and test of time.

6.4.6 Time Efficiency

Users could be discouraged from running a software system if excessive time is going to be expended in its operation to produce the desired result. An application should be time-efficient in producing/achieving end results from the initial launching/calling of the application. The logical flow of the various components of a system can help users to smartly and easily get through an operation in good time. An efficiently enhanced data input and output system is one of the contributory factors in achieving adequate operation time. The increasing improvement in computing power has been an advantage in this requirement. However, the ingenuity of the programmer in the representation of information in the form of objects, classes, and their associated attributes and governing rules remains key in the time-efficient performance of a system.

6.5   Trends and Innovations in Digital Information Management

In the growth of digital information management, the storage and exchange of data that has been generated remain important determinants of levels of advancement. Storage, on one hand, requires space, which in turn is affected by factors such as the format and quality (pixels) of the data. For example, an image file will occupy more space in JPEG format, usually of a better quality, than PNG format. The information technology (IT) industry has seen steady progress in innovation regarding storage media. In addition to hard drives, floppy disks, and compact discs (CDs) recently, flash drives and external hard drives have been developed. Also, hard drives have now been joined by solid state drives (SSDs) creating room to exploit quicker system response time, portability, and noiseless levels. While earlier media, such as floppy disks and CDs, had restrictions in capacity, innovations have made it possible for contemporary flash and external drives to come in varying capacities and this is yet to be exhausted. Besides storage, these media aid wireless-independent information transfer from one system to another. Using wireless means is a rather more convenient approach to information transfer and requires a network or service. The common approaches in the early 1990s combined the internet and file transfer protocols (FTPs) (Vanier and Rahman, 2004). Such earlier systems could not efficiently cope with the volume, speed, and variety of the exponential growth of data generated in more recent times and these data advancements warranted the development of cloud-based storage systems.

Data exchange, on the other hand, covers the important aspect of how transferred data can be utilised. Factors that come into play are first, how seamlessly have the data been transferred without loss of information, and second, the compatibility of other software packages that will be exploiting the data. In the built environment and estates that thrive on teamwork and a trail of supply chain services, it is inevitable to have specialist software package bespoke to professional fields collaborating on a project. While interoperable exchange of data across software platforms exists, the industry has looked to explore neutral file formats that software platforms can read from to overcome the challenge. An example is the Industry Foundation Classes (IFC) developed by buildingSMART (buildingSMART, 2016). A more advanced approach to collaboration is the exploitation of dynamic internet technology which provides an interactive platform for repository and access of project partners (Germani *et al.*, 2013; Abanda *et al.*, 2018). The platform, contemporarily known as the common data environment (CDE), serves as a central server system for dynamic management of project documents and the interactions of partners. Many commercial applications now exist for deployment on projects in the built environment and estates. Table 6.1 shows a list of some popular CDE packages and their vendors.

Table 6.1

S/N	CDEpackaged	Developer/ Vendor	Key features
1	BIM 360	Autodesk	It aids the users to reduce risk, improve the quality of projects, and enable projects to be delivered on time and within budget. It does this by predicting potential safety hazards, managing quality, automatically doing tasks, and reducing rework needed.
2	PlanGrid	Autodesk	An Autodesk Construction Cloud serving as a mobile unified platform for field collaboration, allowing real-time access to information, providing actionable insights, and improving predictability on job sites. Noted for Supercharge collaboration, streamline work company wide and share data across secure platforms
3	Connect	Trimble	Provides a wide range of tech solutions for each stage in the project. Also provides a full range of tools and content to maintain efficient teamwork. Makes collaboration easy via making connections.
4	ProjectWise	Bentley	Provides foundation in a company's drive to digital delivery. Creates and synchs digital twins during design and mobilises data. Improves design quality and brings context to project – combines engineering with reality data. Reduces project risk and solves any design issues. Uses company's infrastructure schemas, explores analysis options.
5	Procore	Procore	Minimises risk but maintains profit with company's construction management platform. Has products that will simplify work from tendering to close out. Has 24/7 customer support, on-demand training.
6	Bimplus	Allplan	Open BIM-based data and platform for project collaborations. Uses cloud technology across full extent of project and into operation. Can access project data anytime, anywhere. All information efficiently communicated and collaboration with partners in real time. Effortlessly includes project data from construction industry (any). Effectively manages, coordinates, reviews, and merges in a centralised model. Manages and controls BIM-based projects, uses issue management and powerful visualisation tools.
7	Fieldwire	Fieldwire	Coordinates productively, tracks performance, and reduces risk. Provides for general and speciality contractors.
8	OceanBIM	OceanBIM	Drawing, clash, quantity, and phasing management. Data management and connection platform for engineers in OceanBIM cloud application. Allows creation of comments and markups, 3D-model views, and plan submissions. Customisable extraction of materials for variable purposes, clash resolution services, and accelerated cost.

(Continued)

Table 6.1 (*Continued*)

S/N	CDEpackaged	Developer/ Vendor	Key features
9	Asite	Asite	Contract Management from one central location, integrated financial information management on Project Financials software, and simplified on-site project management through Field for Site
10	Bluebeam Revu	Bluebeam	Gives team flexibility to work together from anywhere. Claims to be essential communication tool. Can manage projects on the cloud. Builds better tenders and maintains order of documents. Has three levels: Basics, Core, and Complete.
11	Projectmates	Systemates–Hexagon	Provides access to modules on project planning and design collaboration with pre-built tools to configure reports, execute digital bidding, process submittals, generate and configure punch lists, etc. Assists with streamlining building processes and provides a single source of truth for construction documentation with the aim of improving efficiency and reducing costly errors.
12	StratusVue	StratusVue	A collaboration platform with modules for Project Management, Job Cost Management, Document Management, Bid Management, and managing/linking Closeout, Turnover and Build Data. Therefore, useful for clients, project managers, cost managers, document managers, and bid managers for integrated work delivery, using one system from the design phase, through construction, to operation.
13	Viewpoint	Trimble	A centralised document and information management platform that allows the creation of one version of the truth. Can be used to manage project documents, drawings, and photos, and implement workflows and approvals across wider teams. It is part of Trimble software solutions which allows better management of projects, processes, and people.
14	Newforma	Newforma	Brings everything building professionals need to deliver great projects to one place. Allows tracking and managing of all project information – including emails, drawings, models, contracts, etc. – from a single dashboard. Incorporates Project Information Management (PIM) software category aimed at improving efficient information management, and communication across the project life cycle.
15	Thinkproject	Thinkproject	Flexibility CDE, that can be used to collect, manage, and disseminate all project information. Easily adaptable specialised processes, with smart configurable opportunities and insights for collaborative working. Useful for integrating automatic schedule management, data management, and reporting for civil engineering projects including rail, road, and infrastructure projects.

Popular CDEs used for project coordination.

It is important to emphasise here that the CDE remains an integral part of building information modelling (BIM), one of the contemporary innovations of digitalisation in the built environment. Other innovations in these areas include the following:

- artificial intelligence (AI) and machine learning
- innovative resources and workforce management
- 3D and 4D printing services
- augmented and virtual reality and metaverse
- digital twinning
- truly connected construction and estates
- advanced takeoff and estimating tools.

6.6 Summary

In this chapter, the importance of collaborative digital information management is established in the context of the built environment as a sector that is knowledge management dependent. Collaborative digital information management is central to acquiring, processing, and exploiting information that is valuable to businesses and establishments across various sectors. Digital information management scope can vary but generally encompasses some or all of the nine aspects of creation, representation, organisation, maintenance, visualisation, reuse, sharing, communication, and disposal. Depending on the organisation, the workflow for each of these aspects may vary within an organisation or across organisations. Also, processes have improved over time based on the technologies available to aid inherent tasks. This book adopts the definition of digital information as 'the process by which an organisation collects, structures, stores, uses and shares its data to perform its core business across asset lifecycle activities'. The process described by this definition is built on the advances made in information technology (IT) with origins in the inventions of early hardware like giant calculators to the EDVAC and the launching of the World Wide Web. At centre stage of the development of digital information are the target requirements to meet. Although requirements may vary, stakeholders' needs are key in driving the requirement analysis process of digital applications. The fit-for-purpose factors identified in this book include generality, formality, flexibility, ease-of-use, scalability, and time efficiency. The chapter concludes by examining trends in digital information management looking at collaboration hubs of various common data environment tools and identifying building information modelling (BIM), artificial intelligence (AI), machine learning, and digital twinning as some of the trending innovations.

References

Abanda, F., Mzyece, D., Oti, A. and Manjia, M. (2018). A study of the potential of cloud/mobile bim for the management of construction projects. *Applied System Innovation* 1(2): 9.

Aouad, G. and Arayici, Y. (2010). *Requirements Engineering for Computer Integrated Environments in Construction*. Oxford: Wiley-Blackwell.

Bergren, M.D. and Murphy, E.A. (2005). Data destruction. *The Journal of School Nursing* 21(4): 243–246.

buildingSMART (2016). Home. **https://technical.buildingsmart.org/e** (accessed 31 October 2023).

Fahdah, I. (2008). Distributed IT for integration and communication of engineering information for collaborative building design. PhD thesis. *School of Civil Engineering. University of Nottingham.*

Germani, M., Mandolini, M., Mengoni, M. and Peruzzini, M. (2013). Platform to support dynamic collaborative design processes in virtual enterprises. *International Journal of Computer Integrated Manufacturing* 26(11): 1003–1020.

Graham, I. (1998). *Requirements Engineering and Rapid Development: An Object-Oriented Approach.* Boston, MA: Addison-Wesley Longman.

Haymaker, J., Fischer, M., Kunz, J. and Suter, B. (2004). Engineering test cases to motivate the formalization of an AEC project model as a directed acyclic graph of views and dependencies. *Information Technology in Construction* 9: 419–441.

Hicks, B.J. (2007). Lean information management: Understanding and eliminating waste. *International Journal of Information Management* 27(4): 233–249.

Institute of Asset Management (2015). *Asset Information, Strategy, Standards and Data Management.* Bristol: Institute of Asset Management.

KPMG (2021). The value of information management in the construction and infrastructure sector. A report commissioned by the University of Cambridge's Centre for Digital Built Britain (CDBB).

Li, M. (2009). Diagnosing construction performance by using causal models. PhD thesis. Civil Engineering, University of British Columbia.

Meadow, C., Boyce, B. and Kraft, D. (2000). *Text Information Retrieval Systems.* London: Academic Press.

Mitchell, K. (2000). Knowledge management: The next big thing. *Public Manager* 29(2): 57–60.

Nepal, M.P. (2011). Automated extraction and querying of construction-specific design features from a building information model. PhD thesis. Civil Engineering, Graduate Studies, Unversity of British Columbia.

Nuseibeh, B. and Easterbrook, S. (2000). Requirements engineering: A roadmap. *Proceedings of the Conference on The Future of Software Engineering*, June 04–11. Limerick, Ireland, ACM.

Oti, A.H. and Tizani, W. (2015). BIM extension for the sustainability appraisal of conceptual steel design. *Advanced Engineering Informatics* 29(1): 28–46.

Press, G. (2013). A very short history of information technology (IT). https://www.forbes. com/sites/gilpress/2013/04/08/a-very-short-history-of-information-technology-it/?sh=cf63ca62440b (accessed 3 October 2023).

Robillard, P.N., Kruchten, P. and d'Astous, P. (2002). *Software Engineering Process with the UPEDU.* Boston, MA: Addison-Wesley.

Van Leeuwen, J.P. and Wagter, H. (1997). Architectural design-by-features. *Proceedings of the 7th International Conference on Computer Aided Architectural Design Futures*, Munich, Germany. Dordrecht, Netherlands: Kluwer Academic Publishers.

Vanier, D. and Rahman, S. (2004). MIIP report: Survey on municipal infrastructure assets. *NRC Client Report No. B-5123.2*, National Research Council Canada, Ottawa.

7

Technologies for Collaborative Digital Information Management in Estates and Construction

Real estate is the stage on which life is lived, and its value can be maximized if it is designed to enhance those experiences.

Diane Hoskins, Co-Chief Executive Officer, Gensler, USA.

7.1 Introduction

Chapter 6 concluded by examining the emerging digital technology innovations in digital information management in engineering and construction. Although many of these innovations are applicable in estates operations, there are variations in the way applications are implemented. The reason can be attributed to the peculiar nature of estates operations as being different from other sectors in the built environment. By extension, the nature of estates operations also adds additional complexities and challenges regarding the uptake and diffusion of innovations. In this chapter, we examine these intricacies in the digital transformation of estates.

The chapter commences by examining different technologies that feature in estates. First, the future cities' four interconnected pillars of liveability, sustainability, resilience, and affordability, attributed to the discourse organised by the World Economic Forum, are reviewed. The relationship between the enhancement of well-being and productivity in natural/physical and social environments are juxtaposed with the economic constraints of affordability, as well as the enablers of these pillars. While systems and technologies for facilities can be interconnected, the important aspect of risk accompanying digitalisation, focusing on security, is highlighted in this chapter. Cybersecurity remains essential for all digital infrastructure, whether uptake is at individual, company/institutional, or national levels. The chapter further examines what the uptake of digital technologies in facilities management (FM) and estates is like amid the scarce information available in the literature. Important aspects of actors' uptake and promulgation of relevant policies, as well as their continuous review, are further highlighted in the chapter. The chapter concludes by looking at the Technology Adoption Model used for analysing factors that affect adoption of digital technology applications in estates.

The Smart Estate, First Edition. Edited by Jason Challender/Akponanabofa Henry Oti.
© 2024 John Wiley & Sons, Ltd. Published 2024 by John Wiley & Sons, Ltd.

7.2 Technologies Featuring in the Digital Transformation of Estates

The World Economic Forum (2021) suggested four pillars on which a framework for the future vision of cities and buildings is based. The pillars are liveability, sustainability, resilience, and affordability. Liveability concerns the enhancement of well-being and productivity through healthy living, and high-quality, human-centric development of smart spaces. Sustainability should be embodied in the life cycle of spaces through high-level decarbonisation and efficient utilisation that delivers expected social, environmental, and economic benefits for present and future generations. By implication, spaces should exhibit resilience, delivering similar levels of benefits in mitigating risks and preserving cultural identity, from their creation and into the future. In the contemporary world, affordability is key to the accessibility of the vision and gives place for considerations of equality, diversity, and inclusivity. By the dictates of human rights and equality, future estates should be accessible by all, financially and in terms of the asset standard or quality. Further, five key enablers for the pillars were identified as: (i) digitalisation and innovation; (ii) talent and knowledge; (iii) a value-proof business case; (iv) stakeholder engagement; and (v) a regulatory framework (World Economic Forum, 2021). While these five enablers remain interlinked, the aspect of digitalisation and innovation is of interest in this book because of the theme of its discussions.

Digital transformation for future cities is hinged on advances in technology and digital solutions. Digitalisation and associated innovations make room for the development of smart data-driven systems and autonomous buildings that can dynamically adapt to changes in environmental conditions. Interconnected systems of buildings can also be developed to operate together and improve efficiencies with the right balance in energy use. Such levels of performance are products of innovative design and construction, utilising optimised materials and techniques in assembling elements and components. Innovations in design and construction have the tendency to drive down project costs. It is important to mention that digitalisation does come with security risks, so provisions for protecting processes and products from infringement must be considered. This calls for adequate cybersecurity and privacy arrangements to define ownership of data and streamlining usage according to inherent restriction.

The usage and functions of digital technologies vary across the countless software packages used in estates. Some examples of software platforms are Moxo, Monday.com, Pipedrive, Respacio, and Hippo Video. Selection of a software platform for estates operations depends on the functions and goals of the deploying organisation. Some important features considered in real estates are calendar management, contact management, document management, email marketing, lead management, listing management, and property management (Capterra, 2023). The key elements that determine the level of satisfaction entrenched in these features are the extent of elevated and frictionless human experience, real-time dynamic relationships, data-informed decision-making, on-demand delivery, and technology-enabled actions and processes (Uptech, 2022).

7.3   The Uptake of Digital Technologies in Estates

Like other sectors of the built environment, estates is characterised by a series of operational activities and processes; the day-to-day operation of services, maintenance of building spaces, and the landscape. They involve management of people, products, and services to the satisfaction of a range of customers. Many of these operations can be optimised to various levels of granularity to achieve improvements with the right uptake of digital technologies. However, information on the extent to which digital technologies are used in various sectors of estates is scarce (Pärn *et al.*, 2017). The level of digital transformation regarding uptake of innovative digital technologies will be evident in the degree of diffusion inherent in the sector. Evidence should show how facilities management (FM) policies have integrated digital technology provisions in stipulations, levels of digital literacy, and transformation championed by leadership structures in organisations, and how the FM workforce has embraced digital technologies in daily operations, as well as in their direction of professional development. While these aspects remain the overarching evidence to be noted, in this book we examine the uptake of technologies in line with FM core services: hard services and soft services (Government Property Function, 2022)

7.3.1   Digital Transformation in FM Hard Services

The operation of many FM hard services is technically inclined. It entails the act of maintaining the minimum requirement to ensure assets remain continuously operational, compliant with statutory requirements, and prolong their useful life sustainably (Government Property Function, 2022). The key aspects of hard services include mechanical and electrical maintenance, fabric maintenance, portable appliance testing, and furniture, fixtures, and equipment. There is evidence of a high level of digital transformation associated with the design of mechanical and electrical systems. By nature, FM hard services at field level are instrument-based, encompassing a wide range of meters to check that systems and subsystems are within the stipulated acceptable levels of safe operation. For example, gas or plumbing engineers have various meters for ascertaining parameters such as operating pressure, combustion rates, and flue performance associated with any gas boiler installed on a property. At the basic level, many of these modern instruments are electronic with numeric or graphical displays, but are largely standalone devices with little or no dynamic synchronisation with a digitalised, computer-based network of systems. At best in this basic level, data from such FM hard service activities are entered into spreadsheets as records of completed job routines.

In more sophisticated arrangements, advanced computer-based systems (see Table 7.1), in the form of computerised maintenance management systems (CMMS), computer-aided facilities management (CAFM) tools, building management systems (BMS) and building automation systems (BAS), are exploited to achieve effectiveness and better efficiencies (Parsanezhad and Dimyadi, 2013; Wetzel and Thabet, 2015). The functions of these computer-based systems complement each other and may sometimes overlap owing to the proprietors' goals of cumulative development of versions over the years. Some common tools

Table 7.1

Computer-based systems FM tool	Description of functions	Areas of use
Computerised maintenance management systems (CMMS)	For recording, managing, and communicating day-to-day operations.	• Asset management • Inventory control • Generating service requests • Managing work orders • Resource tracking (time and costs) • Materials use
Computer-aided facilities management (CAFM)	For the integration of computer-aided design (CAD) graphics modules and relational database software to provide various FM tasks such as space management.	• Administering room numbers • Demarcating departments • Ascertaining usable heights • Determining room areas
Integrated workplace management systems (IWMS)	Integrates computer-aided design (CAD) graphics modules and relational database software to provide space management.	• Visitor management • Contact tracing • Desk and room booking/scheduling • Floor planning and move management • IT service desk/ticketing • Mail and deliveries management
Building automation systems (BAS)	For monitoring and controlling facility environments through centralised and interlinked networks of hardware and software to enhance operational performance, safety, and comfort of users.	• Monitoring and controlling room temperatures • Remotely controlling air conditioning/heating • Optimising air condition and operation costs
Building management systems (BMS)	Records, monitors and manages building energy consumption.	• Recording and streaming daily energy consumption rates • Prospects for remote collection of energy use data
Building information modelling (BIM)	Wide range of application with tendencies for extension, expansion, and integrations. A digital representation of physical and functional characteristics of assets or facilities and serves as a shared knowledge resource for decision-making during assets' life cycle.	• Design and construction of assets • Collaboration of teams and parties • For storing and sharing information relating to assets • In asset operation and maintenance activities when integrated

Facilities management (FM) software packages.

include: BigChange, Joblogic, Protean, Asset Panda, Fiix, Infraspeak, and MaintainX. Hardware devices, in the form of thermostats, sensors, and automatic switches associated with computer-based systems, may be mounted on the equipment in question or concealed in the walls, above the ceilings, or under the floors of room spaces. In advanced applications, outputs are transferred through electronic and wireless means to centralised computer systems for real-time monitoring. Despite strides in the deployment of computer-based systems, researchers have stressed that there has been no single tool able to cater for all the diverse requirements in FM (Wetzel and Thabet, 2015). However, building information modelling (BIM) applications have been hailed as possessing the capability to take computer-based systems to a more advanced level (Arayici *et al.*, 2012; Wetzel and Thabet, 2015; Hu *et al.*, 2018).

A well executed BIM process will be able to allow a smooth and easy transfer of data for FM requirements from the planning and concept stages through to design, construction, and handover. Currently, the COBie (Construction Operation and Building Information Exchange) protocol is the channel through which expected FM data transfer requirements are achieved (Hu *et al.*, 2018). COBie has its own international standard specification for implementation. This standardisation is a welcome development expected to enhance the implementation of COBie and its diffusion in the built environment sector. There have been pilot studies (Pishdad-Bozorgi *et al.*, 2018) on using COBie on projects to pass on information to FM teams, albeit not without their challenges relating to interoperability and a lack of completeness of the information entities transferred. Other efforts to integrate BIM in FM have looked at aspects of rule-based safety practices in maintenance and repair works (Wetzel and Thabet, 2015), integrated delivery of intelligent mechanical, electrical, and plumbing (MEP) services using logic chain to respond to operations and maintenance (O&M) tasks and emergencies (Hu *et al.*, 2018), and utilising mobile BIM and 2D barcoding to automate updates of FM services, maintenance works, and transfer of items/materials (Lin *et al.*, 2014). Finally, in a case study of the Mediacity affiliated to the BBC, Arayici *et al.* (2012) demonstrated scenarios of how BIM could be integrated into enhancing both soft and hard FM tasks. While aspects of soft FM tasks will be covered in Section 7.3.2, the hard tasks covered included electrical power systems, supporting BAS with locks and keeping the building secured, design and installation of sprinklers, fitting of windows, and checking completion of works.

7.3.2 Digital Transformation in FM Soft Services

The right efficient combination of FM hard and soft services is a panacea for achieving the satisfaction expected in the use of facilities in the built environment. FM soft services, as focused on here, are concerned with ensuring that the environment where people work and live is clean, secure, and able to encourage productivity (Government Property Function, 2022). Government Property Function (2022) rightly advocates that standards should guide operations in FM soft services to achieve continuous desired improvements, and consistency and quality of services across estates. Examples of FM soft services include cleaning, pest control, landscaping/horticultural services, gritting/snow clearance, waste management, mail room, internal planting, catering and vending, security, reception, and audio-visual services/equipment. These services are rather trickier to digitalise into computer-based systems, even taking into consideration the emerging BIM. As such, there is scarce literature focusing on digital transformation of FM soft services. Soft services FM is highly social and human-oriented and largely a function of the behavioural tendencies of perceptions, responses to issues, background and orientation, and knowledge and understanding of concepts and processes which vary widely in FM staff. As noted by Lin *et al.* (2014), FM staff in such services usually record inspection and soft service results on hard copies and depend on information from checklists, paper specifications, and maintenance reports. Gaps in data capture and entry consequently result in appreciable levels of ineffectiveness and inefficiencies in overall service delivery. The deployment of quick-response (QR) codes and mobile BIM can contribute to overcoming such gaps (Lin *et al.*, 2014).

Among the scarce literature on integrating BIM in FM soft services, the study by Arayici *et al.* (2012) is of further interest. In the Mediacity case study, the integration of BIM in FM soft services was suggested for a series of tasks including office space management (regarding use and furniture arrangements and rearrangements) and cleaning the entire fabric of the building during operational life, aided by information and attributes including the manufacturer's specifications attached to components/elements of the model. The BIM model will need to be highly realistic and incorporate a live/real-time dynamic to be able to keep up with directing and planning the soft services related to reception, security, catering, mail, archiving, cleaning, waste disposal, and recycling. Although there are some useful suggestions for how BIM could be used in FM soft services, these are mostly at concept stage with no actual full-scale implementation evident in the literature. However, with the wide awareness of the benefits of BIM in the FM domain, it should not be too long before full-scale integrations proliferate evidence in the literature.

7.4 Factors Affecting Adoption of Digital Technology Applications in Estates

When it comes to the uptake and diffusion of technology, the systems information concept at the centre of discourse suggested by many researchers (Ma and Liu, 2004; Ullah *et al.*, 2018) is the Technology Acceptance Model (TAM) introduced by Fred Davis in 1989. There are five key components of the model shown in the empirical relationship depicted by Figure 7.1. These components are as follows: (i) perceived usefulness relates to the degree of improvement in a user's job performance; (ii) perceived ease-of-use is associated with a system's usage being free of effort; (iii) the pleasure or accomplishment derived from usage is embodied in a user's attitude toward use; (iv) a user may be influenced toward greater use of the system, thereby affecting their behavioural intention to use it; and (v) acting on this intention becomes evidence of an actual increase in system usage. As noted by Ullah *et al.* (2018), TAM is used to analysing the uptake of information technology (IT) in several fields/disciplines including: supply chain management to investigate operational resources and the theoretical factors of operations; gauge the effects of social networks in agriculture; the failure of IT adoption drivers in small businesses; business adoption of smartphone technology in China; and investigation of the correlation of customer decision-making processes and the use of construction equipment. In information systems, TAM has been used to predict and explain user acceptance of various information technologies, and to explain the determinants of acceptance of computer use by a broad range of end-users and user populations (Patel and Connolly, 2008).

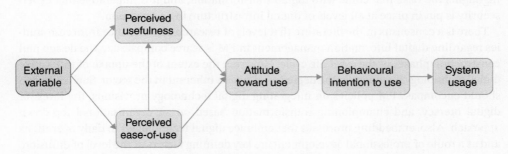

Figure 7.1 The Technology Acceptance Model (Davis *et al.*, 1989).

TAM has been developed into different versions with further detail and in some cases adapted to suit the intended objectives of studies (Chuttur, 2009). Regarding digital technology adoption in estates, the authors choose to examine the subject in line with the global factors considered by Ulla *et al.* (2018). Factors that can significantly influence technology adoption are aggregated into the following seven categories:

- network readiness
- availability of the latest technologies
- individuals using the Internet
- firm-level technology absorption
- capacity for innovation based on adoption capabilities
- successful use of the Internet for business-to-consumer transfer
- government success in Internet and communication technologies (ICT) promotion.

These factors are key and applicable to the estates industry regarding the adoption of smart systems and all aspects of technology uptake.

7.5 Summary

Having examined emerging digital technology innovations in Chapter 6, Chapter 7 focused on reviewing applications in facilities management (FM) and estates. As a result of the peculiar nature of tasks in FM, there is a need to align with job routines in this area of the built environment. The chapter established that there are variations in the way applications are implemented in estates. Based on the vision of future cities, liveability, sustainability, resilience, and affordability are identified as the essential pillars. These pillars are enabled by the five main interlinked factors: digitalisation and innovation; talent and knowledge; a value-proof business case; stakeholder engagement; and a regulatory framework. Among the five, digitalisation and innovation aligns with the theme of this book and covers aspects of smart data-driven systems and autonomous building developments that can dynamically respond to stimuli such as changes in environmental conditions and movements.

Another essential aspect is the achievement of interconnected systems of buildings, taking advantage of technologies such as the Internet of things (IoT), to improve efficiencies and balance energy consumption as well as other performance measures. The chapter also highlights the risks that come with digital transformation, and it is imperative that cybersecurity is put in place at all levels of digital infrastructure in an operation.

There is a consensus in the literature that levels of research and evidence from case studies regarding digital information management in FM is scarce compared to the design and construction phases of the asset life cycle. However, the extent of the uptake of innovative digital technology is evident in the degree of diffusion inherent in the sector. Such diffusion should encompass FM policies on integrating digital technology provisions, the levels of digital literacy, and championing transformation based on an organisational top-down approach. Also, embedding processes that embrace digital technologies in daily operations and as a route of professional development are key defining factors of the level of diffusion. The two core areas of FM, hard services and soft services, have different levels of diffusion in digital transformation due to their disparate associated functions and tasks. By nature in FM hard services, mechanical, electrical, and fabric maintenance are highly instrument/gadget reliant and have a greater tendency for adopting trends in digital information management. However, aspects of FM soft services, such as help desk applications, are moving up the ladder in their level of digital sophistication. Whether FM hard or soft services, the rudimentary elements of perceived usefulness, perceived ease-of-use, attitude toward use, behavioural intention to use, and behavioural change in system usage, as identified in the Technology Acceptance Model (TAM) constitute key influential factors.

References

Arayici, Y., Onyenobi, T. and Egbu, C. (2012). Building information modelling (BIM) for facilities management (FM): The Mediacity case study approach. *International Journal of 3D Information Modelling* 1(1): 55–73.

Capterra (2023). Estate Agency Software. https://www.capterra.co.uk/directory/20049/real-estate-agency/software (accessed 4 October 2023).

Chuttur, M. (2009). Overview of the Technology Acceptance Model: Origins, developments and future directions. *Sprouts: Working Papers on Information Systems* 9(37).

Davis, F.D., Bagozzi, R.P. and Warshaw, P.R. (1989). User acceptance of computer technology: A comparison of two theoretical models. *Management Science* 35(8): 982–1003.

Government Property Function (2022). Facilities Management Standard 001: Management and Services. HM Government.

Hu Z.Z., Tian P.L., Li S.W. and Zhang J.P. (2018). BIM-based integrated delivery technologies for intelligent MEP management in the operation and maintenance phase. *Advances in Engineering Software* 115(6): 1–16.

Lin Y.C., Su Y.C. and Chen Y.P. (2014). Developing mobile BIM/2D barcode-based automated facility management system. *The Scientific World Journal* 2014(4): 374735.

Ma Q. and Liu L. (2004). The Technology Acceptance Model: A meta-analysis of empirical findings. *Journal of Organizational and End User Computing* 16(1): 59–72.

Pärn, E.A., Edwards, D.J. and Sing, M.C. (2017). The building information modelling trajectory in facilities management: A review. *Automation in Construction* 75: 45–55.

Parsanezhad, P. and Dimyadi, J. (2013). Effective facility management and operations via a BIM-based integrated information system. *CIB Facilities Management Conference*, 21–23 May 2014, Copenhagen, Denmark.

Patel, H. and Connolly, R. (2008). Challenges in implementation and promotion of e-government services: A developing country perspective. *Scandinavian Workshop on E-Government 2008*. Copenhagen, Denmark.

Pishdad-Bozorgi, P., Gao X., Eastman, C. and Self, A.P. (2018). Planning and developing facility management-enabled building information model (FM-enabled BIM). *Automation in Construction* 87: 22–38.

Ullah, F., Sepasgozar, S.M. and Wang C. (2018). A systematic review of smart real estate technology: Drivers of, and barriers to, the use of digital disruptive technologies and online platforms. *Sustainability* 10(9): 3142.

Uptech (2022). Digital transformation in real estate: Examples and technologies. https://www.uptech.team/blog/digital-transformation-in-real-estate (accessed 4 October 2023).

Wetzel, E.M. and Thabet, W.Y. (2015). The use of a BIM-based framework to support safe facility management processes. *Automation in Construction* 60: 12–24.

World Economic Forum (2021). *Building a Common Language for Skills at Work: A Global Taxonomy*. World Economic Forum:, Geneva, Switzerland.

8

Infrastructures for Collaborative Digital Information Management for Estates

The built environment is becoming smarter, with the rise of intelligent infrastructure enabled by the use of techniques such as machine learning and artificial intelligence.

KPMG, 2021

8.1 Introduction

In the Chapter 7, applications in facilities management (FM) and estates were examined. The systems examined were considered in a focused perspective looking at individual system performance or local levels of operation. By default, such levels of operation are within certain constraints which may prevent large-scale application and expansion to cope with increasing demands from ever-evolving data variety, volume, and velocity. The solution is to combine systems to form data infrastructure, which is examined in the context of estates in this Chapter 8. The Internet, communication satellites, wi-fi, data centres, cloud computing, and the Internet of things (IoT) are examples of such data infrastructure. How this infrastructure is generally characterised is discussed in this chapter. Also important are the processes in which digital infrastructure are deployed. These processes include FM relating to buildings, people, services, and resources; management of assets in the form of buildings, plants, and equipment; property and space management; flexible workspace and hot-desk management; resource management; and environmental management and control. The chapter also covers tools that aid data acquisition in digital transformation processes, examining the important role of Construction Operation and Building Information Exchange (COBie) and specific energy management tools. Further, best practice cases in using computer-aided facilities management (CAFM), as implemented by a popular vendor in built environment applications, are reviewed to identify lessons.

8.2 Elements of Digital Transformation Infrastructure

Digital transformation, whether organisational or large-scale, involving business at city, regional, and national levels, requires infrastructure in the form of a network of services to enable the functioning of required operations. Common examples are the Internet,

The Smart Estate, First Edition. Edited by Jason Challender/Akponanabofa Henry Oti.
© 2024 John Wiley & Sons, Ltd. Published 2024 by John Wiley & Sons, Ltd.

communication satellites, wi-fi, data centres, cloud computing, and the Internet of things (IoT). Andriushchenko *et al.* (2019) posited that there are four key pillars that have characterised information infrastructure in recent times. These are socialism, mobility, analytics, and clouds. A more detailed delineation of the roles and implications of these pillars is essential for deeper insight, as laid out in Table 8.1. The implementation of service relationships, such as business-to-consumer (B2C) and business-to-business (B2B), are hinged on a combination of these four digital infrastructure pillars. It is essential to emphasise that it takes more than just deploying any one of the pillars, or a combination, for an enterprise or company to become truly digitally transformed. Some redefinition and rebuilding of information infrastructure to align with the contemporary requirements of digitalisation will have to be initiated by that enterprise. Requirements will be defined by external factors such as positive customer experience (Samuels, 2018) and market forces.

Table 8.1 Pillars of digital transformation.

Pillar	Description	Examples
Socialism	The socialism pillar focuses on how the marketing of knowledge and people management matter in a digital space through the improvement of details and personalised offers to customer. It encompasses managing people with intuition, skills, and different levels of competencies. As a pillar, socialism has a direct effect on organisational hierarchy by allowing communication to foster at any level, encouraging a level playing field. An advantage is the ease with which management concepts and principles can spread due to the contagious nature of experience.	In 2022, monthly users were (Barnhart, 2023): • 2.91 billion for Facebook • 2 billion for Instagram • 211 million for Twitter • 810 million for LinkedIn • 431 million for Pinterest • 319 million for Snapchat
Mobility	Mobile technology is now widely used for both personal and corporate communications operations. Almost every adult worthy of employment has a mobile device of some kind. This implies that managing contemporary enterprises is increasingly reliant on the digital need to harness mobile applications to the maximum. The advantage is the exchange and availability of information anywhere, anytime, and in real time. The interconnection of computer devices via the Internet, known as Internet of things (IoT), is important for enabling mobility to attain its full potential. Via the Internet, or other electronic communication networks, smart-enabled devices are able to send and receive data in a range of varieties, volumes, and velocities (big data). Sensors are the key components facilitating the smartness of devices. Well-developed mobile systems can become valuable infrastructure for the service industry with better controlled business process management, workflows, and B2B or B2C collaborations.	Businesses and employees now have a record number of mobile devices which prove invaluable in both personal and corporate transactions. Examples of useful mobile devices include: • phones • tablets • e-readers • personal digital assistant scanners • laptops • cameras with sensors

(Continued)

Table 8.1 Pillars of digital transformation (*Continued*)

Pillar	Description	Examples
Analytics	Data analytics remain the extra step to help make sense of large volumes of unstructured information, big data, streaming across various business enterprises. A welcome scenario will be data analytics applications integrated with enterprise content management or document management systems to provide user-defined flexible outputs to satisfy business objectives. The benefits of such digital infrastructure are now evident from the migration of hard copy paper and file/folder-based documentation processes to digitalisation in computerised electronic devices. Popularly referred to as digital transformation, wholesale adoption by business is required to achieve the full potential capabilities entrenched in digital systems, taking advantage of elements of automation, artificial intelligence, and robotics.	Businesses are getting more dependent on data analytics tools to study existing markets in a more extensive way. Actions on findings go a long way to determine how business can stay relevant in contemporary markets. Data analytics tools may have different areas where they perform better. Haan (2023) suggest the following top tools with specific strengths: • Microsoft Power BI: data visualisation • Tableau: business intelligence • Qlik Sense: machine learning • Looker: data exploration • Klipfolio: instant metrics • Zoho Analytics: robust insights • Domo: streamlining workflows
Clouds	Cloud technology has helped to alleviate the inefficiencies and ineffectiveness associated with managing and storing the increased volume of data from information streaming across networks. Cloud technology is a good companion for social and mobile technologies to cater for huge data management requirements. Sitting on a robust digital system, platforms such as Enterprise Resource Planning are able to explore business intelligence to harness new opportunities, new customers, and new markets. Essential features of interest in cloud management software packages include permission levels, billing, analytical capacity, cost management, demand and supply monitoring, cloud monitoring and performance analysis, service-level agreement management, and workflow approval capability.	Cloud management software packages are numerous in the market. Pricing options can be a one-time license, annual subscription, monthly subscription, or free. Capterra (2022) filtered 478 products including the selected few listed: • Operations Hub – by HubSpot • Google Cloud – by Google • Oracle Cloud Infrastructure – by Oracle • Dell EMC Storage Resource Manager – by Dell EMC • AWS Cost Explorer – by Amazon Web Services • Cisco Cloudlock – by Cisco • IBM WebSphere Application Server – by IBM

In fact, Bonnet *et al.* (2021) in a 2014 report of 'The Nine Elements of Digital Transformation' recommend that companies need to become digital masters to continuously create the required pervasive business advantage. To be digital masters, companies must have both leadership and digital capabilities. While leadership capability will help to envision and champion a profitable systematic organisational change, digital capability will stir and steer the innovative use of contemporary technologies to enhance business processes and products to become more efficient and effective. Digital mastery creates business advantage for companies reducing the risks of falling behind competitors in the market sphere. There have been different levels of value creation in the business environment with the advent of and progress made by a host of technologies including IoT, artificial intelligence (AI), virtual reality, augmented reality, and 5G in the last decade. These applications are embodiments of the current technologies required to usher various economies into the digitally smart future.

8.3 Digital Transformation Processes in Estates

While elements of digital transformation are important, how and where they can be harnessed in the facility and its inherent processes remain relevant in understanding digitalisation in estates. Facilities management (FM) processes are key to maintaining a well-functioning workplace. The main areas with defined activities forming a process are discussed here.

8.3.1 FM in Relation to Buildings, People, Services, and Resources

In many corporate organisations, services such as help desks have been involved in the process of providing necessary advice to customers and other service users to smoothen their experience and improve satisfaction. With increased digitalisation and the use of smart applications, self-service systems have sprung up enabling service users to complete information requirements independently, with little or no guidance from the help desk team. The role of the help desk team is therefore reduced to the task of validating or monitoring data entered by service users. Automation of processes and the use of artificial intelligence (AI) can make the experience of updating of records and creating alerts more rewarding and satisfying to help desk operators, customers, and contractors alike.

8.3.2 Asset Management: Buildings, Plant, and Equipment

Typical business assets include buildings, plants, and equipment. There have been significant technological advancements in the manufacture, creation, construction, operation, and maintenance of assets. Assets are becoming increasingly digitalisation-dependent allowing various degrees of smartness that take advantage of innovative sensor capabilities. It is therefore not out of place to include digital assets under the definition of 'typical business assets'. Digital systems make the operation of associated equipment groups more efficient including capturing information about cost coding and managing repairs and maintenance. BIM applications, radio frequency identification (RFID), barcodes, quick-response (QR) codes, and sensors are useful tools in asset management within estates. Bespoke maintenance planning can explore AI to work out maintenance regimes for systems with more reliable outcomes in the servicing and repair of plants and equipment. Applications can extend to the periodic and whole-life costs of assets.

8.3.3 Property and Space Management

One important function of estates is space planning and management, whether internal or the external surrounding space. Depending on the objectives to be met and functionality to achieve, software packages can be of great assistance in modelling spaces, allowing arrangement and rearrangement of components to compare options when choosing an optimum configuration. Software can deploy different levels of sophistication to simulate security provisions against possible attacks. Also, egress procedure, in case of emergencies such as fire incidents, can be covered in digital simulations.

Other bespoke software packages can be used for moving the positions of desks and equipment to alternative areas or rooms. The measurement and assessment of space utilisation can also be achieved for the purposes of optimisation. It is possible to integrate software packages with computer-aided design (CAD) and building information modelling (BIM) applications for more synchronous analysis of space utilisation. Such integration can extend to human resources (HR) and financial analysis packages to achieve a more holistic output of corporate goals.

8.3.4 Flexible Workspace and Hot-Desk Management

The popularity of flexible and hot-desk approaches to working has continuously increased in corporate organisations. The COVID-19 pandemic, which hit the world in 2019, exacerbated the reliance on such work patterns. Hot-desking has helped organisations manage their facilities in a more effective and efficient way in terms of energy consumption, operating costs, and employee productivity. The viability of the hot-desking approach includes an analysis of the cost of a desk per year or financial period and a comparison of the spaces required with those available. The patterns of work for various employees will also need to be studied vis-à-vis the tasks that need to be performed at a particular time in conjunction with the organisational goals. RFID tags, sensors, and barcodes are useful in setting up systems for abstracting information about holistic work patterns for simulation in hot-desking and flexible working software. Again, the level of sophistication associated with the digital systems deployed by organisations can be of immense benefit to those organisations in keeping on top of flexible workspace management.

8.3.5 Resource Management

Resource management is an essential aspect of FM in estates. Since many businesses are dynamic and entail the operation of systems in the form of services, resource allocation will need to be updated from time to time to balance the varying demands of peak periods and times of less use. For example, in educational facility settings, resources will include office spaces, classrooms, lecture theatres, conference rooms, and car parking for staff, students, and visitors. In many cases, resources are shared and therefore 'scarce'. The solution is to manage available resources optimally, so they are available when needed for different purposes at varying times and for varying durations. Depending on the type of resource being managed, there is a better chance of satisfying an organisation's internal requirements and also its external demands of hire, to generate income as may be applicable.

In any case, two facets of FM exist. These are providing appropriate building space as required by an organisation to carry out its core business and the ongoing management, servicing, and maintenance of the workspace environment in use. Successful resource management should consider these two interwoven facets with the common objective of providing a conducive workplace environment that meets organisational goals comparable to anywhere else (Then, 1999). Depending on the organisation, these two facets can be spread over more functional departments. What is important in any situation is for FM models to identify clear distinction between the facets to allow due representation and for holistic resource management and analysis.

8.3.6 Environmental Management and Control

The goal of these FM processes and activities is to achieve desirable sustainability credentials such as target emissions and footprint information. At the stage of completion of assets and handover, certain levels of sustainability would have been designed into a project. Features such as energy saving electrical elements, including lights and sensors to take advantage of daylight, ingress and egress, and water usage, could be part of the delivery. The use of solar panels to augment energy use can also be considered. The performance of these features and gadgets during the use/operation phase is another important aspect managed by FM in estates. A well-structured digitalised approach will have automated building management systems (BMS) to capture data in real time on performance over time. It is then possible to analyse levels of performance and use the capacities for optimisation purposes. The report of such performance outputs is good for marketing purposes and for creating a desirable image in the public domain. In some cases, data can show external relationships regarding the performance of contractors' response times in mitigation downtimes and the frequencies of components/systems rectifications.

8.4 Aspects and Tools of Data Acquisition Aiding Digital Transformation

The level of dependency of the creation and running of the built environment on technology and hardware is ever-increasing. The associated stages and processes produce a large amount of data which require computer and digital technologies for efficient processing and to produce timely results that users can make sense of. The generation of data for the operation stage starts from the design and construction stages. When the asset is delivered, this vital information is passed on in standard formats to aid the operation of the facilities. The Construction Operation and Building Information Exchange (COBie) data is a recognised format (Pärn *et al.*, 2017) which has been widely discussed but the application is still not extensively used. Data will continue to be generated throughout the lifetime of the asset. Some of the areas for which data is generated include maintenance, in the discharge of core asset functions, occupancy levels, and energy consumption. If standard records are kept, energy consumption remains one the largest sources of data generated in the later stages of the facility. The overall performance of a facility is dependent on a number of factors of which energy consumption is one. An efficient energy consumption system is among the important factors that should be considered in judging the economic value of an asset (Fuerst and McAllister, 2011; Kok and Jennen, 2012; Popescu *et al.*, 2012). Generally, energy-efficient properties cost less to operate and are preferred by clients and tenants, although they may be accompanied by a higher cost to construct or rent. Oti *et al.* (2016) suggested that integrating BMS data from energy consumption in BIM may assist in making sense of records and reduce consumption levels.

Although building management systems (BMS) data may show how much energy is being consumed, additional functionality is required to determine why that much energy is being consumed. The factors that influence total energy consumption, according to Yu *et al.* (2011), include: (i) climate; (ii) building-related characteristics (type, area, orientation, etc.); (iii) building services systems and operation (space cooling/heating, hot water, etc.); (iv) user-related characteristics (user presence/occupancy); and (v) building occupants' behaviour, influenced by social and economic status as well as preferences for indoor environmental quality. While it is possible to model the first four factors into building energy simulation programmes, there are certain limitations with the levels and characteristics of occupants' behaviour. BMS can be used to collate energy data on operational performance. However, it is difficult to accurately capture data regarding occupants' behaviour and its influence on energy consumption, when automating the data collection process. To make better sense of energy consumption levels in building information modelling (BIM) applications, Oti *et al.* (2016) suggested integrating the modelling of these five factors that influence energy consumption into BIM. However, it is difficult to achieve because of the cost of automating data collection in areas like occupancy, and the variability of the rich and detailed data on occupants' behaviour required to make sense of energy consumption levels. An awareness of what tools and systems are available to aid such data collection is important.

Table 8.2 shows building energy consumption modelling tools that can be used to track energy consumption and allow for integration with BIM applications in managing a facility. Conceptual design information, including volumetric and spatial data of assets, is useful input data used by these tools in their respective data gathering and analysis functions. BIM provides a single source of truth by automatically accessing such input data, which can sometimes be provided in popular Green Building XML (gbXML) file formats. Although historical analysis of data may require additional functionality, the integration with BIM can enhance the provision of requisite feedback on performance histories. Usually, entering raw or refined BMS data into these tools for the purposes of analysis and linking such performance data back to a building information model is challenging because of large volume of data involved (Bazjanac, 2003; Bazjanac, 2004; Hand *et al.*, 2008), as is getting the right configuration for the required communication/exchange of energy performance data, in a manner that allows the seamless operation of individual buildings. The adequate

Table 8.2 Facilities and building energy management tools (adapted from Oti *et al.* (2016).

Tool	Functional description
Building energy performance tools for design purposes	
Autodesk Green Building Studio	Cloud-based energy analysis software used for whole-building analysis optimisation of energy consumption and carbon-neutral building designs in early project phases. Functions include whole-building energy analysis, detailed weather data, Energy Star and LEED support, carbon emissions reporting, daylighting, water usage and costs, and natural ventilation potential.
DOE-2	A building energy analysis programme that can predict the energy use and cost for all types of buildings. DOE-2 uses a description of the building layout, construction, operating schedules, conditioning systems (lighting, HVAC, etc.), and utility rates provided by the user, along with weather data, to perform an hourly simulation of the building and to estimate utility bills.
eQUEST	A building energy use analysis tool that allows comparison of building designs and technologies by applying sophisticated building energy use simulation techniques.
BEopt	The BEopt™ (Building Energy Optimisation) software can be used to evaluate residential building designs and identify cost-optimal efficiency. It can be used to analyse both new construction and existing home retrofits. It provides detailed simulation-based analysis based on specific house characteristics such as size, architecture, occupancy, vintage, location, and utility rates.
Facilities management (FM) tools	
ArtrA (Trimble)	ArtrA provides seamless information links between the multiple engineering systems. It enables information to be provided in the relevant format for jobs and has mobile capability for delivering complex data.
Onuma Planning Systems	A web-based BIM tool that can be used for early planning, project programme development, charrettes (BIMStorms), schematic design, connecting to other BIM applications, cost estimating, energy analysis, life cycle costing, FM, and portfolio and programme management.
Autodesk Project Dasher	Project Dasher is a web-based application that helps to augment existing Autodesk® Revit® design models with real-time building submeter and sensor data on electricity and occupancy. It presents a comprehensive framework for monitoring building performance using a visualisation hub where collected data from various sources is intuitively aggregated and presented in 3D to enhance the ability to infer more complex causal relationships pertaining to building performance and overall operational requirements.
QFM	QFM is computer-aided facilities maintenance and management software useful for control and monitoring of a wide range of facilities, assets, and resources. It is a product of Service Works Global (SWG) which helps in streamlining the management of assets, buildings, and maintenance activities to achieve optimum efficiency and rapid return on investment. It is comprehensive with an easy-to-use suite of tools that provide essential insight and critical performance information across an entire building, estate, or portfolio.

consideration of energy design and analysis at early project phases goes a long way in improving the capability of capturing and reporting data generated by an asset, either in the field or during building operation, especially when taking advantage of Internet and cloud services.

The integration of BMS in BIM is developing rapidly and there are a few early examples to examine. Speculation exists in the literature that data acquisition technology (DAT) has been integrated into Onuma Planning Systems (Ozturk *et al.*, 2012). Autodesk Project Dasher is suggested as a BIM and energy consumption integration platform with 3D visualisation capabilities (Ozturk *et al.*, 2012). Autodesk Project Dasher is also demonstrated to be a visualisation tool overlaying energy performance data (Attar *et al.*, 2010; Khan and Hornbæk, 2011). Licences are likely to be costly for Onuma Planning Systems and Autodesk Project Dasher as they are commercial products and dependent on cloud services. Challenges that such energy analysis tools need to address include user targets concerning post-occupancy evaluation, required bespoke reconfigurations, and lack of familiarity with the processes of operations.

8.5 Digital Information Management Cases in Healthcare Facilities

When it comes to digitalisation in the built environment and related activities, best practice examples on concept through design to construction stages appear to dominate the repositories of published materials in circulation. Many case studies dwell on how digital transformation regarding the application of building information modelling (BIM) has improved the design or construction processes (Manning and Messner, 2008; Barlish and Sullivan, 2012; Alshorafa and Ergen, 2021; KPMG, 2021). A few case studies are beginning to crop up for the asset operation phase (Lavy *et al.*, 2019; Kula and Ergen, 2021). For example, at Northumbria University's campus, the value of BIM in enhancing the space management aspect of the facilities management (FM) function was realised from conducting a case study on 32 non-residential buildings. The case study revealed evidence of improvement in the efficiencies of FM work orders and the accuracy of records kept on the geometric information of the assets (Kelly *et al.*, 2013; Kassem *et al.*, 2015). Another interesting example is the case where an integrated BIM–FM platform was deployed and observed for four years on an international airport project for tracking maintainable elements, with lessons on how the integration can be propagated onto other projects (Kula and Ergen, 2021). There are also case studies by Service Works Global, who operate the QFM computerised maintenance management system. The key software packages within QFM include Facility and Maintenance Management featuring the modules Asset Management and Lifecycle, Bookings Management and Self-Service, and Property Management, and Space and Move Management featuring the module Strategic Space Planning. Further, the capability of FM packages, such as QFM, to integrate with BIM tools, as illustrated in Figure 8.1, will help to improve seamless operations in data acquisition, processing, and exchange on the digital transformation journey. Some case studies, courtesy of Service Works Global, are included here to help provide a good insight to what currently existsand the trajectory of future expectations.

Building information can be uploaded into the BIM database tool to form an asset register

Assets that need to be maintained are uploaded into the CAFM tool

Asset information can be bulk uploaded into the CAFM tool

API link enables asset information to be updated in either system for one version of the truth

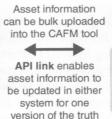

Building information is uploaded via IFC™, Revit™, COBie™ or Excel™

The asset is maintained in the CAFM tool either via the web or mobile app - the 3D web viewer tool allows you to see where the asset is located

Service Works Global, 2023

Figure 8.1 QFM-BIM integration process.

8.5.1 Peterborough Hospital – Computer-Aided Facilities Management (CAFM) System for Service Desk and Hard FM Delivery (Case Study 1)

Case Study 1 Multiplex Europe

Project: To implement an integrated workplace management system (IWMS) to manage the service desk and hard FM service delivery at the new, state-of-the-art Peterborough Hospital.

Objectives: Centralization of reactive and planned maintenance requests to support optimum service delivery.

Results: Centralization of information, visibility of performance and comprehensive, automated PFI concession management.

Service Works Global,2023

(Continued)

Case Study 1 Multiplex Europe (Continued)

A Future-Proof IWMS Solution for a Modern Healthcare Facility

One of the largest PFI (Public Finance Initiative) projects undertaken within the NHS, the £335 million development of the new Peterborough Hospital delivers three NHS Trusts (Peterborough and Stamford Hospitals NHS Foundation Trust, Cambridgeshire and Peterborough Mental Health Trust, and North Peterborough Primary Care Trust) with state-of-the-art facilities designed to meet a wide range of healthcare needs. The hospital has been constructed on the site of the former Edith Cavell Hospital and includes 612 inpatient beds, an emergency care centre, a high-tech diagnostics unit, women and children's unit, cancer unit, specialist rehabilitation unit, renal dialysis and a multidisciplinary training centre.

Whilst the new hospital was being built, interim services were offered via 2 buildings, the Cavell Centre and the City Care Centre. Both facilities were already operational as part of the PFI project. The 102-bed Cavell Centre provides adult acute and psychiatric intensive care, services for older people and patients with learning disabilities, and includes centralized dining, fitness, recreational, and staff facilities. Built on Edith Cavell Hospital site, the first phase of the Cavell Centre opened in November 2008 and the second phase in April 2009. The City Care Centre opened in May 2009 and includes an outpatient diagnostic and treatment centre, rehabilitation services and a children's care centre. Following project completion, the Edith Cavell Hospital site became known as the Edith Cavell Healthcare Campus and the existing Edith Cavell Hospital was demolished.

A Proven IWMS Solution

The scope of the contract includes reactive and planned maintenance for both hard and selected soft services across all hospital buildings. In parallel with the construction of the new hospital, the search began for a new IWMS which could deliver a comprehensive solution to centralize the management of all facilities operations. Maintenance for the previous hospital had been controlled via a legacy system, but the construction of the new PFI hospital demanded a new solution which could handle the inherently complex demands of PFI projects. A shortlist of 5 potential suppliers was identified and following a comprehensive system review process, QFM from Service Works Global was chosen. Martin Payne, Estates Director, Healthcare Projects, at Multiplex explains: "Multiplex is committed to delivering an optimum level of service at the new Peterborough Hospital. It was therefore imperative that we selected a technology partner that understood our needs and could meet the demands of this contract effectively."

> "Through our Australian operation we have collaborated with Service Works on a number of successful PFI projects. This proven experience, combined with Service Works' extensive expertise in delivering software across the healthcare industry provided us with the reassurance that we needed when selecting QFM."

(Continued)

Case Study 1 Multiplex Europe (Continued)
QFM was implemented at Peterborough Hospital in October 2008, initially to manage reactive maintenance requests within the mental health unit at the Cavell Centre. Following a phased roll-out, QFM is now used to centralize and manage reactive and planned maintenance across all operational hospital buildings. The system provides a centralized facilities help desk solution across all sites, allowing staff in any location to log a job via QFM's intuitive interface. Jobs are instantly assigned to the most appropriate in-house or, where applicable, external contractor and closed upon completion. Planned preventative maintenance and health and safety schedules are also managed through the QFM system. Once construction of all three hospital buildings was completed, the Trust's central help desk moved to the main hospital site, and QFM was installed there along with all other infrastructure. **Comprehensive PFI Performance Reporting** With QFM in place, Multiplex are able to effectively manage service delivery. QFM's inbuilt PFI Payment Mechanism functionality has been configured to exactly match the parameters specific to the Peterborough Hospital PFI contract. The performance data needed for the payment mechanism calculation is seamlessly entered into QFM as part of the normal daily help desk workflow activities. Multiplex takes advantage of QFM Event Director, a strategic management tool that delivers real-time event information via a graphical interface. Event Director utilizes traffic light colour coding to highlight deadlines and enable early identification of potentially costly service failures. Events that are approaching their deadline are highlighted in amber and those that are overdue are highlighted in red. Martin Payne comments: "QFM's Event Director is a vital tool for us. It enables us to view critical event progress via one graphical screen and monitor service performance against the contractual PFI service level agreements. Event Director instantly highlights potential failures, allowing us to take remedial action and avoid incurring deduction payments." Comprehensive event reporting enables Multiplex to see at the touch of a button whether events were completed within the required timeframe and if a failed event, details of the deduction incurred. In the occurrence of an overdue event, QFM calculates the service fee quickly and accurately. QFM's PFI reporting capabilities ensure that time sensitive reports can be efficiently produced on demand, giving details of potential and actual performance failures – information that would normally take days or weeks to provide manually. **Future Focus** Multiplex is currently evaluating the possibility of extending their usage of QFM, via QFM Mobile. This will enable the company to deploy the QFM system to field-based staff, allowing the instant dispatch of jobs via a handheld device in real time. Contractors can then update details of the job on their mobile device, reducing administrative load on the help desk and providing a fully integrated help desk, mobile and PFI concession management solution. Since completion, Peterborough Hospital is providing a

(Continued)

Case Study 1 Multiplex Europe (Continued)

truly modern healthcare service for the community. Martin Payne concludes: 'Peterborough Hospital is a key project for Multiplex. We see it as a flagship for future UK contracts and therefore we are keen to be as forward-thinking as possible. Technology plays a vital role in our operations, and QFM is central in supporting optimum levels of service delivery at Peterborough Hospital.'

The beauty of QFM is its ability to mould to meet the unique demands of this comprehensive PFI scheme. The system is robust and flexible and delivers a comprehensive tried and tested solution for facilities management. QFM has provided us with a benchmark for future PFI projects and we look forward to continuing our successful relationship with Service Works during the life cycle of this and other projects.

8.5.2   Implementation of a Comprehensive FM Software Solution for Reactive and Planned Maintenance in an Educational Facility (Case Study 2)

Case Study 2 Calvary Mater Newcastle Hospital

Project: To implement a comprehensive integrated workplace management solution to manage a prestigious PPP contract.

Objectives: To tightly monitor and manage performance utilising 870 KPIs.

Results: A centralised help desk solution offering multi-site and multiservice functionality with integrated performance management and automated abatement calculations, ensuring high levels of service, and time and cost savings.

Service Works Global.2023

(Continued)

Case Study 2 Calvary Mater Newcastle Hospital (Continued)

Providing Healthcare Excellence

The Calvary Mater Newcastle Hospital was the first hospital in New South Wales (NSW) to be built, maintained, and operated by the private sector under a 28-year PPP arrangement between the NSW Government and private sector consortium partner Novacare, a special purpose company for the Calvary Mater Hospital PPP contract. Novacare comprised four companies; Westpac Banking, as equity investor and financier, Abigroup, the design and construction contractor, Honeywell the hard and Medirest, the soft facilities management contractiors. This project was a major undertaking and has been delivered in three phases involving the construction of new hospital buildings, refurbishment of the existing building and transfer of local mental health services onto the site.

The result is a wonderful achievement. The hospital has now increased its occupancy from 196 to 300 beds, has 3 new operating theatres, a day surgery unit and new Intensive Care and Coronary Care Units. With the addition of a new chemotherapy suite, it has also become the largest provider of radiation oncology services in NSW. The Department of Health has estimated that the cancer therapy and mental health facilities have become available several years earlier than would have been possible had the traditional public sector funding approach been taken.

Integrated Facilities Management for Soft Services Medirest is responsible for managing the diverse soft services element of the contract. It includes catering, cleaning, security, linen services, waste management, materials management, retail management and function catering and the provision of general management services.

Help Desk Capability

Medirest's help desk team of 5 staff is also responsible for running the facilities help desk for the campus, which is the cornerstone to Medirest's and Novacare's support services. They use the computer aided facilities management software, QFM, from Service Works International. In 2009, in excess of 20,000 hard and soft service calls were logged by Medirest on QFM; from the usual hospital spillages and asset-related issues through to confirmation of patient meal numbers for the day, dietary changes, and bed-making requirements. John Richardson, General Services Manager for Medirest explains, "QFM is a sophisticated application and we use it to manage the entire Calvary Mater Hospital PPP contract. It is crucial that the performance is tightly monitored and managed. QFM is a completely integrated application, so if there was to be a performance failure, then the system will automatically flag it and calculate the abatement, because the application integrates measurement into daily maintenance operations."

Transparency & Accountability

There are 870 KPIs that Medirest needs to meet at the hospital across two services, all of which are managed by QFM. The KPIs range from a minor event failure (for example, not emptying a rubbish bag) through to complete loss of functionality. The services that Medirest provides at Calvary Mater Hospital are linked to complex performance-based payments and there are a range of performance deductions which are

(Continued)

Case Study 2 Calvary Mater Newcastle Hospital (Continued)

based on functionality and the weighting of an area. John Richardson illustrates, "For example, the operating theatres have a much higher weighting for functionality than office space. Deductions are calculated on the number of periods that something or somewhere is out of use; it ratchets up and there's not a break until it's rectified, therefore providing continuity, safe service and high standards within the facility, as well as ensuring patient, client, customer and employee satisfaction and providing the highest level of confidence to all users."

Depth & Breadth of Technology Experience

Service Works International has extensive experience in the PPP market sector and its QFM software manages in excess of 120 PPP contracts worldwide. It customises each payment mechanism solution to meet the performance demands of individual contracts and the application automates the calculation of any unitary charge that may be due. "Both Medirest and the client have a high level of confidence in QFM", comments John Richardson. "The client was proactively involved in developing and testing the customised payment mechanism solution with Service Works, including entering data to build the initial database and testing formulas, so they feel that they were part of building the system and have therefore bought into it because they were part of the process", he says.

> "The greatest challenge is the calculation of the performance deduction and it's not one that's easy to do manually. QFM has made a very difficult task much more user friendly and makes the complex payment deduction calculations within the contract appear very straightforward and transparent."

Flexibility

If required, QFM can provide flexibility if a time extension is required for a particular task. For example, with hard services, if the service provider goes to fix something and identifies that the original event is related to another problem that they identify, then they may need a time extension for full rectification. The project director or designate for the hospital can see these events in QFM and also has the final sign off for extensions, which, as John Richardson explains, "keeps the integrity behind the function."

The Hub

The help desk provided by Medirest has been very successful and as a result the services and standards at the hospital are well maintained. There is one help desk phone number across the campus and the help desk is easy to access by phone, email or fax, 24/7. "QFM ensures that events are dealt with in a timely fashion," says John Richardson, "and the success is largely due to the help desk and the way in which QFM coordinates the functions."

The help desk service at Newcastle also provides an offsite service for a defence contract. "QFM enables us to manage more than one site from the help desk," explains John Richardson. "It provides a scalable solution that has the capability to provide multi-site, multi-service functionality. If you have regular callers, QFM software can self-populate all

(Continued)

Case Study 2 Calvary Mater Newcastle Hospital (Continued)

the relevant information about them," he says, "which makes it possible to track how often people call and any particular service trends. This is an excellent facility for tracking important callers. Using QFM's reporting tools it is possible to view the top 10 callers and how often they call so that genuine concerns can be addressed in a timely manner."

There are 270 reports that Medirest can use in QFM, and Medirest uses them regularly for monthly reporting and to extract statistical information for annual reports. They run reports on a variety of criteria such as bed making, meal numbers, and response and rectification times so they are confident that they have responded and rectified 95% of tasks within 24 hours. "QFM enables us to slice and dice the information in a number of ways which ensures that we tightly control and manage the various elements of customer service," comments John Richardson. "Because all the jobs in the Calvary Mater Hospital contract are time-lined with clear rectification times managed by QFM, we are able to provide an excellent service which has a positive outcome for staff and patients," he says. "It ensures they have a level of comfort that work is going to be responded to and completed in a timely manner. We are committed to achieving operational excellence through delivering the highest level of services, aligned with Calvary Mater Hospital's operating practices, to ensure the ongoing success of the contract."

8.6 Summary

In this chapter, digital transformation infrastructure designed to cope with data variety, volume, and velocity was examined. The review of individualised and localised systems in Chapter 7 established the background for discussing services such as the Internet, communication satellites, wi-fi, data centres, cloud computing, and the Internet of things (IoT). Four key trends characterising information infrastructure in recent times are socialism, mobility, analytics, and clouds, which to large extent form the foundations for B2C and B2B networks. For enterprises to continue maintaining their relevance and competitive edge, they must possess leadership and digital capabilities along the lines of these key trends. Aspects of digital capability entail establishing strategic areas and processes so that digital transformation can be harnessed in FM and estates. Well-functioning processes in FM are key to maintaining an efficient workplace. The main areas with defined processes discussed in this chapter include: FM in relation to buildings, people, services, and resources; asset management of buildings, plant, and equipment; property and space management; flexible workspace and hot-desk management; resource management; and environmental management and control.

Further aspects and tools for data acquisition aiding digital transformation are examined with the acknowledgement that the level of dependency on information technology (IT) hardware across economic sectors, including the built environment, is ever-increasing. The implication is that established digital systems will require constant improvement and refinement for better efficiencies. In the project life cycle, COBie data has been widely recognised as a standard format for producing and transferring information from the earlier stages of design and construction to the asset operation stage. Such information is vital for the reactive and planned asset maintenance regimes. Another important aspect extensively discussed in this chapter are systems relating to energy consumption in buildings with a focus on building management systems (BMS). Some of the technologies covered among existing systems include Autodesk Green Building Studio, DOE-2, eQUEST, BEopt, Artra (Trimble), Onuma Planning Systems, Autodesk Project Dasher, and QFM. A recount of best practice cases of using computer-aided facilities management (CAFM) implemented in estates wraps up the chapter and sets the stage for Chapter 9, dedicated to examining associated actors in estates.

References

Alshorafa, R. and Ergen, E. (2021). Determining the level of development for BIM implementation in large-scale projects: A multi-case study. *Engineering, Construction and Architectural Management* 28(1): 397–423.

Andriushchenko, K., Rudyk, V., Riabchenko, O., *et al*. (2019). Processes of managing information infrastructure of a digital enterprise in the framework of the «industry 4.0» concept. *Eastern-European Journal of Enterprise Technologies* 1/3(97): 60–72.

Attar, R., Hailemariam, E., Glueck, M., *et al*. (2010). BIM-based building performance monitor. SimAUD 2010-Orlando, FL, USA.

Barlish, K. and Sullivan, K. (2012). How to measure the benefits of BIM: A case study approach. *Automation in Construction* 24: 149–159.

Barnhart, B. (2023). Social media demographics to inform your brand's strategy in 2023. https://sproutsocial.com/insights/new-social-media-demographics/ (accessed 11 October 2023).

Bazjanac, V. (2003). Improving building energy performance simulation with software interoperability. In: *Eighth International IBPSA Conference*, (eds) G. Augenbroe and J. Hensen, August 11–14, Eindhoven, Netherlands, 3: 11–14.

Bazjanac, V. (2004). Building energy performance simulation as part of interoperable software environments. *Building and Environment* 39(8): 879–883.

Bonnet, D., Westerman, G., Sebastian, I.M., *et al*. (2021). How to embrace digital transformation: First steps. MITSloan Management Review.

Capterra (2022). Cloud Management Software. https://www.capterra.com/cloud-management-software/?sortOrder=highest_rated (accessed 11 October 2023).

Fuerst, F. and McAllister, P. (2011). The impact of energy performance certificates on the rental and capital values of commercial property assets. *Energy Policy* 39(10): 6608–6614.

Haan, K. (2023). "Best data analytics tools of 2023, Forbes Advisor https://www.forbes.com/advisor/business/software/best-data-analytics-tools/ (accessed 11 October 2023).

Hand, J.W., Crawley, D.B., Donn, M. and Lawrie, L.K. (2008). Improving non-geometric data available to simulation programs. *Building and Environment* 43(4): 674–685.

Kassem, M., Kelly, G., Dawood, N., *et al.* (2015). BIM in facilities management applications: A case study of a large university complex. Built Environment Project and Asset Management 5(3).

Kelly, G., Serginson, M., Lockley, S., *et al.* (2013). BIM for facility management: A review and a case study investigating the value and challenges. *Proceedings of the 13th International Conference on Construction Applications of Virtual Reality*. 30–31 October, London, UK.

Khan, A. and Hornbæk, K. (2011). Big data from the built environment. *Proceedings of the 2nd International Workshop on Research in the Large*, ACM Digital Library.

Kok, N. and Jennen, M. (2012). The impact of energy labels and accessibility on office rents. *Energy Policy* 46(C): 489–497.

KPMG (2021). The value of information management in the construction and infrastructure sector. A report commissioned by the University of Cambridge's Centre for Digital Built Britain (CDBB).

Kula, B. and Ergen, E. (2021). Implementation of a BIM-FMm platform at an international airport project: *Case study. Journal of Construction Engineering and Management* 147(4): 05021002.

Lavy, S., Saxena, N. and Dixit, M. (2019). Effects of BIM and COBobie database facility management on work order processing times: Case study. *Journal of Performance of Constructed Facilities* 33(6): 04019069.

Manning, R. and Messner, J.I. (2008). Case studies in BIM implementation for programming of healthcare facilities. *Electronic Journal of Information Technology in Construction* 13: 446–457.

Oti, A., Kurul, E., Cheung, F. and Tah, J. (2016). A framework for the utilization of building management system data in building information models for building design and operation. *Automation in Construction* 72(2): 195–210.

Ozturk, Z., Arayici, Y. and Coates, S. (2012). Post occupancy evaluation (POEoe) in residential buildings utilizing BIM and sensing devices: Salford energy house example. *Proceedings of the Retrofit*. 9eds) R. Aspin and S. Bowden. Greater Manchester, UK.

Pärn, E.A., Edwards, D.J. and Sing, M.C. (2017). The building information modelling trajectory in facilities management: A review. *Automation in Construction* 75: 45–55.

Popescu, D., Bienert, S., Schützenhofer, C. and Boazu, R. (2012). Impact of energy efficiency measures on the economic value of buildings. *Applied Energy* 89(1): 454–463.

Samuels, M. (2018). What is digital transformation? Everything you need to know about how technology is reshaping business. https://www.zdnet.com/article/what-is-digital-transformation-everything-you-need-to-know-about-how-technology-is-reshaping (accessed 11 October 2023).

Then, D.S.S. (1999). An integrated resource management view of facilities management. *Facilities* 17(12/13): 462–469.

Yu Z., Fung B.C., Haghighat, F., *et al.* (2011). A systematic procedure to study the influence of occupant behavior on building energy consumption. *Energy and Buildings* 43(6): 1409–1417.

9

Actors in Digital Information Management for Estates

In digital transformation, managing the people and their skills is more important than even identifying the technology.

Alec Wang, Founder, Tana Investment Group

9.1 Introduction

Chapter 9 emphasises the importance of actors in the digital information management process. It suggests that the roles of actors are yet to be clearly defined as information technology (IT) roles cut across different sectors of the economy. The fact that many IT roles are connected to existing processes, which vary from one organisation to another, compounds the complexities in arriving at clearly defined roles. To gain contemporary insight of the situation, a few roles in the job market, related to digital information management, have been identified and reviewed. Emerging roles include asset data exploitation technician, document controller, data quality control in computer-aided facilities management (CAFM) and energy solutions manager. It is not out of place for professional institutions in facilities management (FM) and estates to assist in defining roles and to promulgate guiding policies, as examined in this chapter.

9.2 Key Actors in Digital Information Management and Transformation

The roles of actors in digital information management and transformation are not yet clearly defined. Despite the myriad of activities and apparent progress made in terms of development and inventions, no particular attention appears to have been paid to the roles and actors in these disciplines. A likely reason is that they cut across all economic and business sectors and tend to be bolted onto already existing roles. Also, the lack of a niche definition carved out for roles and the indistinct nature of the impact being made in them must be considered. Related job roles advertised in the early 2020s market have descriptions such as digital director/lead, digital manager, or digital coordinator of the area of activity concerned (e.g., library service, marketing, music, construction/built environ-ment). Digital-related roles tend to be associated with aspects of campaigning and imple-menting digital marketing projects with regard to developing strategies for boosting business goals around sales and branding, benchmarking, monitoring achievements, and evaluating performance. In a more general sense, they are about ensuring how digital tools and systems used in businesses can be more efficient and effective in achieving particular tasks, making continuous improvements, and meeting overall business targets. However, the importance of digital roles can sometimes be overlooked and not given the deserved attention, as noted by Hernández-Dionis *et al.* (2022) in music. Hernández-Dionis *et al.* (2022) suggested that the very vital role of coordinator of information and communication at Spanish music centres is in many cases unknown, unregulated, and could be casually designated to any individual or group to perform. It is rather different in the built environ-ment where a niche for digitalisation has been established around BIM. Thus, the impor-tance of BIM is increasingly changing the construction industry landscape (Eastman, 2018) regarding work processes, phases of the project life cycle, and the emerging roles of actors.

Researchers (Wu and Issa, 2014; Uhm *et al.*, 2017; Bosch-Sijtsema and Gluch, 2021) have identified a range of BIM-related roles with varying nomenclatures. In considering 242 job adverts across the USA, UK, and China. Uhm *et al.* (2017) classified the BIM roles into 35 job types as shown in Figure 9.1. The 'manager' role, used in relation to a mix of comput-er-aided design (CAD), Revit, building information modelling (BIM), or virtual design and construction (VDC), dominated. Other popular keywords denoting roles are engineer, coordinator, technician, and designer. There have been attempts to define the BIM/infor-mation manager, coordinator, and modeller/technician roles in early versions of BIM pro-tocols (AEC (UK) BIM Protocol and CIC Protocol). More contemporary protocols, such as the UK BIM Framework Documents, aligned with the EN BS19650, recognise that these emerging roles are still maturing, so they advocate associating processes/responsibilities with the appointed project parties. It is worth noting here that there have been suggestions of an inherent confusion of responsibilities, functions, and competencies of these roles by researchers (Uhm *et al.*, 2017; Hosseini *et al.*, 2018; Bosch-Sijtsema and Gluch, 2021). In terms of hierarchy, it is expected that the manager occupies a higher place of responsibility than the coordinator who in turn is placed above the modeller or technician. This expecta-tion is corroborated by suggestions (see Figure 9.2) that the professional platform BIM spe-cialists are being overseen by the BIM coordinator, who in turn works under the BIM manager (ACCA, 2021). In some set-ups, it is possible to have the BIM manager report to a lead or director. A similar suggestion is put forward by Autodesk University where the director may oversee business strategy, finance, and budgets (Autodesk, 2022). The man-ager, in this case, has a broad and shallow function of overseeing the training and standards of a wide range of activities, with the specialist involved in the narrow and more focused depth of technical responsibilities relating to tools, systems, or processes. In any case, rec-ommended habits to achieve effectiveness include being proactive, having a continuous vision of the end or completion goal, and prioritising sequencing – putting first things first (Autodesk, 2022). Further habits include keeping a positive win–win mindset, taking advantage of synergies, and seeking to understand situations first before being understood by others in a team. These are general characteristics that are relevant to leadership or other roles, even specific digital roles in facilities management (FM) and estates which currently do not have any clear definitions.

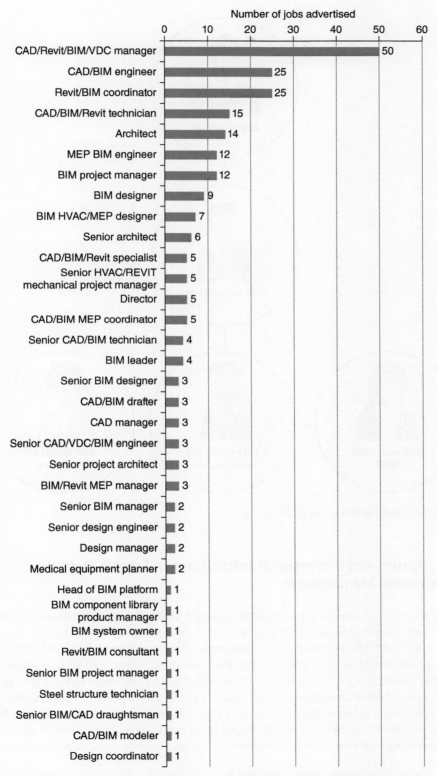

Figure 9.1 Types of BIM jobs advertised in the USA, UK, and China (Uhm *et al.*, 2017).

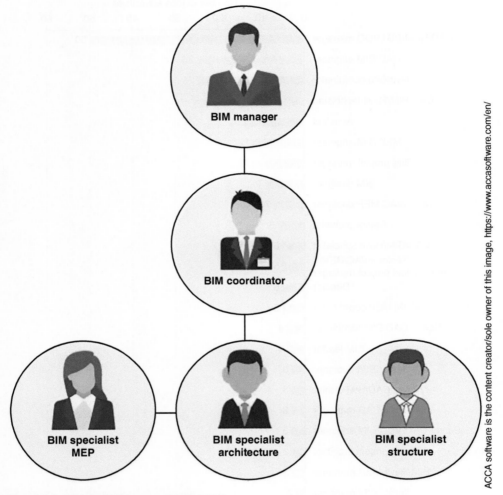

Figure 9.2 Roles of BIM actors (ACCA, 2021).

9.3 Actors and Professional Institutions in Estates Digital Information Management

There are vast numbers of actors in estates, cutting across different professional fields of endeavour. Common actors include human resources (HR) personnel, property lawyers, accountants and valuers, quantity surveyors, architects, interior decorators, and other technical professionals in mechanical, electrical, communications, and civil engineering. Another interesting group of actors are those in facilities management (FM), which is this book's point of focus in relation to smart estates. Facilities management (FM) is a relatively young profession in terms of standardisation. The organisational structures often vary from one institution to another and are influenced by elements such as the sector of operation, the prevailing function of the FM services, the institution's organisational structure, location and the localisation/internationalisation of operations (Pala and Melzi, 2009). Facilities management (FM) organisation models analysed by Cotts and Lee (1999) are useful points to start from in examining improvements to accommodate emerging roles and actors. Cotts and Lee (1999) differentiated five models based on location: (i) the office manager model; (ii) the one-location, one-site model; (iii) the one-location, multiple-sites model; (iv) the multiple-locations, strong-regional, or divisional-headquarters model; and (v) the fully international model. Examination of these models shows that there is need to incorporate an FM digital services unit. The point of integration and approach to integrating FM digital services may differ from one model to the other. From the view of FM functions (see Figure 9.3), points of integration can become clearer. The two approaches suggested by this book are: (i) fusing FM digital services with building systems management (BMS); or (ii) establishing FM digital services as a separate function.

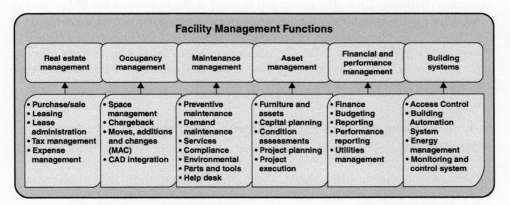

Figure 9.3 FM functions (Limble CMMS, 2020).

Regarding digital information management in estates, there are currently no indications of a significant change in the titles of professionals as discussed in Section 9.2. There are likely to be BIM managers, coordinators, or specialists in FM digital services defined according to the functions performed. Although the Institute of Workplace and Facilities Management (IWFM), the popular FM professional institution in the UK, recognises the advent of digital transformation in the industry and has provided reports on guidance of adoption (Gales, 2017), there are yet to be special definitions of roles related to digital services. The IWFM, as a professional institution, is also young. Perhaps, a look at the history of professional institutions is relevant here.

Following the argument of Drion *et al.* (2012) that there is a lack of an accurate, detailed, historical account of FM development, Nor and Azman (2014) and Wiggins (2020) have attempted to bridge this gap. The consensus is that FM has its origin in the USA and it is suggested that its development is closely tied to the development of information technology (IT) systems and office-based work in the 1960s (Wiggins, 2020). Ross Perot first coined the words 'facility management' in relation to IT and network systems but the expression soon widened to include furniture and office space designs (Wiggins, 2020). In 1979, Herman Miller founded the Facility Management Institute (FMI) and then the National Facility Management Association (NFMA) was formed in 1980 to establish some independence from traditional furniture and space planning inclinations. An international body rapidly developed from the national body and became known as the International Facility Management Association (IFMA), with its base in the USA. IFMA has its own education programme and is able to award chartered and fellow professional status. Similar development in FM followed in the UK ahead of other countries in Europe. The Association of Facility Managers (AFM) was respectively registered and launched in 1985 and 1986. In 1990, the Institute of Facilities Management (IFM), which grew from the Institute of Administrative Management (IAM), was launched. By 1994, the AFM and IFM formalised a merger to become the British Institute of Facilities Management (BIFM). BIFM operated four membership categories: associate, member, certified, and fellow. Having been in operation for about 25 years, there were concerns that BIFM was yet to achieve its full potential due to certain bottlenecks. Consequently in 2018, BIFM changed its name to the Institute of Workplace and Facility Management (IWFM) and also attained chartered body status. Integrating 'Workplace' into the new name was intentional, as mentioned by the CEO, Linda Hausmanis (OBeirne, 2018). The reason was to build on the routines of the FM profession, recognising the key component of future development through the mutual collaboration of FM, IT, and HR to optimise performance in any type of workplace environment. It is interesting to note the recognition given to IT here. IT, in encompassing all facets of digital transformation, is rapidly evolving and requires professional attention with regard to achieving standardisation in applications, processes, and roles.

9.4 Emerging Roles in Estates Digital Information Management

Advances in information technology (IT) have given rise to new roles in facilities management (FM) and more generally in estates. In some cases, responsibilities associated with existing roles have been extended to include knowledge and proficiency of specialised software packages. Many establishments design roles to align with digital transformation processes already taking root or envisaged future expansion. Currently, there is a mix of roles in the job market but these roles will metamorphose according to advances in various IT infrastructure. The common roles in the current dispensation are related to common data environment (CDE) administration, document management, data quality control and assurance, energy solutions, and building management systems (BMS).

9.4.1 Asset Data Exploitation Technician

This role can vary depending on the type of data in question. For FM and estates, the role may be tailored toward management of asset information in CDEs. The key responsibility is to ensure one source of truth of data is generated and maintained. Such technicians are expected to have a versatile knowledge of different data types, data exchange processes and protocols, and means of data conversion where required. Aspects of generating and reporting business intelligence information may be required as part of this role. The technician may be required to have an analytical capability in data manipulation to produce insights for businesses to make evidence-based decisions. Working in the asset information management team, the technician manages collaboration with external parties and project partners, while looking after the asset information model and all building information modelling (BIM) information exchange implementation. Functions of the role includes configuring the CDE and making sure users are comfortable in its use, attending to queries that might result and finding ways to resolve them, providing technical support and training to users within the software provisions. Where and when required, such technicians are involved in liaising with vendors for updates and the procurement of new versions of the software. Many establishments have begun recruiting professionals in this capacity. For example, the UK Ministry of Defence advertised for the role 'Data Exploitation – Asset Information Management Common Data Environment (CDE) Technician' to be part of their ongoing technology change programme in 2023 following the mandatory use of BIM across UK government establishments.

9.4.2 Data Quality Controller in Computer-Aided Facilities Management (CAFM)

Data quality controller is a common role in all establishments that depend on IT infrastructure for their primary functions, such as managing a warehouse, from major processes to sales fulfilment. For example, JLL Sports, London, was looking to employ a CAFM data quality controller. The role was to ensure their CAFM system always held quality data to support the job of the performance manager. With the advent of BIM, CAFM is included as part of asset information models. Also included as part of the role was reporting on data quality exceptions to highlight non-conformance and correction activity; the analysis and dissemination of data depicting the establishment's performance, location of assets, maintenance regimes, and work order governance; the extraction of data required for ad hoc reporting; and the maintenance of CAFM systems, including updates and upgrades.

Specific responsibilities should include the following:

- business management system data monitoring, control, and maintenance
- performance information recording, auditing, and anomaly resolution
- ensuring accuracy in all CAFM data in conjunction with those who generate the data
- ensuring new data is of required standard – in quality and efficiency
- supporting others/users, and investigating data anomalies and proffering solutions
- supporting asset maintenance plans and positive change processes.

9.4.3 Document Controller

Office equipment and stationery manufacturing companies, such as Xerox, require document controllers. This role, however, is to support estates teams in managing their documents in a structured way. The controller will help to define document standards and requirements during ongoing FM projects and aspects of capital improvements. Functions include ensuring quality and integrity in collecting, maintaining, and distributing documents. The role expects a high level of proficiency in the operation of computer, experience of document management on the Web or in cloud-based environments, and interaction with third parties and customers. Further, systems administration, data governance, and project management skills are useful in this role. Good knowledge of electronic document management systems (EDMS), such as Constructware, Prolog, Primavera, PM Web, Newforma, Aconex, and Asite, is expected in this role, as well as good experience of using computer-aided design (CAD) and BIM software packages.

Specific areas of responsibility include the following:

- timely delivery of pre-established document submission to meet target requirements
- maintaining electronic documents, files, and folders, and counterpart hard copy as required, including engineering drawings, project reports, specifications, and proposals
- ensuring prepared documents meet the standard requirements in terms of numbering, versioning, approval conditions/signatures, and storage and retrieval, as well as security
- managing schedules for information/document delivery, anomalies in documents, escalation of discrepancies, and providing solutions.
- data reporting with regard to quality, quantity, tracking, logs, requisition tickets, or resolutions.
- making the querying of documents possible and easy to implement
- supporting the closeout processes and project workflows adopted by the project management team
- being able to understand and use bespoke estate document management
- facilitating the integration of data from the design, fabrication, and construction phases with real estate document management and FM practices
- managing document control risks and ensuring adherence to data protection requirements.

9.4.4 Energy Solutions Manager

The energy solutions manager is a highly technically inclined role involved in organising energy supply contracts. Responsibilities include maintaining the security and uninterrupted supply of energy infrastructure, monitoring energy use and systems/building performance, and keeping accurate records of performance. Advising on optimising consumption levels will be part of the responsibilities in the job description. This extends to life-cycle planning in the maintenance of energy assets and carrying out risk assessment and associated mitigation as an essential part this role. The role oversees the installation of BMS and its operation and maintenance, including updates when required. In addition, tasks might include reporting of performance indices, resolving complaints, and efficiently managing response systems to internal job requests. A likely employer is Mitie, which runs multiple services across hospitals and higher education institutions.

A variation of the energy solutions manager role is BMS manager, with more focused responsibilities. The role can be designed to support specialist built estate managers and IT systems linked to building services on a project that are used for the monitoring and evaluating of performance. Promotion of health and safety and environmental standards, and observing statutory legislations are important aspects of this role. Other more specific tasks include monitoring of building energy management systems (BEMS), voice alarm systems, and fire alarm systems in an efficient manner; providing timely assistance to facility users; dealing with complaints; and systems maintenance. The role also oversees services rendered by specialists and the supply chain members. Keeping accurate records and overseeing how this is achieved is crucial to this role. The UK Ministry of Defence has been keen to employ such professionals to support the digital transformation drive going on in government in the 2020s. A more general role is data manager, who is responsible for overseeing, managing, and maintaining data integrity, BIM data, and information management across projects.

9.5 Digital Information Management Case in an Educational Institution

The case studies from Service Works Global discussed in Section 8.5 are projects on healthcare institutions. The case study featured in this section is on an educational institution, giving the opportunity to examine a different range of operations. The case study detailed here is on the National Oceanography Centre at Southampton.

9.5.1 Implementation of a Software Solution for Controlling Maintenance and Asset Reliability at the National Oceanography Centre (Case Study 3)

Case Study 3 National Oceanography Centre

Project: To procure a software solution to perform the critical role of controlling maintenance and asset reliability across the site.

Objectives: To control Planned Preventative Maintenance (PPM) and ensure the smooth running of the complex equipment that the building houses.

Results: Improved efficiency, asset reliability, utilisation of staff and an informed decision-making process, resulting in measurable cost savings

Service Works Global, 2023

(Continued)

Case Study 3 National Oceanography Centre (Continued)

QFM Software - Supporting a Leading Research Facility

The National Oceanography Centre (NOC) is one of the world's top oceanographic institutions, working with government, business, and scientists to provide essential knowledge and resources. The Centre operates on two sites, one located in Southampton and the other in Liverpool. The Southampton site is operated by the NOC but is shared with the University of Southampton. Approximately 1,700 persons are based at the Southampton site, a mixture of scientists, engineers, support staff, and students. NOC additionally welcomes several thousand visitors from the wider science and research community through an extensive programme of seminars and conferences which are held at the centre each year.

Due to the nature of the activities which take place in the building, NOC houses a broad range of complex technology and equipment, from sea floor survey systems to pressure testing facilities, laboratories, clean rooms, workshops, lecture theatres, and classrooms. Covering in excess of 50,000 square metres, on a site of about 5.25 hectares, NOC has two oceangoing vessels and accommodates a range of intricate equipment. NOC's estates department is responsible for all the building services on the site, including mechanical, electrical, and fabric maintenance. In addition, they are responsible for the soft FM services, such as cleaning and security, as well as the management of meeting and conference rooms, reception, and mail and porterage services.

Since the building's inception, all building services have been controlled using QFM, the award-winning CAFM software from Service Works Global. The software was originally run via a third-party FM service provider, who controlled facilities operations at the site until 2000, when the contract was subsequently brought in-house. NOC's own estates department assumed responsibility for facilities management at the site and considered it vital to retain QFM to perform the critical role of controlling maintenance across the site. Lewis Rennison, Head of Estates at NOC, explains: "QFM had performed extremely effectively since the Centre opened and we therefore viewed it as an important tool to retain when we took over the responsibility for the building's estates management ourselves."

> "Due to the vast array of complex equipment that is housed at NOC, it is important to have a reliable CAFM system in place to control planned preventative maintenance (PPM) and ensure the smooth running of the equipment that the building houses."

NOC's estates team comprises over 40 staff including help desk staff, plumbers, electricians, cleaners, security, and reception staff, who use QFM to control both planned maintenance routines and also to enable a quick response to job requests from building users. All reactive maintenance requests are logged in QFM, prioritised, and subsequently assigned to the most appropriate engineer. NOC's team of in-house contractors have "contractor level" access to the QFM system, enabling them to update details of current jobs from notification through to completion. Full details of each job are recorded and can be fully audited and reported upon. NOC's Deputy Head of Estates, Simon Stone adds: "QFM tracks labour and efficiency. It allows us to improve efficiency and utilisation of staff, and enables us to make informed decisions, which result in measurable cost savings."

(Continued)

Case Study 3 National Oceanography Centre (Continued)

Optimising Service Delivery
Because of the nature of activities and study undertaken at NOC, a significant portion of staff and students' time is dedicated to practical work, involving the use of specialist equipment. For the Estates team, this means that ensuring the reliability of assets is critical. Rennison explains, "One of the most important routines is the need to control the calibration of certain pieces of apparatus. We log this requirement on QFM as a PPM and run preventative maintenance schedules weekly through the software which is completely integrated with our unique needs. It delivers complete control and accuracy within such a key area." A key benefit of QFM for Rennison are the reporting facilities that the system provides. "The reporting offered by QFM is comprehensive, accurate and informative. We run regular performance reports through QFM, from which we are able to identify at a quick glance where there are repetitive problems onsite."

He continues: "Should a particular piece of equipment encounter multiple failures, we can investigate the underlying cause and address the issue promptly. QFM allows us to maintain control, not just from a cost perspective, but also environmentally."

World-Class Conference Facilities
Throughout the year, the building plays host to a range of events and conferences (such as the biennial Ocean Business exhibition) in addition to educational days for schools and open days for the public. NOC's estates team is responsible for coordinating the management of meeting and conference rooms across the site, and this process is largely controlled using QFM. Rennison explains: "Because of the busy educational and research programme that we support, we cannot afford to encounter potential scheduling problems or double-booked rooms. QFM helps us to avoid these pitfalls by providing a centralised facility from which all bookings are controlled." NOC uses the web-based QFM Room Bookings application, which has enabled it to provide all building users with view-only system access, allowing them to view meeting room availability at a glance. Rennison states: "QFM has brought consistency to the room booking process. It has increased meeting room utilisation and enabled us to deliver a professional experience for visitors."

Supporting Sustainability
As one of the leading centres of its kind in the world, NOC is committed to minimising environmental impact and has been awarded ISO 14001 accreditation. This accreditation has been maintained for several years. Rennison says, "QFM supports us in managing our environmental risks and reducing environmental impact by ensuring the reliability of our assets and equipment. The QFM app further allows us to reduce notification and rectification times for maintenance work. It not only helps us improve efficiency but also eliminates the unnecessary paper trail and supports the sustainability strategies to which we are committed." As cost and energy efficiency concerns continue to be top of the agenda for facilities managers, Rennison firmly believes that in QFM, NOC has invested in a system that will fully support their functional and environmental objectives and reaffirm the Oceanography Centre's position as a leading

(Continued)

Case Study 3 National Oceanography Centre (Continued)

research institute for years to come. "Our mission is to maintain our position as the national focus for oceanography in the UK, and remain within the top five centres for Ocean and Earth Sciences and Marine Technology globally. We are committed to delivering world class education and research facilities and QFM allows the facilities team to demonstrate to our own staff, students, and the wider community, the first rate educational and research facilities for which NOC is renowned."

Managing Safety

The site also went on to achieve the ISO 45001 accreditation for occupational health and safety management, which represents NOC's ongoing commitment to eliminating workplace hazards and supporting employee wellness. Stone comments: "QFM has given us great support in achieving this important certification, and also confidence in retaining it. We can now easily provide records that show our annual servicing plans for each asset and when the PPM took place. That level of auditability is really making a difference."

Future Focus

As an organisation striving for continuous improvement, NOC seeks user feedback around its estates' services. This previously took the format of an annual survey, but QFM's Dynamic Forms are being introduced to improve this process. Those who request a service are now automatically emailed a short survey after the work is completed, allowing them to provide feedback on aspects like service and communication quality. "Regular feedback helps us monitor and improve performance across the estates team. These surveys are a more targeted approach to our communications and we expect to see a greater response due to their timeliness," says Stone. "The team at SWG were happy to help us set up the initial forms, and provided training so we can continue to collect information we need as our services evolve." Dynamic Forms can also be attached to PPMs on the mobile app, which NOC is looking into for the future. The form will show a checklist of items that require completion to finish the job, helping standardise service across the team and also make completion easier as all information is at hand.

9.6 Summary

In Chapter 9, key actors in digital information management and transformation were examined together with roles of the professional institutions in digital information management in estates. Since digital information management is still developing in facilities management (FM) and estates, it was crucial to look at the emerging roles in this area of the built environment. The commonly identified roles in the job market of the 2020s include digital director/lead, digital manager, or digital coordinator of the area of activity concerned. These roles can relate to areas of activity such as library services, marketing, music, or construction/built environment. Many tasks on these roles relate to benchmarking, monitoring achievements, and evaluating performance. On a more general basis, the chapter identified the existence of some levels of confusion in the responsibilities and functions of roles in digital information management. However, a suggested hierarchy is that digital managers oversee coordinators who may in turn direct modellers, technicians, or specialists. Slight variations exist in such relationships in different establishments which are typically tailored according to the organisational functions. In any case, the crucial point is the adoption of arrangements that are most suitable for meeting organisational objectives.

The chapter also examined professional institutions as essential supporting resources for actors in estates in the same way as other professional areas of work in the built environment. The historical context of professional bodies in FM traces its origin to the 1960s in the USA. Professional bodies have seen different phases of development and refinement to reach their contemporary states. There have been mergers and change of names, and redefining of areas of operation as evident with UK's IWFM, all with the view to improve operation efficiencies and effectiveness. There is a clear recognition of the prowess and awareness of possibilities with digital information management in professional bodies covering FM. However, a clearer definition of standard roles and hierarchy will be useful. Some roles identified and discussed included asset data exploitation technician, data quality controller in computer-aided facilities management (CAFM), document controller, and energy solutions manager, needed by employers from the public and private sectors alike. What is clear from the chapter is that roles are still developing and early definitions by professional institutions will help with standardisations for general adoption.

References

ACCA (2021). BIM manager, BIM specialist and BIM coordinator roles and responsibilities. https://biblus.accasoftware.com/en/bim-manager-bim-specialist-and-bim-coordinator-roles-and-responsibilities/ (accessed 18 October 2023).

Autodesk (2022). Digital information management roles, Autodesk Inc. https://www.autodesk.com/autodesk-university/article/Habits-Highly-Effective-BIM-Managers-2017 (accessed 2 November 2023).

Bosch-Sijtsema, P. and Gluch, P. (2021). Challenging construction project management institutions: The role and agency of BIM actors. *International journal of Construction Management 21(11):* 1077–1087.

Cotts, D. and Lee, M. (1999). *The Facility Management Handbook.* New York: AMACOM Press.

Drion, B., Melissen, F. and Wood, R. (2012). Facilities management: Lost, or regained? *Facilities* 30(5/6): 254–261.

Eastman, C.M. (2018). *Building Product Models: Computer Environments, Supporting Design and Construction.* Boca Raton, FL: CRC Press.

Gales, A. (2017). *Good Practice Guide: Selecting FM Software*, London: Institute of Workplace and Facilities Management (IWFM).

Hernández-Dionis, P., Pérez-Jorge, D., Curbelo-González, O. and Alegre de la Rosa, O.M. (2022). The coordinator of information and communication technologies: Its implication for open innovation. *Journal of Open Innovation: Technology, Market, and Complexity* 8(1): 42.

Hosseini, M.R., Martek, I., Papadonikolaki, E., *et al.* *(2018). Viability of the BIM manager enduring as a distinct role: Association rule mining of job advertisements. Journal of Construction Engineering and Management 144(9): 04018085.*

Limble CMMS (2023). Complete Guide to Facilities Management. https://limblecmms.com/blog/facilities-management/ (accessed 22 November 2023).

Nor, M. and Azman, N. (2014). Facility management history and evolution. *International Journal of Facility Management 5(1).*

OBeirne, S. (2018). FM clinic: Debate on BIFM's proposed rebrand and application for chartered body status. *Facility Management Journal.*

Pala, F. and Melzi, E. (2009). Facility management organizational models. *Open Facility Management.* Milan: IFMA.

Uhm, M., Lee, G. and Jeon, B. (2017). An analysis of BIM jobs and competencies based on the use of terms in the industry. *Automation in Construction 81: 67–98.*

Wiggins, J. M. (2020). *Facilities Manager's Desk Reference.* Oxford: John Wiley & Sons.

Wu W. and Issa, R.R. (2014). Key issues in workforce planning and adaptation strategies for BIM implementation in construction industry. Construction Research Congress 2014: Construction in a Global Network.

10

The Role of Digital Technology in Healthcare Facilities Management

It is not the strongest of the species that survives, nor the most intelligent that survives it is the one that is the most adaptable to change.

Charles Darwen (1809–1882)

10.1 Introduction

Although the above quotation relates to evolution, it can also be used in an organisational sense as it exemplifies the importance of changing to meet future needs. The chapter is based on the MSc research of Ben Lyre, University of Bolton, and looks specifically at the role of digital technology in healthcare facilities management (FM). Accordingly, while the chapter articulates and discusses the role of digital technology in the built environment, it is geared specifically to case studies around the healthcare sector. The use of digital twins for the built environment is just beginning to take place and yet to catch up with healthcare, which was the motivation for choosing this sector as a model of good practice for the future.

The chapter starts by considering the importance FM in the healthcare sector and examining the different digital technologies that can be used to streamline estates services. For this reason, it considers such digital technologies as the enablers to overcoming problems, creating efficiencies, and generating other benefits for managing large complex healthcare estates. It introduces the concept of artificial intelligence (AI) in estates management and the crucial role that this can play. In addition, it discusses the knowledge management technologies required to effectively manage healthcare facilities with an emphasis on achieving organisational objectives. In this sense it articulates the benefits that knowledge management can provide in identifying knowledge and skill gaps. It then explains how to build competencies to improve the understanding of human resource (HR) professionals and for establishing a knowledge-driven culture to facilitate the success of the innovation framework or process. Accordingly, this chapter investigates the knowledge management technologies required to effectively manage healthcare facilities with an emphasis on achieving organisational objectives. This provides an overview of the significant research efforts on digital technology that apply to improving the FM processes for the management

The Smart Estate, First Edition. Edited by Jason Challender/Akponanabofa Henry Oti.
© 2024 John Wiley & Sons, Ltd. Published 2024 by John Wiley & Sons, Ltd.

of infrastructural assets and to present a roadmap for future research on digital FM applications.

In addition, the chapter explains the various digital technologies, systems, and software currently being used within healthcare facilities management. These include the following:

- Geographic information systems (GIS)
- Internet of things (IoT)
- mobile-first
- Machine learning and predictive analytics
- Building information modelling (BIM).

Finally, the chapter provides some conclusions based around the future of digital technologies and a brief overview on the aspects covered.

10.2 The Advancement of Digital Technology in Healthcare Facilities Management (FM)

Facilities management (FM) is a set of multidisciplinary services and activities integrating people, place, process, and technology to ensure proper management of an asset during its life cycle (Abdullah *et al.*, 2013). Thus, FM has extensive information requirements and the use of innovative digital technologies and tools such as building information modelling (BIM), computer-aided FM (CAFM) systems, and building automation systems (BAS) has significantly improved FM efficiency (Araszkiewicz, 2017). However, it is highly complex to integrate different software and systems with heterogeneous devices from various vendors using different communication protocols. Although academic efforts like Construction Operation and Building Information Exchange (COBie) and Industry Foundation Classes (IFC) have been made, the industry has been slow to embrace interoperability.

The provision of healthcare FM services, which are considered non-core services in healthcare organisations, has emerged as a critical ability in delivering effective inpatient care and running productive healthcare FM. It is believed that both technologies and the physical environment are critical in bringing about the changes needed in the healthcare sector. The opportunities offered by technology range from more efficient administrative processes to a shift in how people interact with services (Wenzel and Evans, 2019). Rodriguez *et al.*, (2014) have argued that hospitals' infrastructural assets should no longer be considered as passive objects. Instead, they should act as a group of motivated agents meshed in a culture of continuous quality improvement in healthcare delivery processes. Several UK National Health Service (NHS) policies acknowledge the importance of technology and real estate as change enablers. For example, the NHS's long-term plan (NHS England, 2019) places a strong emphasis on technology and its role in delivering on some of the most ambitious commitments to safe and efficient healthcare delivery.

Technology and social changes have altered how facilities are managed, and many tasks previously performed by hand are now done automatically including building operations, comfort, safety, and efficiency in estates management. Every industry, including FM, has undergone digital transformation. Facilities are encouraged to transform for various reasons, including the associated improvements in process transparency, data performance analysis, workplace productivity, and sustainability (Leaman and Bordass, 2006). This technology has also had an impact on healthcare FM. While business leaders see endless applications for increasingly powerful technologies, they worry that they lack the talent to capitalise on artificial intelligence (AI). At the same time, workers fear having fewer opportunities for their human contributions due to AI. AI refers to machines or systems that exhibit humanlike behaviour and the basic form of it involves computers' mimicking human behaviour based on extensive data from previous examples. Many different types of tasks can be performed by AI, from recognising the differences between cats and birds to complex organisational activities (Riedl, 2019). Furthermore, organisations working on building new strategic capabilities frequently disregard employees' concerns about new systems as stubbornness or a lack of ability to learn. This narrative of change-resistant workers is reinforced when AI implementation stalls, as it often does, due to slow user adoption.

Even though technology is rapidly evolving, the FM profession is relatively risk-averse (Aloisio, 2019). Furthermore, the unexpected rate of technological change and the uncertainties it brings are challenging those in charge of healthcare FM to gain a better understanding of the body of knowledge, procedures, and processes related to the management of infrastructural assets. Perhaps, this is why many academics believe that advances in information technology (IT) provide greater data-processing capabilities applicable at all stages of the life cycle of built assets (Shohet and Lavy, 2004). Currently, the healthcare FM discipline lacks quantitative models that support strategic and tactical decision-making; thus, this insight is deemed necessary. Perhaps for this reason, within the healthcare context, it can be argued that knowledge management is the formal management of knowledge for facilitating the creation, identification, acquisition, development, dissemination, use, and preservation of a healthcare enterprise's knowledge using advanced technology (Abecker *et al.*, 1998; O'Leary and O'Leary, 1998). Accordingly, this chapter investigates the knowledge management technologies required to effectively manage healthcare facilities with an emphasis on achieving organisational objectives. The goal of this investigation is twofold: (i) to provide an overview of the significant research efforts on digital technology that apply to improving the FM process for the management of infrastructural assets; and (ii) to identify gaps in the research and present a roadmap for future research on digital FM applications.

It is more evident than ever that global issues, such as the COVID-19 crisis, necessitate global solutions and that digitalisation of all activities, remote operations, and digital readiness must be explored. Digital technology refers to innovative workplaces with digitally ready employees and the emergence of the fourth industrial revolution, which is driven by rapid technological advancements and has somewhat disrupted the current environment for various industries. According to Anshari and Almunawar (2021), the fourth industrial revolution offers speed of innovation that enables rapid deployment of digital technologies, reduces turnaround times for products and services, expands organisations by developing new products and services, and improves developmental processes.

Seeing relevant problem features in existing knowledge has become the essential component of innovation in an organisation to improve performance and solve problems (McAdam, 2000). For this reason, knowledge management plays an instrumental role in innovation. Temel *et al.* (2021) describe knowledge management as creating and utilising knowledge within an organisation to foster innovation, develop new skills, and create a positive work environment. Conversely, López-Nicolás and Meroño-Cerdán (2011) highlighted that the creation of novel and valuable knowledge could be converted into products, services, and processes by transforming general knowledge into specific knowledge. In addition, Darroch (2005) argued that leveraging the potential for competitive advantage through fourth industrial revolution technology can further drive organisational interest in knowledge management.

In the innovation process, knowledge management has several values. According to Du Plessis (2007), knowledge management aids in developing platforms and processes for sharing tacit knowledge. In this regard, it aids in converting tacit to explicit knowledge and facilitates collaborative work to spark workplace innovation and allows knowledge to flow freely throughout the organisation to improve information accessibility during innovation (Temel *et al.*, 2021). It also provides high-level, specialised assistance in specific areas, such as identifying knowledge and skill gaps to build competencies to improve the understanding of human resource professionals and for establishing a knowledge-driven culture to facilitate the success of the innovation framework or process.

The healthcare sector is constantly changing, with evolving technology and advances in patient care driving demands for the quick delivery of state-of-the-art facilities. Medical equipment advancements have prompted the industry to seek novel approaches to incorporating technology into the delivery of modern healthcare FM (Wilson, 2015). Healthcare facilities frequently deal with dynamic external forces, such as market changes, stringent regulation, and a variety of stakeholders, all of which add to the variability of the process (Okada *et al.*, 2017). Such services are undergoing a technological transformation to improve functions, such as facilities control and performance, as well as to reduce costs. The adoption of new information and communications technologies (ICT), such as the Internet of things (IoT) and BIM, referred to later in this chapter, will enable healthcare facilities to access real-time information via interconnected sensors, allowing them to better manage their operations. The IoT paradigm allows physical objects to communicate with one another over the Internet (Patel *et al.*, 2016; Usak *et al.*, 2020). The IoT is rapidly gaining popularity, and its application spans a wide range of industries, including energy, water, transportation, defence, aerospace, shopping, health, and agriculture (Matta *et al.*, 2017).

The provision of equitable, high-quality, and cost-effective healthcare necessitates an extraordinary array of well-balanced and managed resource inputs. Physical resources, such as fixed assets and consumables, also known as healthcare technology, are among the most common types of inputs. Technology serves as the foundation for healthcare delivery and the delivery of all health interventions, and has become a more visible policy issue in recent years, where healthcare technology management (HTM) strategies have been repeatedly scrutinised (Rasoulifar *et al.*, 2008). While the need for improved HTM practise has long been recognised and addressed at numerous international forums, healthcare facilities continue to face a variety of challenges, including non-functioning medical equipment, because of various factors. These factors include inadequate planning, inappropriate procurement, poorly organised and managed healthcare technical services, and skilled personnel shortages (Lenel *et al.*, 2005). Buildings, plants and machinery, furniture and fixtures, communication and information systems, catering and laundry equipment, waste disposal, and vehicles all face the same issues (Temple-Bird *et al.*, 2005). Consequently, both technology and real estate are essential for the modification of healthcare organisations. The opportunities offered by technologies range from more efficient administrative processes to transformation in the interaction and care of patients. Although its capability to bring about transforming changes may seem low, the NHS estate also plays a substantial role in supporting developments in healthcare and, crucially, in improving patient experience (Department of Health, 2012; Kelsey *et al.*, 2014).

Grimshaw (2000) argued that revolutionary changes in the demand side of organisational structures would result in a fundamental shift in the relationship between businesses and their supporting infrastructure in terms of the attempts to identify the fundamental forces shaping the global growth of FM. As a prerequisite for FM to generate opportunities to increase business efficiency through the successful application of infrastructure assets, it must respond to the new environment proactively. This will necessitate a review of the system that supports the growth of FM, including the system that generates facilities knowledge and the development of new models that combine research and practice. Accordingly, healthcare FM services, considered non-core services in healthcare organisations, have emerged as critical resources in delivering effective inpatient care and running productive healthcare facilities.

The advancement of digital technologies has had a significant impact on how traditional industries carry out their daily functions. Most knowledge-based industries, including construction and healthcare FM, have been transformed by easy access to information and faster communication speeds (Wong *et al.*, 2018). Advances in computer-aided design (CAD) software and BIM have gradually changed traditional design practices and communication methods, according to studies by Gandhi *et al.* (2016). Furthermore, Manyika *et al.* (2016) argued that the architecture, engineering, and construction (AEC) sector has a slow rate of digitalisation, particularly in terms of building digital assets, expanding digital usage, and creating a highly digital workforce, compared to other sectors, such as manufacturing and distribution. Both researchers and practitioners have acknowledged the need for faster digitalisation of the AEC sector (Boland *et al.*, 2007; Lu *et al.*, 2015). Studies have also been conducted to promote and transfer digitalisation to the design and construction stages (Zhou *et al.*, 2011), promote the use of radio frequency identification (RFID) in construction (Valero *et al.*, 2015), and encourage the use of BIM in construction processes. Notwithstanding this premise, there has been relatively little research on using digital technologies in the operations and maintenance stage of the building life cycle. Renovation, retrofitting, maintenance, and refurbishment are critical components of FM, but there has been far less research and implementation into this stage when compared to the design and construction stages. Interest in digital technologies in FM has grown in recent years, and many governments (e.g., Australia and the UK) have emphasised the need to revolutionise the FM sector by increasing their adoption. For FM, a growing number of studies have examined the potential implementation of BIM (Parsanezhad and Dimyadi, 2014; Oti *et al.*, 2016) and other digital technologies applications, such as: geographic information systems (GISs); the IoT, RFID, and sensor network technologies; and reality capture technology (e.g., 3D laser scanning and point clouds) (see Figure 10.1). Building information modelling (BIM) employs computer programmes to create, share, exchange, and manage information among all stakeholders throughout the life cycle of a building. Furthermore, photogrammetry and 3D laser scanning are used as capture technology to acquire accurate geometrical/spatial information and generate point cloud data for the creation of a digital model of existing facilities (Flanagan *et al.*, 2014; Barazzetti, 2016).

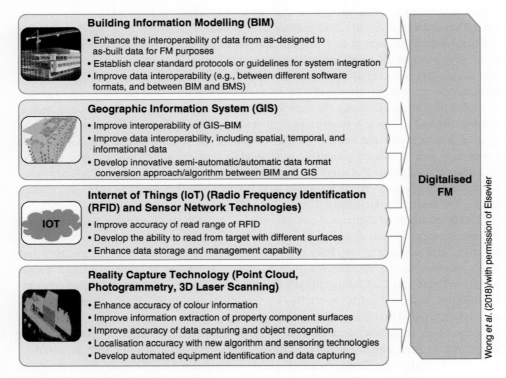

Figure 10.1 Future digital technology and facilities management (FM) research roadmap (Wong *et al.*, 2018/with permission of Elsevier).

The IoT enables the rapid collection, transmission, and exchange of data using embedded sensors and wireless technologies (Morgan, 2014). Sensor network technologies and RFID are two of the most rapidly growing information and communication technologies among the IoT, with RFID being made up of four basic components: a tag, a reader (antenna), software, and a computer network (Kumar *et al.*, 2010). Additionally, GIS aid in the comprehension and visualisation of data in a variety of ways, revealing the relationships using maps, globes, reports, and charts (Meerow *et al.*, 2016).

10.3 Digital Technologies within Healthcare Facilities Management (FM)

Generally speaking, digital technologies can be described as scientific or engineering knowledge that deals with the establishment and application of computerised or digital devices, methods, or systems that can improve the immediacy, accuracy, and flexibility of communication (Puolitaival *et al.*, 2018; Wong *et al.*, 2018). Many traditional industry practices have been altered because of technological advancement. For example, large corporations in the automotive (e.g., BMW and Bosch) and aerospace (e.g., Boeing) industries have been digitalised to improve operations, increase revenue, and drive research and development innovation. According to the McKinsey Report, the global construction industry is the least digitalised and technologically innovative of all industries (Manyika *et al.*, 2016). In general, its research and development investment are less than 1% of revenue, which is much lower than that in other sectors, including the automotive and aerospace industries. The construction and building industry has yet to embrace new digital technologies and has thus remained uncoordinated between offices and sites, with paper still being frequently used to manage processes and deliverables, such as design drawings and daily management (Agarwal *et al.*, 2016). The operation and maintenance stage accounts for most of the total life cycle costs of the building process. Overall, the costs of operation and maintenance account for 50–70% of total annual facility operating costs (Rondeau *et al.*, 2012), while FM accounts for 85% of total life cycle costs (Teicholz, 2013).

Maintenance management and energy consumption are two critical aspects of daily property management (Lewis *et al.*, 2011). Building maintenance decisions necessitate analysing and integrating various types of information and knowledge, such as maintenance records, work orders, and failure causes and consequences, generated by various stakeholders on project teams (Motawa and Almarshad, 2013). If project team members' information/ knowledge is not captured, ineffective decisions may be made, and high costs may be incurred. A well-integrated data system is becoming increasingly important for healthcare FM organisations to manage the massive number of staff and facilities data as well as to accommodate the constant changes occurring in facilities. Despite this, many FM systems are separate from and independent of one another, meaning FM relies heavily on a variety of incompatible systems to manage building maintenance and asset value management.

The variety of software tools and interoperability issues continue to be barriers to the adoption of digital technologies in the FM sector (Becerik-Gerher *et al.*, 2012). Data (or information) from various FM processes are frequently organised and managed in disparate information systems, such as computerised maintenance management systems (CMMS) or computer-aided FM (CAFM). While both CMMS and CAFM help organisations manage and record a database of daily maintenance operations (e.g., asset management, inventory control, service request generation, and work order management), CAFM provides additional functions, such as reactive maintenance, planned preventative maintenance (PPM) management, space and move management, and resource scheduling (Cheng *et al.*, 2016). To meet FM requirements, a wide range of commercial software applications are available on the market, including Archibus, BIM 360 Ops/BIM 360 Field, Ecodomus,

Onuma (Onuma Software, 2018), QFM Facilities Management Software (Service Works Global, 2018), and IBM TRIRIGA (IBM, 2018). Many of these applications perform similar asset and maintenance management functions, but most current FM software falls short of meeting the basic digital technological requirements (Cheng *et al.*, 2016).

Current FM systems fail to capture and retrieve the detailed information and knowledge generated by building operation and maintenance, such as causes of failure, reasons for selecting specific maintenance methods, specialist contractor selection, and the ripple effects on other building elements (Motawa and Almarshad, 2013). A building maintenance data management system that can support and integrate the data and information generated by project team members can have a significant impact on building performance. Accordingly, the potential for extending the application of major digital technologies, such as BIM, reality capture technology (including 3D laser scanning, point cloud, and photogrammetry), RFID and GIS, for the purposes of capturing, transferring, and storing big data/information from the design and construction stages to building operation and maintenance stages has piqued the interest of many researchers and professionals. As a result, an increasing number of innovations have been developed in recent years (Chen *et al.*, 2015).

10.4   Geographic Information Systems (GIS)

Maintaining links between GIS and building information modelling (BIM) applications is an ongoing issue that must be addressed on a large scale. With the growing use of GIS-integrated BIM in facilities management (FM), future research could focus on improving the interoperability of GIS and BIM-based data. The interoperability of various data forms, such as spatial, temporal, and informational data, remains an unresolved issue. Improved architecture should be developed to support data interoperability among various GIS, BIM, and FM tools. New prototypes for effective data integration should also be developed. More research is required in future to improve the automated integration of heterogeneous BIM, GIS, and FM data (Wong *et al.*, 2018; Altıntaş and Ilal, 2021). According to Kang and Hong (2015), one of the significant challenges in the application of BIM–GIS systems to FM is the inherent variation in datasets in terms of semantics, geometry, and level of development (LOD) in GIS and BIM models. The Industry Foundation Classes (IFC) and city geography markup language (CityGML) are chosen as the representative schemas for the BIM and GIS domains, respectively. Unlike GIS, the current IFC lack the LOD system, meaning converting a shape from IFC to CityGML necessitates LOD mapping using a unique mapping algorithm (Kang and Hong, 2015).

While most current research focuses on improving the semantic aspects of GIS–BIM integration, the spatial and geometric data issue remains unresolved. More research is required to reduce the occurrence of information mismatch during and after the integration of BIM and GIS. It is also necessary to develop semi-automatic or automatic data format conversion to reduce the time-consuming manual conversion and translation between IFC and CityGML (Liu *et al.*, 2017). Furthermore, storing large facilities asset databases generated in an integrated BIM–GIS platform remains a challenge. Healthcare organisations and facilities managers would benefit greatly from the effective integration of a BIM–GIS asset database with energy management and a building automation system (BAS)/building management system (BMS) for monitoring building energy consumption (Fosu *et al.*, 2015).

10.5 The Internet of Things (IoT)

The IoT is a popular trend in the field of facilities management (FM). It comprises objects with technology built into them, such as sensors or machinery, that allow employees to control, connect, and share data with other devices connected to the Internet. IoT-based FM can be achieved based on this method of operation. The digital transformation of FM makes it easier to collect accurate and efficient data about facilities, which helps in determining how well they are performing. Another advantage of using the IoT is that it saves energy and costs by reducing manual labour and allowing tasks to be completed quickly (Vermesan and Friess, 2013; Patel *et al.*, 2016).

Although the use of radio frequency identification (RFID) technology has grown, the distance between the tag and the reader is a critical factor in ensuring successful RFID signal reading. Furthermore, indoor localisation technologies based on RFID also have several flaws and frequently provide low accuracy for identifying indoor locations. For this reason, improving the reliability of target readings when there are different surfaces in the facility is another area that should be investigated in the future, as this would greatly improve the application of RFID in FM and the management of existing buildings (Kim *et al.*, 2013). Future research should focus on the automatic and timely delivery of spatial information as well as the context of building components, equipment objects (including maintenance history), work orders, and inspection records to on-site mobile FM or maintenance personnel using RFID-based technology (Costin *et al.*, 2014; Li and Becerik-Gerber, 2011). Improvements in the efficiency and reliability of context-aware information delivery (e.g., location, time, and 3D space) have the potential to eliminate time-consuming manual location identification processes and facilitate FM personnel maintenance work. Future research should investigate how to store, process, manage, and maintain the massive amount of data generated by the RFID system and integrate the collected data with FM systems. With reference to Figure 10.2 this should seek to overcome some of the documentation management issues that can be experienced by organisations.

Figure 10.2 Pictures of document storage for FM information after a turnover by the contractor.

10.6   Mobile-First

The rapid advancement of technology is also altering how people use mobile devices at work. With everyone working on mobile devices, work will be easier to complete, and workplace estates costs can be reduced. For this reason, the trend of mobile management has begun to benefit organisations, particularly in facilities management (FM) (Hassani *et al.*, 2020). With this approach, employees can monitor facilities at any time from anywhere, allowing them to react more quickly.

10.7   Machine Learning and Predictive Analytics

Many systems in today's organisations use machine learning to make work easier. One way machine learning simplifies work is by assisting in decision-making. Machine learning trends are becoming more prevalent in facilities management (FM), particularly in combination with predictive analytics. Both Hassani *et al.* (2020) and Nosratabadi *et al.* (2020) agreed that learning encompasses more than simply employing pre-programmed algorithms and entails reviewing the data the systems collect and searching through large amounts of data for patterns, trends, and new ideas. Consequently, organisations frequently use semantic segmentation methods to make visual data easier to use for their artificial intelligence (AI) models, ensuring the success of the automation processes. Machine learning usually forecasts how each facility will perform using data from Internet of things (IoT) sensors. Due to its efficiency, organisations employing this strategy do not need to look at their dashboards very often; instead, they can view the results of machine learning analyses (Raju and Laxmi, 2020).

10.8   Building Information Modelling (BIM)

Broadly speaking, facilities management (FM) refers to an integrated set of services and activities that integrate people, places, processes, and technologies to ensure proper asset management during a facility's life cycle (Abdullah *et al.*, 2013), and for this reason it requires access to extensive information (Becerik-Gerber *et al.*, 2012). There have been many innovations in digital technology over recent years, including BIM, computer-aided FM (CAFM) systems, and building automation systems (BAS), which have significantly enhanced FM efficiency (Araszkiewicz, 2017). In addition, BIM provides an improved means of describing a building, as shown in Figure 10.3, leading to improved process efficiencies brought about by early contractor involvement and knowledge exchange. However, this has generated a large amount of complexity in terms of the different software and systems, which can cause challenges in synchronising devices coming from a variety of vendors.

Several efforts have been made to promote interoperability, such as the Construction Operations and Building Information Exchange (COBie). However, the adoption of this technology is still lagging. In part, this is the result of a lack of a semantically complete mapping between entities and relationships in these standards, which significantly limits

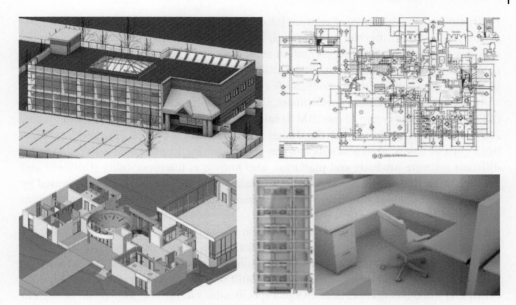

Figure 10.3 3D and 4D BIM provide an improved means of describing a building, leading to improved process efficiencies.

their application. One way to achieve semantic clarity is to use a knowledge map to map a dataset's unknown terms into general terms. The requirement for clear and straightforward mapping between data structures and knowledge structures can be satisfied if the meaning of each data element is clearly defined (Jiang *et al.*, 2022).

In FM, BIM refers to the operation and maintenance activities that ensure end-users receive the services for which a facility was designed. A facility's FM cost is estimated at approximately 71% of its total life-cycle cost over a 40-year period (Kuda and Berankova 2014; Song, 2018). Furthermore, a practical FM project necessitates collaboration among actors from various domains, such as designers, contractors and operators, as well as understanding and engaging multiple stakeholders, including both end-users and owners (Niskanen *et al.*, 2014).

According to the International Facility Management Association, there are 11 core competencies for FM: communications, emergency preparedness and business continuity, environmental stewardship and sustainability, finance and business, human factors, leadership and strategy, operation and maintenance, project management, quality, real estate and property management, and technology. An increasing number of digital technologies and tools, including BIM, building automation systems (BAS), and environmental management systems (EMS), are being used to assist FM in meeting different tasks and improving efficiency. As a result of the many heterogeneous systems involved, FM-related data formats can vary greatly, increasing the difficulty of sharing information and integrating them among the involved systems. For this reason, facilities managers face a challenge in integrating and interpreting heterogeneous facility data and homogenising a representation of the exchange of building knowledge throughout a facility's life cycle (Pittet *et al.*, 2014).

Furthermore, the availability of relevant information is critical to an efficient FM and operations practice (Parsanezhad and Tarandi, 2013). There is evidence that BIM can solve problems caused by a lack of information at all stages of a building's life cycle, including maintenance. In addition, an integrated BIM system provides a solid knowledge base for facility decision-making throughout its life cycle (Golabchi and Kamat, 2013).

After years of research and development, the architecture, engineering, and construction (AEC) industry has begun to use BIM to integrate and interoperate (Halfawy and Froese, 2007). BIM is primarily used in the design and construction phases. However, organisations must be able to represent data in a way that allows for accurate data exchange among different software products and platforms, also known as interoperability (Golabchi and Kamat, 2013). BIM acts as a reservoir for all design and construction information used by FM while BIM-enabled information systems seamlessly transfer design and construction models to FM systems.

As previously stated, the Industry Foundation Classes (IFC) is the current standard for representing, accessing, and sharing BIM information (Karshenas and Niknam 2013). BuildingSMART facilitates interoperability among various processes in AEC/FM projects by developing IFC and its implementation is built on a product data modelling language called EXPRESS (Jiang *et al.*, 2022). Object specifications in the IFC format can be used to share data between applications. For example, the definition of a door in IFC goes beyond just lines and geometries. However, IFC provides only a generalised BIM data structure that is not supported by the project's stakeholders (Kang and Hong, 2015) and this is due to a lack of semantic clarity in mapping entities and relationships, which severely limits its application (Jiang *et al.*, 2022).

Various functions, such as financial management, human resource (HR) management, health risk management, maintenance management, and supply management can be provided by FM, in addition to property management (Pittet *et al.*, 2014). Given the various areas and functions involved in the FM phase, FM systems do not have to be managed by a public data model (Kim *et al.*, 2018). The National Institute of Building Sciences developed COBie as a standard data exchange system for use throughout the life cycle of a building to ensure the interoperability of BIM data for an FM service during the operation and maintenance phase. In essence, it determines how information can be collected during design and construction and distributed to facility operators while eliminating the current process of transferring massive amounts of paper documents to facility operators once construction is completed. Overall, COBie reduces operational costs by eliminating the need for post hoc as-built data capture and facilitates the transfer of digital information from the process' design and construction phases to FM databases (East, 2007, Lavy and Jawadekar, 2014).

A COBie document outlines guidelines for consistent file naming, storage, indexing, and archiving procedures so that information can be easily retrieved and validated (Smith and Tardif, 2009). The COBie file for a building project contains all phases of the project. At the beginning of operation or for data updates, the facilities manager or organisation can load operation and maintenance data directly into spreadsheet software or a COBie-based maintenance management system. The use of BIM standards, such as IFC and COBie, has been viewed as highly promising by construction and political actors to address data dematerialisation issues and maximise building information interoperability (Farias *et al.*, 2015). At the same time, their application is hampered by a lack of semantic information. Semantic clarity in mapping entities and relationships is required for intelligent functions, such as information integration and ontology reasoning (Jiang *et al.*, 2022). In the last two decades, healthcare has made significant advances in terms of digital transformation. The challenge of healthcare knowledge management is integrating multisource and multiformat healthcare information into a coherent knowledge base that can be used to provide day-to-day service. This is a critical issue that should concern all stakeholders in the broader health ecosystem.

10.9 Conclusions

One of the essential prerequisites for achieving the strategic objectives of healthcare facilities management (FM), broadly defined as interdisciplinary practice related to the management of buildings and facilities designed for building users, is the efficiency of communication and information flow. The economic sense of healthcare FM is to relieve building users of problems not directly related to the organisation's core activities. By linking the quality of available facilities with active cost control, healthcare FM increases the organisation's efficiency and improves the work efficiency of the patients, staff, and visitors. The presented FM concept entails the need to engage advanced technology and information technology (IT) tools that ensure efficient information management and integrate various actions associated with the efficient management of healthcare FM.

10.10 Summary

Facilities management (FM) refers to the management of operation and maintenance activities that ensures end-users receive the services for which a facility was designed. A facility's FM cost is estimated at approximately 71% of its total life-cycle cost over a 40-year period. There are 11 core competencies for FM:

- communications
- emergency preparedness and business continuity
- environmental stewardship and sustainability
- finance and business
- human factors
- leadership and strategy
- operation and maintenance
- project management
- quality
- real estate and property management
- technology.

Conversely, knowledge management is regarded as creating and utilising knowledge within an organisation to foster innovation, develop new skills, and create a positive work environment, and has become the essential component of innovation in an organisation to improve performance and solve problems. It aids in developing platforms and processes for sharing tacit knowledge. The challenge of healthcare knowledge management is integrating multisource and multiformat healthcare information into a coherent knowledge base that can be used to provide day-to-day service. This is a critical issue that should concern all stakeholders in the broader health ecosystem. To address these issues, some governments have emphasised the need to revolutionise the FM sector by increasing the adoption of digital technologies.

Digital technologies can be described as scientific or engineering knowledge that deals with the establishment and application of computerised or digital devices, methods, or systems that can improve the immediacy, accuracy, and flexibility of communication. Advanced digital technology is a source of numerous solutions that can facilitate the acquisition, processing, redundancy, and compression of information about used buildings, making it easier to develop cause-and-effect models, draw conclusions, and make forecasts. Systems that have long been used for FM purposes, such as computer-aided FM (CAFM), computerised maintenance management systems (CMMS), building automation systems (BAS), or electronic document management systems (EDMS), have been proven helpful in practice, despite a lack of interoperability limiting their functionality. They function appropriately as separate systems but cannot communicate because there is no platform for information exchange. As a result, time dedicated to FM actions is inefficiently managed, including the integration of critical information, which can result in both time and financial losses. The provision of healthcare FM services, which are considered non-core services in healthcare organisations, has emerged as a critical service in delivering effective inpatient care and running productive healthcare. To assist these services, both technologies and the physical environment are critical in bringing about the changes needed in healthcare. For instance, technology and social changes have altered how facilities are managed, and many tasks previously performed by hand are now done automatically. Such automation in healthcare can bring about many beneficial outcomes including improvements to patient comfort and safety and greater efficiency in estates management.

Even though technology is now rapidly evolving, the FM profession is relatively risk-averse which might explain why the rate of technological change has been relatively slow. In addition, enacting such changes can bring uncertainties which is challenging for those in charge of healthcare FM. Notwithstanding this premise, FM has extensive information requirements and to effectively manage this, the use of innovative digital technologies and tools such as building information modelling (BIM) has proved useful. In addition, such technologies have provided greater data-processing capabilities applicable at all stages of the life cycle of built assets. This has helped estates personnel to gain a better understanding of the body of knowledge, procedures, and processes related to the management of infrastructural assets.

Healthcare facilities continue to face a variety of challenges, including non-functioning medical equipment, inadequate planning, inappropriate procurement, poorly organised and managed healthcare technical services, and skilled personnel shortages. Consequently, both technology and real estate are essential for the modification of healthcare organisations and have emerged as critical resources in delivering effective inpatient care and running productive healthcare facilities. For this reason, there is a future need for the healthcare sector to constantly change, with evolving technology and advances in patient care driving demands for the quick delivery of state-of-the-art facilities. Accordingly, healthcare services need to undergo a technological transformation to improve functions such as facilities control and performance, as well as to reduce costs. Despite this need for change, the architecture, engineering, and construction (AEC) sectors have yet to embrace new digital technologies. This has had the adverse effect of these industries remaining uncoordinated between offices and sites, with paper still being frequently used to manage processes and deliverables, such as design drawings and daily management. In addition, the variety of software tools and interoperability issues continue to be barriers to the adoption of digital technologies in the FM sector. Other problems are that existing technologies sometimes do not always capture and retrieve the detailed information and knowledge generated by building operation and maintenance, especially when failures arise. Such challenges may explain why there has been a slow rate of digitalisation, particularly in terms of building digital assets, expanding digital usage, and creating a highly digital workforce, compared to other sectors, such as manufacturing and distribution. To compound matters there has been relatively little research on using digital technologies in the operations and maintenance stage of the building life cycle.

Finally, there remains a need to engage advanced technology and information technology (IT) tools that ensure efficient information management and integrate various actions associated with the efficient management of healthcare FM. Otherwise this could lead to continued inefficiencies and excessive FM costs across large estates, such as those in the healthcare sector. Building information modelling (BIM) is a technology that in healthcare is attempting to 'turn the tide' in enabling new technologies to more effectively manage large estates. It acts as a reservoir for all design and construction information used by FM while BIM-enabled information systems seamlessly transfer design and construction models to FM systems. The use of BIM standards, such as Industry Foundation Classes (IFC) and Construction Operations and Building Information Exchange (COBie), has been viewed as highly promising by construction and political actors to address data dematerialisation issues and maximise building information interoperability. Despite this, maintaining links between geographic information systems (GIS) and BIM applications is an ongoing issue that must be addressed on a large scale.

References

Abdullah, S.A., Sulaiman, N., Latiffi, A.A. and Baldry, D. (2013). Integration of facilities management (FM) practices with building information modelling (BIM).

Abecker, A., Bernardi, A., Hinkelmann, K., et al. (1998). Toward a technology for organizational memories. *IEEE Intelligent Systems* 13(3): 40–48, May/June.

Agarwal, R., Chandrasekaran, S. and Sridhar, M. (2016). Imagining construction's digital future. https://www.mckinsey.com/capabilities/operations/our-insights/imagining-constructions-digital-future (accessed 20 October 2023).

Aloisio, M. (2019). Internet of Things for facility management services. An overview of the impact of IoT technologies on the FM services sector. https://www.politesi.polimi.it/handle/10589/149766 (accessed 21 September 2021).

Altnta, Y.D. and Ilal, M.E. (2021). Loose coupling of GIS and BIM data models for automated compliance checking against zoning codes. *Automation in Construction* 128: 103743.

AMI (Advanced Manufacturing International, Inc) (2022). Accelerating the Digital Transformation of Small & Medium Manufacturers. https://advmfg.org/a-change-in-perspective/ (accessed 20 August 2022).

Anshari, M. and Almunawar, M.N. (2021). Adopting open innovation for SMEs and industrial revolution 4.0 *Journal of Science and Technology Policy Management* 13(2): 405–427.

Araszkiewicz, K. (2017). Digital technologies in facility management: he state of practice and research challenges. *Procedia Engineering* 196: 1034–1042.

Barazzetti, L. (2016). Parametric as-built model generation of complex shapes from point clouds. Advanced Engineering Informatics 30(3): 298–311. http://dx.doi.org/10.1016/j.aei.2016.03.005 (accessed 20 October 2023).

Becerik-Gerher, B., Jazizadeh, F., Li N. and Calis, G. (2012). Application areas and data requirements for BIM-enabled facilities management, *Journal of Construction Engineering and Management* 138(3): 431–442. http://dx.doi.org/10.1061/(ASCE) CO.1943-7862.0000433. (accessed 20 October 2023).

Boland Jr, R.J. Lyytinen, K. and Yoo, Y. (2007). Wakes of innovation in project networks: The case of digital 3-D representations in architecture, engineering, and construction. *Organanization Science* 18(4): 631–647.

Chen K., Lu W. S., Peng Y., *et al.* (2015). Bridging BIM and building: From a literature review to an integrated conceptual framework. International Journal of Project Management 33(6): 1405–1416. http://dx.doi.org/10.1016/j.ijproman.2015.03.006 (accessed 20 October 2023).

Cheng, J.C.P., Chen W., Tan Y. and Wang M. (2016). A BIM-based decision support system framework for predictive maintenance management of building facilities. *16th International Conference on Computing in Civil and Building Engineering (ICCCBE2016)*, Osaka, Japan, 6–8 July 2016. http://www.see.eng.osaka-u.ac.jp/seeit/icccbe2016/Proceedings/Full_Papers/090-102.pdf (accessed 20 October 2023).

Costin, A., Pradhananga, N. and Teizer, J. (2014). Passive RFID and BIM for real-time visualization and location tracking, *Proceedings of the Construction Research Congress 2014*, Atlanta, GA, USA, 19–21 May 2014, pp. 169–178. http://dx.doi.org/10.1061/9780784413517.018 accessed 20 October 2023).

Darroch, J. (2005). Knowledge management, innovation and firm performance. *Journal of Knowledge Management* 9(3): 101–115.

Department of Health (2012). The power of information: Putting all of us in control of the health and care information we need. London: Department of Health. https://assets.publishing.service.gov.uk/media/5a7c3e9340f0b67063da7c11/dh_134205.pdf (accessed 20 October 2023).

Du Plessis, M. (2007). The role of knowledge management in innovation. *Journal of Knowledge Management* 11(4): 20–29.

East, E.W. (2007). Construction Operations Building Information Exchange (COBIE): Requirements definition and pilot implementation standard. Champaign, IL, USA: Engineer Research and Development Centre, Construction Engineering Research Lab.

Farias, M., Roxin, A. and Nicolle, C. (2015). COBieOWL, an OWL ontology based on COBie standard. In: *On the Move to Meaningful Internet Systems: OTM 2015 Conferences*, (eds C. Debruyne, H. Panetto, R. Meersman, *et al.*) Cham, Switzerland: Springer, pp. 361–377.

Flanagan, R., Jewell, C., Lu W.S. and Pekericli, K. (2014). Auto ID: Bridging the physical and the digital on construction projects. Chartered Institute of Building, Bracknell, Berkshire, pp. 1–38, (ISBN: 1853800191).

Fosu, R., Suprabhas, K., Rathore, Z. and Cory, C. (2015). Integration of building information modelling (BIM) and geographic information systems (GIS): A literature review and further needs. *Proceedings of the 32nd CIB W78 Conference*, 27–29 October 2015, Eindhoven, Netherlands. https://pdfs.semanticscholar.org/ f9d1/2f14791a7246a61c62c3e58f270d6104c97c.pdf (accessed 26 February 2021).

Gandhi, P., Khanna, S. and Ramaswamy, S. (2016). Which industries are the most digital (and why)? *Harvard Business Review*. https://hbr.org/2016/04/a-chart-that-shows-which-industries-are-the-most-digital-and-why (accessed 20 October 2023).

Golabchi, A. and Kamat, V. R. (2013). Evaluation of industry foundation classes for practical building information modeling interoperability. *Proceedings of the 30th ISARC*, Montreal, Canada, pp. 17–26.

Grimshaw, J. (2000). Locality and extended projection. In: *Amsterdam Studies in the Theory and History of Linguistic Science, Series 4*, (ed. E.F.K. Korner). Amsterdam: John Benjamins Publishing Company, pp. 115–134.

Halfawy, M.M. and Froese, T.M. (2007). Component-based framework for implementing integrated architectural/engineering/construction project systems. *Journal of Computing in Civil Engineering* 21(6): 441–452.

Hassani, H., Silva, E.S., Unger, S., *et al.* (2020). Artificial intelligence (AI) or intelligence augmentation (IA): What is the future? *AI* 1(2): 143–145.

IBM (2018). IBM TRIRIGA. https://www.ibm.com/au-en/marketplace/ibmtririga (accessed 20 October 2023).

Jiang F., Ma L., Broyd, T., *et al.* (2022). Building demolition estimation in urban road widening projects using as-is BIM models. *Automation in Construction* 144: 104601.

Kang T. W. and Hong C. H. (2015). A study on software architecture for effective BIM/GIS-based facility management data integration. *Automation in Construction* 54: 25–38. http://dx.doi.org/10.1016/j.autcon.2015.03.019 (accessed 20 October 2023).

Karshenas, S. and Niknam, M. (2013). Ontology-based building information modeling. *Computing in Civil Engineering* (2013): 476–483.

Kelsey, T., Cavendish, W. and National Information Board (2014). Personalised health and care 2020: Using data and technology to transform outcomes for patients and citizens. A framework for action. London: Department of Health. www.gov.uk/government/ publications/personalisedhealth-and-care-2020 (accessed 20 October 2023).

Kim S.C., Jeong Y.S. and Park S.O. (2013). RFID-based indoor location tracking to ensure the safety of the elderly in smart home environments. *Personal and Ubiquitous Computing* 17(8): 1699–1707.

Kim K., Kim H., Kim W., *et al.* (2018). Integration of IFC objects and facility management work information using Semantic Web. *Automation in Construction* 87: 173–187.

Kuda, F. and Berankova, E. (2014). Integration of facility management and project management as an effective management tool for development projects. *Applied Mechanics and Materials* 501: 2676–2681.

Kumar, S., Livermont, G. and McKewan, G. (2010). Stage implementation of RFID in hospitals. *Technology and Health Care* 18(1): 31–46. https://content.iospress.com/articles/technology-and-health-care/thc00570 (accessed 20 October 2023).

Lavy, S. and Jawadekar, S. (2014). A case study of using BIM and COBie for facility management. *International Journal of Facility Management* 5(2).

Leaman, A. and Bordass, B. (2006). Productivity in buildings: The 'killer' variables. In: *Creating the Productive Workplace*, 2e (ed. D. Clements-Croome). Abingdon, UK: Routledge, pp. 181–208.

Lenel, A., Temple-Bird, C., Kawohl, W. and Kaur, M. (2005). *Guide 1: How to Organize a System of Healthcare Technology Management.* ('How to Manage' Series for Healthcare Technology). St Albans, UK: TALC.

Lewis, A., Elmualim, A. and Riley, D. (2011). Linking energy and maintenance management for sustainability through three American case studies. *Facilities* 29(5/6): 243–254. http://dx.doi.org/10.1108/02632771111120547 (accessed 20 October 2023).

Li N. and Becerik-Gerber, B. (2011). Performance-based evaluation of RFID-based indoor location sensing solutions for the built environment. Advanced Engineering Informatics 25(3): 535–546. http://dx.doi.org/10.1016/j.aei.2011.02.004 (accessed 20 October 2023).

Liu X., Wang X., Wright, G., *et al.* (2017). A state-of-the-art review on the integration of building information modeling (BIM) and geographic information system (GIS). *ISPRS International Journal of Geo-Information* 6(2): 53. https://www.mdpi.com/2220-9964/6/2/53 (accessed 20 October 2023).

López-Nicolás, C. and Meroño-Cerdán, Á.L. (2011). Strategic knowledge management, innovation and performance. International Journal of Information Management 31(6): 502–509.

Lu Y., Li Y., Skibniewski, M., *et al.* (2015). Information and communication technology applications in architecture, engineering, and construction organisations: A 15-year review. Journal of Management in Engineering 31(1): 1–19. http://dx.doi.org/10.1061/(ASCE)ME.1943-5479.0000319 (accessed 20 October 2023).

Manyika, J., Ramaswamy, S., Khana, S., *et al.* (2016). Digital America: A tale of the haves and have-mores. McKinsey Global Institute. https://www.mckinsey.com/industries/technology-media-and-telecommunications/our-insights/digital-america-a-tale-of-the-haves-and-have-mores (accessed 20 October 2023).

Matta, P., Pant, B. and Arora, M. (2017). All you want to know about Internet of Things (IoT). In: *2017 International Conference on Computing, Communication and Automation (ICCCA)*, 5–6 May 2017, Noida, India. New York: IEEE, pp. 1306–1311.

McAdam, R. (2000). Knowledge management as a catalyst for innovation within organizations: A qualitative study. *Knowledge and Process Management.* 7(4): 2–6.

Meerow, S., Newell, J.P. and Stults, M. (2016). Defining urban resilience: A review. *Landscape and Urban Planning* 147: 38–49. https://www.sciencedirect.com/science/article/abs/pii/S0169204615002418 (accessed 20 October 2023).

Morgan, J. (2014). A simple explanation of 'The Internet of Things'. *Forbes*. https://www.forbes.com/sites/jacobmorgan/2014/05/13/simple-explanation-internet-things-that-anyone-can-understand/?sh=76ffb8d11d09 (accessed 20 October 2023).

Motawa, I. and Almarshad, A. (2013). A knowledge-based BIM system for building maintenance. *Automation in Construction* 29: 173–182. https://www.sciencedirect.com/science/article/abs/pii/S0926580512001574?via%3Dihub (accessed 20 October 2023).

NHS England (2019). A five-year framework for GP contract reform to implement The NHS Long Term Plan. www.england.nhs.uk/publication/gp-contract-five-year-framework (accessed 12 March 2020).

Niskanen, I., Purhonen, A., Kuusijärvi, J. and Halmetoja, E. (2014). Towards semantic facility data management. In: *INTELLI 2014: The Third International Conference on Intelligent Systems and Applications*, pp. 85–90

Nosratabadi, S., Mosavi, A., Duan, P., *et al.* (2020). Data science in economics: Comprehensive review of advanced machine learning and deep learning methods. Mathematics 8(10): 1799.

Okada, R.C., Simons, A.E. and Sattineni, A. (2017). Owner-requested changes in the design and construction of government healthcare facilities. *Procedia Engineering* 196: 592–606.

O'Leary, D. and O'Leary, E. (1998). Using AI in knowledge management: Knowledge bases and ontologies. *IEEE Intelligent Systems and their Applications* 13(3) 34–39, May/June.

Onuma Software (2018). onuma-bim.com/ (accessed 27 February /2021).

Oti, A.H., Kurul, E., Cheung, F. and Tah, J.H.M. (2016). A framework for the utilisation of building management system data in building information models for building design and operation. Automation in Construction 72: 195–210. https://www.sciencedirect.com/science/article/abs/pii/S0926580516301972?via%3Dihub *(accessed 20 October 2023).*

Parsanezhad, P. and Dimyadi, J. (2014). Effective facility management and operations via a BIM-based integrated information system. In: *Proceedings of the CIB Facilities Management Conference*, Copenhagen, Denmark, 21–23 May, 2014. https://www.researchgate.net/publication/262362615_Effective_Facility_Management_and_Operations_via_a_BIM-based_Integrated_Information_System (accessed 26 September 2021).

Parsanezhad, P. and Tarandi, V. (2013). Is the age of facility managers' paper boxes over? In: *Proceedings of the 19th CIB World Building Congress, 2013*. http://www.diva-portal.org/smash/record.jsf?pid=diva2%3A665801&dswid=5329 (accessed 26 February 2021).

Patel, K.K., Patel, S.M. and Scholar, P. (2016). Internet of things-IOT: Definition, characteristics, architecture, enabling technologies, application and future challenges. *International Journal of Engineering Science and Computing* 6(5).

Pittet, P., Cruz, C. and Nicolle, C. (2014). An ontology change management approach for facility management. *Computers in Industry* 65(9): 1301–1315.

Puolitaival, T., Kestle, L. and Kähkönen, K. (2018). What's the real story around digital technologies in construction management? https://www.researchbank.ac.nz/handle/10652/4399 (accessed 21 September 2021).

Raju, M.P. and Laxmi, A.J. (2020). IOT based online load forecasting using machine learning algorithms. *Procedia Computer Science* 171: 551–560.

Rasoulifar, R., Dankelman, J., Thomann, G. and Villeneuve, F. (2008). Healthcare management technology: Place of design process and role of the universities. *Euromot*.

Riedl, M.O. (2019). Human-centered artificial intelligence and machine learning. *Human Behaviour and Emerging Technologie*s, 1(1): 33–36.

Rodríguez, J., Dackiewicz, N. and Toer, D. (2014). La gestión hospitalaria centrada en el paciente. *Archivos Argentinos de Pediatría* 112(1): 55–58.

Rondeau, E.P., Brown, R.K. and Lapides, P.D. (2012). *Facility Management*, 2e, New York: Wiley.

Service Works Global (2018). QFM facilities management software. https://www.swg. com/aus/landing-page-qfm-facilities-management-software/?gclid=EAIaIQobChMI49X D7a-V2QIVSgYqCh2PrQHuEAAYASAAEgJjKPD_BwE (accessed 20 September 2023).

Shohet, I.M. and Lavy, S. (2004). Development of an integrated healthcare facilities management model. *Facilities* 22(5/6), 129–140.

Smith, D.K. and Tardif, M. (2009). *Building Information Modelling: A Strategic Implementation Guide for Architects, Engineers, Contractors and Real Estate Asset Management*. Hoboken, NJ: Wiley.

Song, T. (2018). Facilities management knowledge mapping from text documents: A case study for using NLP for facilities management knowledge mapping. Doctoral dissertation. Texas A&M University. https://oaktrust.library.tamu.edu/handle/1969.1/173909 (accessed 21 September 2021).

Teicholz, P. (2013). *BIM for Facility Managers*. Hoboken, NJ: Wiley.

Temel, S., Mention, A.L. and Yurtseven, A.E. (2021). Cooperation for innovation: More is not necessarily merrier. *European Journal of Innovation Management* 26(2): 446–474.

Temple-Bird, C., Kawohl, W., Lenel, A. and Kaur, M. (2005). *Guide 2: How to Plan and Budget for Your Healthcare Technology*. ('How to Manage' Series for Healthcare Technology). St Albans, UK: TALC.

Usak, M., Kubiatko, M., Shabbir, M.S., *et al.* (2020). Health care service delivery based on the Internet of things: A systematic and comprehensive study. *International Journal of Communication Systems 33*(2): e4179.

Valero, E., Adán, A. and Cerrada, C. (2015). Evolution of RFID applications in construction: A literature review. *Sensors* 15(7): 15988–16008. https://www.mdpi. com/1424-8220/15/7/15988# (accessed 20 October 2023).

Vermesan, O. and Friess, P. (eds) (2013). *Internet of Things: Converging Technologies for Smart Environments and Integrated Ecosystems*. Aalborg, Denmark: River Publishers.

Wenzel, L. and Evans, H. (2019). Clicks and mortar. https://www.property.nhs.uk/ media/1680/clicks-and-mortar-kings-fund-report-final.pdf (accessed 21 September 2021).

Wilson, J. (2015). Architecture tomorrow: Healthcare. *Architects' Journal* 241.19: 30–31.

Wong, J.K.W., Ge, J. and He, S.X. (2018). Digitisation in facilities management: A literature review and future research directions. *Automation in Construction* 92: 312–326.

Zhou P., Bundorf, K., Chang J.L., *et al.* (2011). Organisational culture and its relationship with hospital performance in public hospitals in China. *Health Services Research* 46(6pt2):2139–2160. doi: 10.1111/j.1475-6773.2011.01336.x. (accessed 20 October 2023).

11

An Introduction to Smart Estates and Digital Information Management for Collaboration in the Built Environment Using Case Studies

At least 40% of all business will die in the next 10 years if they do not figure out how to change their entire company to accommodate new technologies.

John Charles, CISCO

11.1 Introduction

This chapter of the book discusses the immense potential of digital twins in solving some of the current urbanisation-led challenges for the urban built environment. The research further recommends strategies on how best to derive value from a digital twin to improve the future state of the urban built environment, such as target value design, knowledge sensitisation, continuous upskilling, collaboration, secure and safe data, and infrastructure, and the need for standardisation.

The chapter uses case studies carried out in Singapore and Herrenberg, Germany, which are two examples of where digital twins, albeit on different scales, have proved very influential in promoting this technology globally. It starts by giving context to the digital transformation in the built environment. In this regard, it will discuss how digital technologies have allowed the construction and engineering industries to develop what could not be created before, and to construct new forms of building, therein transforming cities. It then explains the work of the Centre for Digital Built Britain (CDBB) in providing the framework for information management to enable stable, resilient data sharing between digital twins. Furthermore, it refers to the work of the UK government's Digital Framework Task Group (DFTG) which has devised a set of principles to promote the creation of a UK network of the digital twin.

The chapter then provides background and context to digital twins and describes what they are with alternative definitions given. It explains the three virtual models that make up digital twins and their key characteristics as a context for what they represent. An articulation is also made regarding the six recognisable elements that form part of a digital twin's maturity spectrum. The evolution and original concept and history of digital twins is then discussed with reference to certain similar technologies dating back to the Apollo missions 50 years ago. The chapter then proceeds to explain and discuss the importance of digital twins to the built environment and urbanisation on a global scale. The need for urban built environments to pave the way for continuous evolution integrating emerging technologies for more effective global sustainability is then discussed.

The ways and means by which digital twins have been regarded by many as a natural evolution of building information modelling (BIM) are discussed and evaluated. Following on from this, the challenges around the built environment, particularly focusing on fragmentation and low, underachieving productivity levels will be covered. To address these challenges, the use of digital twins in the built environment as a collaborative tool for creating smart cities in terms of urban modelling and planning is analysed. In this sense the chapter explains how digital twins allow a high degree of simulation of urban plans, real-time monitoring, and control of urban transport infrastructure, future mobility, and improved sustainability, with reference to the Singapore case study. Finally, the other benefits of digital twin technologies are described such as efficiency and streamlined information workflows in capital delivery, health and well-being, security, building automation, and predictive maintenance.

11.2 The Digital Revolution

The digital revolution is a generic term to describe the phenomenon of usage of information and automation technologies to allow collaboration between products and their process and supply chain. Since the early 2010s, digital technologies have transformed vast industries, setting in motion the digital revolution. Digital transformation in the built environment is the use of digital technology to allow the industry to develop what could not be created before; to construct new forms of building, to transform cities and towns, and to address urbanisation and sustainability challenges. The digital revolution in this regard promotes growth and development, through its efficiency and versatility, toward productivity (Maskuriy *et al.*, 2019). For this reason, most companies across different sectors, ranging from services to manufacturing, have transformed since the beginning of the twenty-first century and have striven to put product and process innovations at the centre of their operations.

Dramatic shifts in climate, technology, culture, global production, and value chains are forcing governments, companies, and professionals to reconsider not only how they interact with each other but also how they produce, distribute, and consume the environment and its built assets. The advent of broad deployment of emerging technologies, such as artificial intelligence (AI), sensor technology, cloud computing, open data, the Internet of things (IoT), and blockchain, has reinvented the way in which we can handle development and adapt to these challenges. Accordingly, urban built environments need to use innovative technologies to allow them to develop, sustain growth, and exploit high-tech products to serve their people better (ESPON, 2020).

Building information management (BIM) and developing information management in the building industry is a significant move forward, particularly for the UK. Not withstanding this development, it is essential to exploit the full potential of emerging digital technology, such as the IoT, digital twins, AI, and advanced data analytics, throughout the built environment.

11.3   Information Management Framework

The UK took steps toward championing the digital revolution in the built environment through policy and the launch of the Centre for Digital Built Britain (CDBB). The purpose was to maximise the performance, service, and value of UK infrastructure; to generate value to society, industry, the environment, and the economy (IET, 2019). The CDBB provided resources to guide the infrastructure and construction sector toward its digital transformation and also provided the framework for information management to enable stable, resilient data sharing between digital twins. The CDBB introduced 'The pathway towards an Information Management Framework'. This pathway set out a digital framework for secure sharing and coordination of infrastructure data to realise the benefits of data sharing as recommended by 'Data for the Public Good' (NIC, 2017). The digital framework provided a roadmap for industry and government in exploiting their information to enable better decisions as a critical step toward a national digital twin. The vision for 'Digital Built Britain' was to get data right from the start and design better performing homes, buildings, and infrastructure, using best practice. This included secure-by-default, information management, using modern and evolving digital construction, and utilising techniques to enhance safety, efficiency, and productivity during construction. It was also crucial to understand how the built environment would enhance the quality of life and use that information to drive the design and development of the economic and social infrastructure.

The UK government's Digital Framework Task Group (DFTG) issued a set of principles to promote the creation of a UK network of the digital twin. The 'Gemini Principles' guide encouraged the creation of the framework leading to the National Digital Twin (NDT). The Gemini Principles are intended to assist the industry in creating compatible digital twins that can become part of the NDT. The constituent digital twins will have several subordinate functions which will contribute to the NDT's common objective. The Gemini Principles are descriptive of intent but agnostic on solutions, so over time, they are intended to promote flexibility for innovation and development.

The Gemini Principles, as shown in Figure 11.1 categorise the three main mandatory targets of a digital twin; purpose, trust, and function. This is predicated on the digital twin having a clear purpose for the public good, enabling value creation, and performance improvement, while providing determinable insight to the built environment. In addition, the digital twin must be trustworthy while promoting security, openness, and quality of information. Furthermore, it must function effectively, based on a standard connected environment, having clear ownership, governance, and regulation, be able to adapt as technology and society evolve.

'The flourishing systems' set out that infrastructure is intended for human flourishing and thus infrastructure should be perceived and maintained as a network of systems that serve people and the environment. In this way, they develop a system-based focus on infrastructure based on:

- People: an emphasis on outcomes and human flourishing, as infrastructure offers essential services that people, and society, depend on;
- Connections: a focus on existing and proposed integrated infrastructure since the infrastructure is a network of systems;

Purpose	Public good	Value creation	Insight
Must have a clear purpose	Must be used to deliver genuine public benefits in perpetuity	Must enable value creation and performance improvement	Must provide determinable insight into the built environment
Trust	**Security**	**Openness**	**Quality**
Must be trustworthy	Must enable security and be secure itself	Must be as open as possible	Must be built on data of an appropriate quality
Function	**Federation**	**Curation**	**Evolution**
Must function correctly	Must be based on a standard connected environment	Must have clear ownership, governance, and regulation	Must be able to adapt as technology and society evolve

Figure 11.1 The Gemini Principles (adapted from Bolton *et al* 2018).

- Sustainability: an emphasis on long-term infrastructure sustainability, and the society it supports, because infrastructure as a network must be sustainable, secure, and resilient; and
- Digitalisation: a focus on creating infrastructure as a cyber–physical system because digital transformation is necessary to extract greater value from the built environment.

The flourishing systems suggest that infrastructure must get smart. Digital assets, such as data, information, algorithms, and digital twins, must be recognised as genuine assets that are valuable and must be handled efficiently and securely. When data and digital assets are valued in time, data would be seen as infrastructure. By better data collection, curation, and connectivity, it becomes possible to create new digital value assets for owners, operators, and society. In digital twins, technologies such as the Internet of things (IoT), artificial intelligence (AI), and augmented and virtual reality may be incorporated to improve better decision-making. Accurate and open records of our facilities and built environment can also assist decision-makers of the present and future.

11.4 Background and Context to Digital Twins

11.4.1 Description of a Digital Twin

Digital twins represent an open, trusted, and reliable digital representation of the elements and dynamics of a physical system or built assets, such as a building, urban network, or asset portfolio, and can be referred to as a cyber–physical system. Traditionally, they contain feedback loops that allow big data transportation and synchronisation between the virtual replication and physical environment with near-real-time Internet of things (IoT) sensors. In this way, they are embedded into multiple data points to relay structured and big unstructured data flows from physical to virtual. They also offer the ability to incorporate analytics, including machine learning and simulation algorithms, to provide an understanding of the elements and dynamics. In this way, they offer real-time corrective triggers back to the physical asset, or responses, current insights, and the prediction of various potential future scenarios, to promote better decision-making on a built asset or an ecosystem of connected digital twins.

Managing urban areas is now one of the twenty-first century's most significant developmental challenges. Rapid urbanisation does not negate urban areas from the urban growth threats posed to their built environment. It results in an increased demand for the built environment to rethink and change the adverse effects of fast urbanisation, such as climate change, resource scarcity, and a growing urban population, to more positive outcomes. The digitalisation of the built environment is an opportunity to tackle the industry's challenges by taking advantage of the general availability of best practices from other sectors. This encapsulates advanced techniques and tools, digital workflows, and technological expertise to shift to a higher level of efficiency and to become a digital industry.

The use of digital twins for the built environment is just beginning, and yet to catch up with healthcare, manufacturing, aerospace, and the automotive industries. The leverage of this technology for the urban built environment can deliver many positive outcomes. These include mitigating the adverse effects of urbanisation such as pressure on built asset services, climate change, and built environment industry fragmentation. They can also assist in managing COVID-19, and any future pandemics, the impact on organisational estates, and the creation of healthier operations in urban built assets, cities, and towns.

The development of digital twins is in their infancy. Possibly, this can be explained by the array of challenges and risks to their adoption, and these will be identified and discussed more in Chapter 13: Digital Twin Enablers for Collaboration and the Risks and Barriers to Adoption of Digital Twins.

11.4.2 The Digital Twin Concept

A digital twin is a cycle flow between physical and virtual realities (mirroring or twinning), where data flows from the physical to the virtual environment, and information and processes respond from the virtual to the physical state (Jones *et al.*, 2020). Furthermore, it is a digital replica or illustration of a system, process, or place in the real world that mimics its behaviour. A digital twin can also be described as a virtual representation rendered of a product that contains real-time data capable of being captured by big data or sensor technologies. In the built environment, it has sometimes been referred to as an 'integrated product model' that is developed for all assets, issues, and defects and one which is continuously modified to incorporate wear and tear sustained during occupational use. In this sense, it could be deemed to be real-time representation of a physical entity or system that helps to improve business performance. In addition, it is a suitably synchronised body of useful information comprising the structure, function, and behaviour of a physical object in virtual space, with information flows that allow for integration between physical and virtual states. Furthermore, it represents real objects in the digital world, with their data, functions, and communication capabilities.

A digital twin can be described as an evolving digital profile of a physical object or process' historical and current behaviour, which helps optimise business efficiency. It is focused on huge, cumulative, real-time metrics of real-world data over several dimensions. These metrics may establish an emerging object or process profile in the digital world that can provide valuable insights into system operation. One other definition for a digital twin is a 'model of a physical object that can be used to simulate impacts, often in real-time, and track the physical asset' (Duarte, 2019), whereby it communicates, promotes, and co-evolves with the physical asset through bidirectional interactions. In this regard, it assists with the design, operation, and maintenance phase of the built environment, therein making it safer and more effective (Duarte, 2019). The 'Gemini Principles' define a digital twin as a realistic digital representation of a physical object that unlocks value by allowing for better insights that support better decisions, leading to improved outcomes in the physical world. Ultimately, the Gemini Principles also define a digital twin as a realistic digital representation of assets, processes, or systems in the built or natural environment. This technology relies on the ability to combine data from various data sources to optimise the efficiency of data processing and better decision-making.

The digital twin model consists of three virtual models comprising: a physics model, a behaviour model, and a rule model. A digital twin model should be a true replica of the physical object, reproducing the physical geometries, properties, actions, and rules to a 3D geometric model. The 3D geometric models define the shape, scale, tolerance, and structural relationship of a physical object. The physics model represents the physical phenomenon of the body, such as deformation, delamination, fracture, and corrosion, based on physical properties such as speed, wear, and force. Alternatively, the behaviour model defines the behaviour of the object such as state transition, performance, and coordination and reaction mechanisms to outside environment changes. By following the rules derived from historical evidence, the rule model provides the digital twin with analytical abilities such as reasoning, judgment, interpretation, and autonomous decision-making.

The key characteristics of a digital twin are:

- It must be a trusted and reliable digital representation of something physical like a system or a built asset such as a building, network, or asset portfolio.
- It must have feedback loops that allow data transportation and synchronisation between the virtual replication and physical environment in near real-time.
- It must ensure that a common data environment (CDE) enables it to be a secure, unified source of truth. A digital twin incorporates analytics, including machine learning and simulation of algorithms, offering insights that produce multiple potential future scenarios while promoting better decision-making.

A digital twin's maturity spectrum could be divided into six recognisable elements (IET, 2019) as demonstrated in Table 11.1. Each of the elements can increase in complexity and cost in its own right, therefore, it is neither a linear nor a sequential system, in that a twin may possess the early or experimental features of higher order elements before possessing the fundamental lower order elements (IET, 2019). The lower elements are the development of an accurate, as-built asset or system, or asset data model. These models can be tied to static data, metadata, and building information modelling (BIM) and enhanced in real-time with additional sensors and mechanical augmentation, and two-way integration so that interaction can begin. This enables a digital twin to alter physical asset status and condition. This system could gradually become autonomous in its activities, evolving to operate the asset through full integration between the physical and digital worlds (IET, 2019).

Table 11.1 The digital twin maturity spectrum (adapted from IET, 2019).

Element (logarithmic scale of complexity)	Defining principle	Outline usage
0	Reality capture (e.g., point cloud, drone, photogrammetry)	Brownfield (existing) as-built survey
1	2D map/system or 3D model (e.g., object-based, with no metadata or BIM)	Design/asset optimisation and coordination
2	Connect model to persistent (static) data, metadata, and BIM Stage 2 (e.g., documents, drawings, asset management systems)	4D/5D simulation, design/asset management Stage 2
3	Enrich with real-time data (e.g., from IoT sensors)	Operational efficiency
4	Two-way data integration and interaction	Remote and immersive operations
		Control the physical from the digital
5	Autonomous operation and maintenance	Complete autonomous operation and maintenance

A digital twin is a necessary foundation and direction for a cyber–physical system. Cyber–physical systems have been proposed within production systems as smart embedded and networked systems. They work on a virtual and physical level, communicating with and manipulating physical instruments, sensing, and acting on the real world. The cyber–physical system's physical and digital twins are linked reciprocally and synchronised in real time through interconnected sensors and devices. The cyber–physical system acts as a tool for visualising, simulating, manifesting, observing, and controlling the physical object.

Digital twin technology can enable the improvement in performance in the built asset operation process through cyber–physical systems and closed-loop optimisation realisation (Barricelli *et al.*, 2019). A digital twin is dynamically connected to its physical counterpart to enable advanced simulation, operation, and analysis. Connections between physical entities, virtual models, systems, and data enable data-driven, closed-loop optimisation and information exchange for optimum resource allocation, cost management analytics, and avoidance of errors and fatal failure. Furthermore, dynamic information exchange may involve, for example, information on the environment, energy consumption, equipment, and operation.

The transformative power of digital twins lies in their being connected, to provide more information into a broader context (IET, 2019). In this sense, the digital 'golden' thread connects digital twins and physical asset models, or asset groups, and therein offers a continuous, seamless data string that links every stage of a product's life cycle from design, through construction, to field use. This thread also provides the medium through which product data is linked and shared collaboratively between alternate digital twins. Accordingly, they may nurture a national digital twin from those at a more local level, which could open up the possibility of generating even more value from using data for the public good.

11.4.3 The Evolution of Digital Twins

The digital twin idea is not a new phenomenon. The technology is already embedded in some current technologies, such as 3D modelling, simulation, and digital prototyping (including architectural, functional, and behavioural prototyping). The first use of the term digital twin can only be traced back to 2003, in the discipline of manufacturing, as a concept in product life-cycle management. However, the concept had been used by some industries and organisations with various levels of sophistication. It has also existed under several different terminologies, such as the 'mirrored system' first used by NASA to rescue Apollo 13 in 1970 (Jones *et al.*, 2020). Furthermore, digital twins were used in real-time monitoring systems for detecting oil and water pipeline leakage and remote satellite or space station control and maintenance.

The term 'digital twin' was originally coined in the year 2003 by Michael Grieves in his research with NASA's John Vickers. Grieves presented the digital twin concept in a 2003 lecture on product life-cycle management (Jones *et al.*, 2020). Grieves and Vickers envisioned a future where a virtual product model would lay the groundwork for product life-cycle management (Jones *et al.*, 2020). In 2010, NASA presented the idea of digital twin technology. NASA used digital twin technology to create a highly detailed simulated model of a spacecraft or aircraft. Within the virtual world, the simulated model was demonstrated to mimic the spacecraft or aircraft's physical behaviour as closely as possible (Research and Markets, 2020). In addition to NASA, the US Air Force utilised the digital twin idea while introducing new concepts like a digital thread. They detailed an analysis of digital twin technology for the production of weapons systems, showing the need to build a design road map and environment for the creation and deployment of digital twin systems. The US Air Force defined a digital thread as the development and use of a digital surrogate of a product system to allow dynamic, real-time evaluation of the current and future capacities of the system to inform decisions.

The initial definition describes a digital twin as a virtual representation of a physical product with information about a product originating in the domain of product life-cycle management (Jones *et al.*, 2020). Grieves built on this concept by defining the digital twin as consisting of three elements: a physical object, a virtual representation of that object, and bidirectional data links feeding data from physical to virtual representation, and information and processes from virtual to physical representation (Jones *et al.*, 2020). After several years of in-depth work in the field of virtual modelling, simulation methods, data processing, and visualisation digital twins have seen their applications expanded to many fields since the advancement of information and communications technologies. Some of these fields are maintenance and product quality management, real-time tracking, education, production systems, smart grids, energy efficiency, and healthcare.

11.5 Digital Twins, the Built Environment, and Urbanisation

11.5.1 The Importance of the Built Environment and Urbanisation on a Global Scale

The built environment is not just a conglomeration of buildings; it is also the physical result of the different economic, social, and environmental factors that are related to the needs and standards of society (Santamouris, 2001). Furthermore, it is everything humanly created, modified, or constructed, and arranged to serve human needs, desires, and values (Bartuska, 2007). The built environment is designed to help us deal with the overall environment and protect us from it, to meditate, or change it for our comfort and well-being (Bartuska, 2007). Urbanisation refers to increases in the cities' size, density, and heterogeneity over time. It is related to the agglomeration dynamics of people and resources (Ompad *et al.*, 2007). Urban built environments are areas formed by urbanisation and defined by urban morphology as cities, towns, conurbations, or suburbs. Furthermore, urbanisation is a mechanism involving urban development and growth (Ompad *et al.*, 2007) whereby cities and towns are engines for growth and development. These aspects are pivotal to development, significantly contributing to the gross domestic product (GDP) in both low-income and high-income countries. The continuous change in human residences is generated by the fact that cities and towns generate wealth, allow economic functions, and offer the population more meaningful life opportunities.

Urban built environments are formed by deep forces such as population, technology, and infrastructures. According to the World Bank, about 55 % of the world's population, circa 4.2 billion inhabitants, reside in urban areas. We are gradually becoming an urban world, with a projected increase in growth in the urban population to about 70% of the world's population by 2050. Such forces converge, with urbanisation and climate change spurring drastic changes in urban environments. The increase in urban built environments can set a wave of urban challenges in motion. An apparent but often ignored feature is that every component of the built environment is defined and affected by context. Each dimension contributes to the overall quality of both built and natural environments and human–environmental relationships, either positively or negatively. These impacts are most often local and are increasingly experienced at all levels, including global (Bartuska, 2007). There is a need for urban built environments to pave the way for continuous evolution, integrating emerging technologies for a more effective and sustainable set-up. Solutions need to be adjusted to meet local needs and ensure that the best techniques are implemented in the right settings, suited to each environment's unique characteristics (Siemens, 2020).

The critical sector in developed and developing economies is the built environment industry, as it is a major contributor to the production of built assets and responsible for 39% of all carbon emissions in the world. The built environment is also a leading source of job creation that provides job opportunities for millions of unskilled, semi-skilled, and skilled workers. The construction industry, as part of the built environment, contributes 13% of global GDP and employs approximately 7% of the global working-age population (McKinsey and Company, 2020). The construction sector in the UK contributes 6% of economic output and 6.6% of all jobs. In comparison, the property sector is worth about 7% of economic output and contributes to about 7% of all jobs.

The joint strategy for government and industry in the UK, Construction 25, set out three strategic priorities: smart construction and digital design, sustainable design, and improved trade performance (HM Government, 2013). The strategic priorities are aimed at enabling: a reduction of 50% in the average time from commencement to finish for new build and refurbished assets, a 33% drop in both the primary building costs and the asset's total life costs, a 50% reduction in greenhouse gas emissions in the built environment, and a decrease of the trade gap between total exports and total imports of construction products and materials by 50% (HM Government, 2013).

The built environment in the UK is no exception to the prevalent digital revolution and the government is making smooth collective progress on the building information modelling (BIM) action plan since the introducing it on all public sector projects in 2016. Building information modelling (BIM) information enables effective resource management and processes. An industry mandate under Government Construction Strategy 2011–2015 that made BIM level 2 mandatory for use in optimisation, resulting in improved productivity and profitability. The benefits BIM provides to the built environment are limitless, but the implementation has not taken place at the pace desired. The sector is rapidly digitalising, and BIM is becoming an essential part of it. The built environment is already dealing with large volumes of heterogeneous data; information or data is the core of BIM. BIM changes how information is managed and exchanged regarding a project's entire life. Digital twins can be seen as a natural evolution of BIM, which is already beginning to reflect the built environment digitally (BSI Group, 2018). For the improvement of social, economic, and environmental value, the use of BIM has been the focus of digital transformation for years. But quickly appearing in the rear mirror is digital twin technology that could dramatically change the industry if it could understand its potential (Harris, 2019). In and beyond 2020, data creates value and has become the most valuable resource. The idea of harnessing digital twins and data in other sectors such as the healthcare, aerospace, and the automotive industries has been proven to provide more opportunities to use information to make better decisions for improving sustainable value in operations and processes. The latest inclination is to develop systems and solutions that will support it not only during the conceptualisation, prototyping, testing, and design optimisation process but also during the operational phase, with the ultimate goal of using digital twins during the entire product life cycle and perhaps far beyond.

The global digital twin market is expected to be worth US$5.1 billion in 2020, reaching US$115.1 billion by 2035, growing at an estimated compound annual growth rate (CAGR) of 23.2% (Research and Markets, 2020). Digital twins can help mitigate many of today's major problems, like urbanisation, population growth, climate change, infrastructure cost inflation, and sustainable development. Different analysts may express different values to the digital twin market but all expect one aspect – the digital twin's tremendous growth and significance. This research presents the leverage potential for the adoption of digital twins in the built environment as a solution to urban built environment issues.

11.5.2   Challenges around the Built Environment

The built environment sector is now very much a data management business, where concepts like BIM are now essential to driving information-led productivity in capital projects and programmes. Customers understand the value of purchasing not only a physical asset but also the associated data and information sets. Accordingly, the use of data, emerging technologies, materials, and instruments have enormous prospects. Managing urban areas is now one of the twenty-first century's most significant developmental challenges. Rapid urbanisation does not negate the urban growth threats posed to its built environment. It results in an increased demand for the built environment to rethink and change the adverse effects of fast urbanisation, such as climate change, resource scarcity, and a growing urban population, to more positive outcomes. The industry is always under pressure from the government, local authorities, and the public. The industry is the critical player in the retrofitting, rehabilitation, and renovation of existing built assets. Nevertheless, it also has to fill in the deficit in the delivery of new sustainable buildings, services, and infrastructure, such as transport, schools, hospitals, and affordable housing. These problems have ensured the built environment industry continues to rethink and reinvent itself.

Globally, the built environment is one of the most fragmented sectors, hampering sustainable development, particularly in urban settings. It contributes to a myriad of industry challenges in the UK including low and underachieving productivity levels as compared to other developed economies and industries such as manufacturing, aerospace, and the automotive industries. Outdated technologies are prevalent across the industry and they are incapable of meeting industry needs, leading to client dissatisfaction, inefficiencies in process and operations, deficiencies in safety, and a higher than acceptable carbon footprint.

In 2020, the abrupt arrival of the COVID-19 pandemic struck the world, bringing economies and industries to resounding devastation. The pandemic has also had a devastating impact on the built environment with the delay and disruption of the delivery of built assets to meet the urban growing need. This unpredictable phenomenon has placed a steep digital learning curve on the industry to reinvent design and develop digital strategies to create stable urban areas and assets able to function at high capacity during times of severe disruption, *yet also* enhancing liveability and healthy user functionality in the event of social distancing.

The digitalisation of the built environment is an opportunity to tackle industry's challenges by taking advantage of the general availability of best practices from other sectors, for using advanced techniques and tools, digital workflows, and technological expertise to shift to a higher level of efficiency, and to become a digital industry. Despite the vast potential of the industry, increased efficiency and productivity can only result from digitalsation, new construction techniques, and innovations (Maskuriy *et al.*, 2019).

11.6   The Use of Digital Twins in the Built Environment

Digital twin technology is one of the most innovative tools in the digital transformation of the urban built environment today. This chapter, predominantly using a case study of Singapore, articulates the benefits of harnessing digital twins to our urban built assets.

11.6.1 Digital Urban Twins as a Collaborative Tool for Smart Cities

Digital urban twins are sophisticated data models that allow collaborative processes. They are a collaboratively procured digital tool of the built environment containing buildings, a street network model using space syntax theory and method, a simulation of urban mobility, wind flow simulation, and a variety of empirical, quantitative, and qualitative data using volunteered geographic information (Dembski *et al.*, 2020). City-scale digital twins aid in mapping space, people, and their activities in the physical city to a virtual city by establishing a closed-loop, city-level data feed into the virtual city. They make it possible to monitor, predict, and regulate the physical city, and to solve diverse urban lifecycle problems. These problems involve but are not limited to, mitigation and adaptation to climate change, urban sprawl, spatial disparity, air quality, and urban infrastructure and service pressure.

An urban digital twin is an essential tool for smart cities. A smart city denotes an instrumented, interconnected, and intelligent city. Instrumented refers to the ability to capture and incorporate live real-world data by using devices, detectors, appliances, personal computers, and other related sensors (Harrison *et al.*, 2010). Interconnected means incorporating such data into a computing framework that enables this information to be shared between the various city services. Intelligent refers to the use of advanced analytics, modelling, optimisation, and visualisation tools to make better organisational decisions (Harrison, *et al.*, 2010). A city is smart when investments in human and social capital, traditional infrastructure, and disruptive technology drive sustainable economic development and high quality of life through participatory governance, with a wise management of natural resources. A digital twin is a data-rich virtual model of a city in the realm of smart cities, a mirror of the physical world, with layered real-time data sources of buildings, urban infrastructure, services, industries, and movements of people and automobiles. It is increasingly becoming an invaluable resource to visualise the pulse of the city in real time, therein simulating city strategies before they are implemented, and exposing problems before they become a reality.

A national digital twin is an ecosystem of connected digital twins that have the potential not only to mirror but also to help manage and get more out of the existing network of systems that is the national infrastructure. It can also be defined as a virtual model of the national infrastructure that can track real-time infrastructure as well as have predictive capabilities. This is intended to provide a natural resource that utilises data and digital technology to support the management, planning, situational prediction, and understanding of the national infrastructure, providing quality and service, high-performance, and robust and responsive systems in the built environment (NIC, 2017).

11.6.2 Digital Twins in Urban Modelling and Planning

A digital twin can help in urban modelling and planning by combining spatial, electrical, and mechanical models with sensor data to optimise urban planning and city science for the public good, while collaboratively communicating prospective policies and plans to its citizens. Governments and local authorities can leverage a digital twin to plan for existing and future smart urban environments in potentially valuable operations such as land-use optimisation, urban design modelling, strategic planning, geofencing, progress monitoring, monitoring of mobility and traffic, monitoring of climate change, issuance of building permits, monitoring of zoning, and environmental compliance. Digital twins allow high-degree simulation of urban plans or building operations before they are implemented. This exposes problems before they become a reality, allowing for an improved degree of efficiency and precision in a city or a building operation. This enables the use of predictive analytics for scenario and risk assessment, forming a more informed decision-making support system for the urban collective good. This is important in planning for future resilient urban environments, especially in the current post-pandemic times.

Governments can better communicate plans for development to their citizens through the simulation and visualisation of proposed plans. The involvement of citizens in urban planning through the application of digital twin models and data analytics forms human–infrastructure–technology connections for collaboration by creating a real-time intersection of realism and virtual realities. This contributes to the smart city idea and is evidenced across the world in cities such as Singapore. A digital twin, using analytics and immersive visualisation, helps urban planners and designers understand and learn about the effects of planned urban change. It can assist with public engagement by providing people with a voice and an ability to influence public decision-making for a smart, sustainable society. The process of democratic decision-making allows citizens to come to a public consensus on the urban challenges facing their society. In Singapore, public participation aided by an immersive visualisation enhanced public infrastructure and citizen experiences. Open data systems, as part of the digital twin, improved consultation with communities and aided decision-making processes in urban planning. Digital twins thus create better synergies for efficiency, productivity, and collaboration among urban planners and the public.

11.6.3 Real-Time Monitoring and Control of Urban Transport Infrastructure

Digital twin technology can be harnessed to enable more effective real-time monitoring and control of transport infrastructure demand in urban areas, helping significantly as these challenges increase in urban environments. For instance, Singapore's digital twin provides traffic information, such as data on the static location of traffic lights and bus stops, together with dynamic data from sensors such as bus movements. This makes it a resource that offers great potential for urban planning. The digital twin, therefore, understands transport challenges, providing insight to the users to allow them to implement strategic measures to control traffic, incidents, and general transport issues. For example, detection of an incident along a route could open, in real time, an alternative way for people to travel.

11.6.4 Future Mobility

The power of connected digital twins to a national level could bring to life self-driving cars or autonomous transport. Self-driving technology is one of the most advanced illustrations of artificial intelligence (AI) integrated into digital twin technology to reduce accidents that are attributed to human error. Google Maps can be regarded as one of the most advanced digital twins by providing an accurate geographic information system (GIS). Thus, linking single digital twins at an urban scale, and proceeding to a national digital twin along with automobiles, has excellent potential for realising safe autonomous mobility. For instance, a link can be made between an electric vehicle running low on charge and a charging station digital twin to automatically request the amount of energy needed from the grid for your journey. Alternatively, a communication link from the UK's Meteorological Office digital twin can alert a vehicle to an expected flood and re-route it. This would support an eco-friendly, automated, and safe method of transport.

11.6.5 Sustainability Using the Case Study of Singapore

The built environment accounts for over 40% of energy consumption worldwide (IET, 2019). While climate change has dramatically changed the global agenda in the last few years, some cities are working to be the first carbon-neutral cities. Urban digital twins present a real opportunity to realise zero-carbon goals and promote sustainable, healthier built environments. The journey to a competitive, decarbonised, and digitised energy environment includes a transition to low-carbon energy systems, renewable energy integration and storage technologies, and data analytics to measure, predict demand, and empower users.

Digital twin technology provides decision-makers with the insights they need to implement smart solutions by finding the most effective and resource-efficient ways to significantly minimise the use of energy and fossil fuels in an area. As evidenced through the case study of Singapore, buildings in this city-state use up to 90% of the national electricity energy supply. The digital twin of Singapore is harnessed to provide insights into how air temperature and daytime sunlight differ. City designers can see the impact of constructing new buildings or infrastructure, such as the use of green roofs, on temperature and light intensity. In Singapore's digital twin data, such as building height, rooftop level, and amount of sunlight, is collected. This helps city planning to evaluate which buildings have a higher potential for producing solar energy and which areas are more suitable for installing solar panels to harness clean, renewable power from the sun as an alternative to fossil fuels, to reduce the carbon footprint and therefore reduce greenhouse gases.

Digital twins enable various alternatives for target energy use that can be simulated and tested digitally before they are implemented in real life. Urban digital twins allow planners to predict how much energy can be produced on a typical day, as well as the savings in energy and costs. A 3D visualisation and master planning model for Nanyang Technological University (NTU) in Singapore, along with virtual learning, comprehensive operational modelling of 21 buildings, and performance management, revealed campus-wide energy savings of 31% and cost savings of $4.7 million. The interplay between different systems on how urban infrastructure services and energy are connected can be explained by digital twin technology, providing a degree of understanding that allows for wide-ranging improvements among planners, designers, and citizens. The model can be used to simulate adaptation strategies, to foresee ripple effects across different urban assets and services, and to consider future impacts on key urban targets. Critically relevant is the potential for the public to test various scenarios based on alternative approaches to energy management and to reduce emissions.

Digital twins have the leverage of optimisation of asset performance and sustainability to achieve zero-carbon targets. They can interpret physics that determine real-world conditions such as flows of energy, environmental factors, and the properties of a material. In the built environment, digital twins offer a real opportunity to achieve zero-carbon targets and encourage sustainable, safer buildings, and urban environments. The journey to a decentralised, decarbonised, and digitised built environment includes a transformation to low-carbon energy. This promotes intelligent building management systems, renewable energy integration and storage technologies, and data analytics to measure and predict users' demand and resources, to make informed choices about energy usage by creating valuable insights into reducing consumption. Digital twins can be used by building and infrastructure owners to monitor detailed performance and the use of built assets against an accelerated implementation plan on carbon emissions reduction by harnessing real-time data capabilities.

11.6.6 Scenario and Risk Assessments

Digital twins of our built assets can provide scenario and risk assessments through virtual experimentation, using a 'what if' scenario or an incident status. These assessments can enhance and assist emergency services by configuring assets to report, adapt, and respond to extreme events such as natural disasters. For example, Asia had the highest proportion of natural disasters over a 10-year reporting period ending 2017, with over 40% of global natural disasters. The case study of Singapore applies its digital twin to helps users and city officials to conduct simulated test-bedding of everything from population growth to public emergencies to natural disasters and other emergencies to determine the best response. This creates greater efficiency in disaster preparedness leading to better provision for public safety. In addition, digital twins can provide scenario risk and assessment through remote monitoring and control in real time in the event of an incident or disaster. Local authorities and government users can harness urban-scale digital twins in earthquake situations to establish whether hundreds, or even thousands, of buildings or infrastructure are safe or not, as quickly as possible. Sensor output from physical assets can be leveraged, to measure the vibration of a physical asset. Artificial intelligence (AI) can be utilised to detect potentially compromised buildings in real time. On the urban-scale digital twin, the users can identify physical assets that are considered safe, potentially dangerous, and dangerous. This can guide emergency services to the buildings that need responding to first following a disaster, and more effectively distribute resources.

Following the Grenfell fire of 2017 in London, digital building passports and golden threads were recommended by the UK government as a means of providing construction and maintenance information of built assets. Open and live digital twins are considered as more effective digital data tools capable of improving the design resilience of new and existing assets or understanding the current asset state, and tracking the asset's situation as it is through sensor networks. They can also update maintenance activities, run real-time 'what if' models and scenario analytics, or create a digital preview and simulation of potential risk factors. An example of a reliable digital twin would be a fire-experiencing building sending real-time information about where the fire is located, spaces where people are gathering, trapped, or leaving the building, and all related fire suppression and flight data to firefighters, to help them fight the fire better and save those inside.

11.6.7 Security

Urban digital twins enabled by AI and the Internet of things (IoT) can monitor urban security. Singapore, with a more progressive AI-enabled digital twin, incorporates AI-powered facial recognition sensors located throughout the city for security monitoring as part of its broader strategy of smart city-nation. The data has real-time feedback loops to the smart command centre that applies AI to identify criminals and lost persons. Virtual Singapore is also exploring AI's facial recognition towards smart check-ins at its airport terminals, hotels, and subway systems. Digital twins are thereby important in improving security and efficiency in transport systems in urban areas.

11.6.8 Health and Well-Being

Health, well-being, and nature have become the lens that we look through in urban environments. The future urban environment will be as liveable as we choose to make it. Even under the current vulnerabilities revealed by the COVID-19 pandemic on modern infrastructure, we need to rethink urban planning to help us lead healthier lives. Urban environments need a massive transformation in the face of disease. They need transformed by urban planning and design for the creation of healthier, sustainable, and resilient urban living space. This can be achieved by readjusting urban spaces and infrastructure to the new reality in the post-COVID-19 age, for example, by modelling and simulations of an urban environment supporting a more local lifestyle, such as the pandemic-friendly 'hyperlocal micro market'. This will ensure hygiene and social distancing by designing urban environments to reduce high volumes of human traffic, commute times in urban spaces, and congestion in transport infrastructure. Urban digital twins can be leveraged in tracking the COVID-19 virus' progress in real time as they are the perfect platforms to aggregate and distribute information at scale in a crisis. Digital twins can be harnessed in modelling to predict the spread of COVID-19 infections in urban environments. This could help policymakers understand the common impact of coronavirus policies based on a comprehensive analysis of datasets. Already used were AI-driven real-time temperature screening sensors, installed at different sites within Singapore with the advent of COVID-19. The solution provided real-time identification of the key symptom of the infection (high temperature), status reports, and updates on the rate of traffic and how many persons had been identified with a high temperature, whom were then traced and taken in for isolation or treatment, thus controlling the spread of the pandemic.

Urban digital twins can help evaluate and implement economic recovery plans for the cities and urban areas affected. Digital twins also have the potential to provide valuable predictive modelling important in assessing the economic and safety repercussions of policy actions on a city-scale before they are implemented countywide.

11.6.9 Efficiency and Streamlined Information Workflows in Capital Delivery

A significant amount of information, such as drawings, documents, and notes, are produced during the design and construction of an asset. However, capital delivery and operations are disjointed, making finding and maintaining this information after construction often very expensive and time-consuming. A digital twin offers a dynamic, expressive real-time recording system as an 'umbrella' solution to this challenge. This collation of information is embedded with rich information about spaces and assets and can provide significant benefits to asset owners and users in the life cycle of built assets. In addition, digital twins offer great potential and value in the capital delivery of a built asset. They can help break institutional silos, unlocking multidisciplinary productivity and collaboration. Furthermore, digital twins enable teams to plan better and monitor progress against schedule layout, therein providing smarter insights through immersive design visualisation. Such visualisation can include constructability simulation, clash detection to spot and correct flaws, resource planning, and geographic information systematics during the design stages of projects and thus reduce disruption time and costs. Digital twins also present opportunities to test scenarios and constraints, safety monitoring, and training and monitoring of personnel, through simulations in artificial reality and virtual reality-driven digital environments.

11.6.10 Streamlined Asset Operations

Digital twins harness data to prepare the future digital operational life of built assets. At the handover stage, a digital twin provides a single source of truth, through a complete and reliable set of information about the built asset. This creates a uniform, smart built asset database, saving money and time by not having to recreate these applications. During the operational stages of projects, smart assets gather data from their surroundings using IoT networks and sensors, so they can adapt to their environment and change their operating performance accordingly. This enables them to evolve over the lifespan of the assets using machine learning and operational data AI to recognise trends in usage, and where building or network activity does not meet expectations. This not only increases the efficiency, sustainability, and security of buildings and infrastructure but also transforms the management of facilities. Operations decision-making of this kind, led by smart live and static information management, can extend the life cycle of urban built assets and improve their performance. The use of digital twins now also allows asset owners and operators to have greater leverage over their buildings and service networks, with the capacity to enforce and test against specific targets. An example of this could be carbon footprint monitoring and energy controls in buildings and infrastructure, as referred to earlier in this chapter.

11.6.11 Building Automation

Digital twins have the power for building automation operations. A digital twin can integrate complex physical systems and leverage twin and sensor data for an asset to be intelligently operated with transparency and to provide valuable insight to the owners and operators. A digital twin brings together previously unconnected physical systems into real-time IoT integrated systems. These include smart heating, ventilation, air-conditioning (HVAC) systems, digitised pneumatic thermostats, smart plugs, intelligent elevator controls, security sensors, environmentally responsive kinetic facades, and smog-eating facades. This enables a unified building database with optimised processes. Building ventilation systems became more critical following the COVID-19 pandemic. Smart ventilation systems and sensors can be integrated into the physical building and linked to the digital twin to provide simulation, monitoring, and control of airflow to improve air quality and control the level of virus infections. The application of digital twins for building automation enhances aspects such as human comfort, air quality, and overall asset productivity.

11.6.12 Predictive Maintenance

Digital twins can continuously monitor assets and activities, and identify abnormal behaviours, allowing human operators to react rapidly and reduce downtime by managing predictive maintenance. Predictive maintenance incorporates machine learning and sensors to enable the digital twin to inform the facilities management (FM) team that, based on actual user data, a component needs servicing or is near to the end of their life. Sensors provide new insights to the digital twin performance and predictive maintenance of the asset and its integration with smart systems. For this reason, a digital twin can link with users through visualisation web dashboards and provide new insights into improving built asset utilisation and performance. This gives users greater control over their own spaces and environment, thus improving the user experience and reducing maintenance costs.

11.6.13 Remote Assistance Technology

A digital twin can operate autonomously just by being able to evaluate a scenario, formulate tailored solutions, and bring them into a corrective action through the power of remote assistance technology. Remote assistance technology enables users to remotely monitor and control built assets, plant, and machinery. This technology in digital twins can provide decision support and alert users to any potential malfunction, incident, or anomaly in an asset or an ecosystem. In FM, remote monitoring can provide maintenance staff with real-time monitoring to troubleshoot distant sensors systems and perform remote maintenance, enabling operators to fix the issue at hand instantly. Furthermore, remote assistance technology can accelerate the adoption of digital twins, especially in the aftermath of COVID-19. It can achieve this first by minimising the need to have people working from offices, by allowing remote monitoring and control of assets via an IoT platform. Second, it can be developed to remotely show real-time use of critical care beds in a single hospital, with a capability to link them on a national scale. Ionics, a London-based technology company, is running a demo on creating hospital digital twins for the UK's National Health Service (NHS) using metadata from hospitals. This could allow hospital administrators the opportunity to organise resources locally and direct patients to the beds and ventilators accessible, while also having a national view of resources. In addition, the digital twin would also provide real-time insight to both first response teams and the government in crisis management and resource planning.

11.6.14 Research and Development

Digital twins offer platforms for big data, artificial and virtual reality simulation in research, and innovation for a diverse range of problems. For example, when made available to researchers with the requisite access rights, Singapore's digital twin's rich data environment encouraged them to innovate and build new technologies or capabilities. The 3D model of the city with stylometric information provided researchers with enough opportunities to build advanced 3D software. With appropriate security and privacy protections, Singapore's digital twin will allow all stakeholders to use the information and system capabilities for policy and business analysis, decision-making, concept testing, group collaboration, and other information requiring activities. Such stakeholders could be public agencies, academia, the private sector, and the community. Another fascinating aspect of the future of the digital twin is virtual tourism. For example, Herrenberg, Germany is planning to utilise its digital twin to give visitors the chance to experience it virtually with virtual reality (VR) glasses before they arrive in Herrenberg.

11.7 Summary

This chapter of the book has discussed the immense potential of digital twins to mitigate some of the current urbanisation-led challenges in the urban built environment. In this pursuit it has used the case study from Singapore, which is regarded as a model of good practice for transformation through digital twin technology. In this sense, digital transformation in the built environment is the practice of how technology allows the industry to develop what could not be created before; to construct new forms of building, to transform cities and towns, and to address urbanisation and sustainability challenges. Managing urban areas is now one of the twenty-first century's most significant developmental challenges. The digitalisation of the built environment is an opportunity to tackle the industry's challenges by taking advantage of the general availability of best practices from other sectors. The advent of broad deployment of emerging technologies, such as artificial intelligence (AI), sensor technology, cloud computing, open data, the Internet of things (IoT), and blockchain, has reinvented the way in which we can handle development and adapt to these challenges. The UK took steps toward championing the digital revolution in the built environment through policy and launched of the Centre for Digital Built Britain (CDBB). This organisation provided resources to guide the infrastructure and construction sector toward its digital transformation and also provided the framework for information management to enable stable, resilient data sharing between digital twins.

A digital twin is a cycle flow between physical and virtual realities (mirroring or twinning), where data flows from the physical to the virtual environment, and information flows between the two states. Processes in the physical state responding to the virtual state can be described as an evolving digital profile of a physical object or the process' historical and current behaviour, which helps optimise business efficiency. For this to work effectively, the digital model should be a true replica of the physical object, reproducing the physical geometries, properties, actions, and rules in a 3D geometric model. Furthermore, the digital twin must have a clear purpose for the public good, enabling value creation and performance improvement, while providing determinable insight into the built environment. In addition, the digital twin must be trustworthy while promoting security, openness, and quality of information. To allow it to function effectively, based on a standard connected environment, it must have clear ownership, governance, and regulation, and be able to adapt as technology and society evolve.

A digital twin represents open, trusted, and reliable digital representation of the elements and dynamics of a physical system or built asset, such as a building, urban network, or asset portfolio, and can be referred to as a cyber–physical system. It is embedded into multiple data points, to relay structured and big unstructured data flows from physical to virtual states. It offers the ability to incorporate analytics, including machine learning and simulation algorithms, to provide an understanding of the elements and dynamics. The digital twin idea is not a new phenomenon and has already been embedded in some current technologies, such as 3D modelling, simulation, and digital prototyping.

One should not underestimate the importance of the built environment and urbanisation on a global scale. Urban built environments, such as cities and towns, are engines for growth and development and are pivotal to development, significantly contributing to gross domestic product (GDP) in both low-income and high-income countries. The built environment is also a leading source of job creation that provides job opportunities for millions of unskilled, semi-skilled, and skilled workers. To reinforce this point, the construction industry in the UK, as part of the built environment, contributes 13% of global GDP and employs approximately 7% of the global working-age population. The built environment sector is now very much a data management business, where concepts like building information modelling (BIM) are now essential to driving information-led productivity in capital projects and programmes. Managing urban areas is now one of the twenty-first century's most significant developmental challenges. Despite this, in the UK the construction industry is underachieving when compared to the manufacturing, aerospace, and automotive industries. This may be explained by the industry being associated with outdated technologies that are incapable of meeting industry needs, leading to client dissatisfaction, inefficiencies in process and operations, deficiencies in safety, and a higher than acceptable carbon footprint. The digitalisation of the built environment is an opportunity to tackle the industry's challenges by taking advantage of the general availability of best practices from other sectors and of advanced techniques and tools, digital workflows, and technological expertise to shift to a higher level of efficiency and to become a digital industry. A digital urban twin is sophisticated data model that allows collaborative processes at a local and national level. City-scale digital twins aid in mapping space, people, and their activities in the physical city to a virtual city by establishing closed-loop, city-level data feed into the virtual city, as Singapore has demonstrated. These allow high-degree simulation of urban plans or building operations before they are implemented, which exposes problems before they become a reality, allowing for an improved degree of efficiency and precision in a city or a building operation.

The use of digital twins in the built environment has many other applications which can bring about significant benefits for cities and their communities. These include:

- Sophisticated data models that allow collaborative processes across urban environments. Data input into a computing framework enables information to be shared between the various city services.
- Urban modelling and planning allowing governments and authorities to plan for existing and future smart urban environments.
- Better communication of plans for city development allowing communities to understand proposed plans and strategies more fully through simulation and visualisation.
- Real-time monitoring and control of urban transport infrastructure.
- Future mobility improvements that could bring to life self-driving cars or autonomous transport.

- Sustainability improvements through a journey to a competitive, decarbonised, and digitised energy environment. This includes a transition to low-carbon energy systems, renewable energy integration and storage technologies, and data analytics to measure, predict demand, and empower users.
- Scenario and risk assessments with virtual experimentation, using a 'what if' scenario or an incident status.
- Security enhancements, enabled by AI and the IoT to monitor urban security more effectively.
- Health and well-being improvements, enabled by the creation of healthier, sustainable, and resilient urban environments through readjusting urban spaces and infrastructure.
- Efficiency and streamlined information workflows in capital delivery, offering a dynamic, expressive real-time recording system. This can embed rich information about spaces and assets and can provide significant benefits to asset owners and users in the life cycle of built assets.
- Streamlined asset operations by harnessing data to prepare the future digital operational life of built assets.
- Building automation by integrating sensor data within complex physical systems to enable an asset to be intelligently operated with transparency.
- Predictive maintenance by continuously monitoring assets and activities, and identifying abnormal behaviour, allowing human operators to react rapidly and reduce downtime.
- Remote assistance technology to enable users to remotely monitor and control built assets, plant, and machinery.
- Research and development by creating the platforms for big data, artificial and virtual reality simulation, and innovation for a diverse range of applications.

References

Barricelli, B.R., Casiraghi, E. and Fogli, D. (2019). A Survey on digital twin: Definitions, characteristics, applications, and design implications. *IEEE Access* 7: 167653–167671.

McClure, W.R. and Bartuska, T.J. (2007). The Built Environment: Definition and Scope.

BSI Group (2018). Digital Twins for the Built Environment. London: BSI Group.

Dembski, F., Wössner, U., Letzgus, M., *et al.* (2020). Urban digital twins for smart cities and citizens: The case study of Herrenberg, Germany. *Sustainability* 12(6): 2307.

Duarte, S. (2019). Digital twins: needs, challenges, and understanding. London: Open Data Institute.

ESPON (2020). Digital Innovation in Urban Environments. Luxembourg: ESPON.

Harris, J. (2019). As important as the internet: Are digital twins the next big thing for construction? https://www.building.co.uk/digital-transformation/as-important-as-the-internet-are-digital-twins-the-next-big-thing-for-construction/5102682. article (accessed 24 October 2023).

Harrison, C., Eckman, B., Hamilton, R., *et al.* (2010). Foundations for smarter cities. *IBM Journal of Research and Development* 54(4): 1–16.

HM Government (2013). *Construction 2025. Industrial Strategy: Government and Industry in Partnership.* London: HM Government.

IET (2019). Digital Twins for the Built Environment. London: The Institution of Engineering and Technology (IET).

Jones, D., Snider, C., Nassehi, A., et al. (2020). Characterising the digital twin: A systematic literature review. *CIRP Journal of Manufacturing Science and Technology* 29: 36–52.

Maskuriy, R., Selamat, A., Ali, K.N., and Krejcar, O. (2019). Industry 4.0 for the construction industry: How ready is the industry? Applied Sciences 9(14): 2819.

McKinsey and Company (2020). How construction can emerge stronger after coronavirus. https://www.mckinsey.com/industries/capital-projects-and-infrastructure/our-insights/how-construction-can-emerge-stronger-after-coronavirus# (accessed 19 June 2020).

NIC (2017). Data for the Public Good. London: National Infrastructure Commission.

Ompad, D.C., Galea, S. and Vlahov, D. (2007). Urbanicity, urbanization, and the urban environment. In: *Macro Determinants of Population Health*. New York: Springer, pp. 53–69.

Research and Markets (2020). Global Digital Twin Market (2020 to 2035): Opportunity and Trend Analysis. Dublin: Research and Markets Press.

Santamouris, M. (2001). Energy and Climate in the Urban Built Environment. New York: Routledge.

Siemens (2020). A Worldwide Challenge. Retrieved July 13, 2020, from https://new.siemens.com/global/en/products/services/Internet of things-siemens/public-sector/city-performance-tool.html

12

The Benefits and Value of Digital Twin Technologies for Collaborative Information Management

Think of digital transformation less as a technology project to be finished than as a state of perpetual agility, always ready to evolve for whatever customers want next, and you'll be pointed down the right path.

Amit Zavery, VP and Head of Platform, Google Cloud

12.1 Introduction

The above quotation hopefully persuades us that technology will give us a chance to change the world in which we all live and work. With this in mind this chapter discusses the full value and benefits of digital twins, especially linked to collaboration and information management using Singapore and Herrenberg, Germany as case studies. With reference to these case studies, the chapter articulates how Herrenberg established an 'Integrated Mobility Plan' and formed a digital twin pilot to reduce its high levels of traffic, while improving its environmental sustainability through reduced carbon and noise emissions. Conversely, it explains how Singapore, developed 'Virtual Singapore', a city-state digital twin and collaborative data platform designed to allow users from government and different industries to create and test new technologies, applications, and services.

The chapter discusses collaborative insights for the built environment by enhancing live real-time capabilities and data capture. It then explains how digital twin-related technologies are maturing to deliver intelligent solutions for urban planning and city science. Virtual technologies to help us manage demands on transport infrastructure, emissions, increasing energy use, and other challenges in urban areas more effectively are discussed. In addition, the chapter explores the means to address the ever-growing challenges around environmental sustainability through digital technologies. It then assesses the ability of digital twins to monitor and control real-time asset outputs and how this technology can boost any number of adaptable services. The chapter then covers scenario planning and risk assessments and the notion of 'digital siblings' to understand the 'what if' scenarios, where things go wrong, and systems and assets fail. Predictive analytics and scheduling are discussed and how a digital twin can act as a validation model framework with data from the real world. It then looks at how this technology can provide a more effective and informed support system for decision-making, with the aim of transforming decision-making and investment.

The Smart Estate, First Edition. Edited by Jason Challender/Akponanabofa Henry Oti.
© 2024 John Wiley & Sons, Ltd. Published 2024 by John Wiley & Sons, Ltd.

Better synergies in intra- and inter-team collaboration are then explored. From this angle, the chapter explains how digital twins allow information and data flow to enhance collaboration across the supply chain, reduce silos, and increase the understanding of existing built asset projects. This is followed by an insight into the optimisation of asset performance and sustainability. This covers the measures to improve future building performance through sensor networks linked to building elements and components. A case study in this context is discussed, namely the Energy House research by the University of Salford in the UK.

In addition to the above, greater efficiency in safety from digital technologies is examined whereby individuals can get real-time monitoring and warnings, including updates of dangers and guidance for responding to emergencies. Finally, the ecosystem of connected networks, portfolios, and sectors is discussed. This includes examples whereby sensors, using Internet of things (IoT) technology linked to physical assets, can be utilised to evaluate their performance, condition, and status in real time.

12.2 Improvement to the Quality of Life

Digital twin technologies represent a new opportunity for the built environment and the 'Gemini Principles', referred to in Chapter 11, specify the public good as one of their three main benefits. The framework that builds digital twins focuses on people and emphasises performance and human prosperity. This notion is largely predicated on buildings and infrastructure as the main enablers to providing the essential services on which people and society rely for well-being and quality of life. This is unified and justified through both of the case studies for Herrenberg and Singapore. The Herrenberg region was not only vulnerable to high levels of traffic but also to carbon and noise emissions from its urban environment. To face this urban challenge, Herrenberg established an Integrated Mobility Plan (IMEP 2030). The town's digital twin was part of a pilot project on how the novel application of 3D visualisation can be useful in promoting collaborative urban development for improved outcomes, leading to an overall better quality of life. Conversely, Singapore, developed 'Virtual Singapore', a city-state digital twin and collaborative data platform designed to allow users from government and different industries to create and test new technologies, applications, and services. The platform, as illustrated by the highly accurate and detailed virtual image in Figure 12.1, was proven to enhance planning and decision-making, and to find ways to tackle urban challenges in real time to improve the standard of living.

Figure 12.1 Singapore's digital twin visualisation (Government of Singapore, 2020).

12.3 Creation of Value

A digital twin is a purposed tool allowing value creation and performance improvement, while providing the built environment with determinable insights to foster a collaborative approach as provided by the Gemini Principles. The Herrenberg digital twin demonstrates this through the development of a 3D solid town model, augmented by 3D scans and 360° stereoscopic videos, which form the basis of a digital representation model of the town. Modern digital tools, including sensors, were used to compile high-quality network asset data on various factors, including the effects of pedestrian and traffic flows on air quality. Such big datasets were then combined with the aid of supercomputers and advanced analytics, enabling researchers to display them in a virtual reality environment, providing a real-time overview of the town's complex interactions. In this way, the Herrenberg model can conduct simulations of urban mobility and air flows to gain a better understanding of the quantity and distribution of pollution and its relationship with the urban grid, morphology, topography, and geometry. This allows decision-makers to see abstract data in a more user-friendly and condensed manner, enabling the town to be more accurately visualised for planning purposes. Conversely, the Virtual Singapore digital twin was designed to operate on Internet of things (IoT) sensors, big data, and cloud computing, in conjunction with 3D models, geospatial datasets, and building information modelling (BIM). Data sources included in the detailed development of 3D city models drilled right down to encapsulating the construction materials of buildings and their structure, terrain characteristics, city data, the sensor network, and real-time operating data. The platform was also designed to integrate other real-time variables including demographic, environmental, or traffic information, making it a resource that offered excellent opportunities to improve the city's environmental credentials.

12.4 Collaborative Insights

For digital twin technologies to be successful they must provide determinable insights for the built environment by enhancing live capabilities. The 'Gemini Principles' outline that such technologies must be trustworthy while enabling security, openness, and quality of information. Open and live data generation allows collaboration to enable improved service and support through simulation of city strategies before they are implemented. Such collaboration platforms facilitate improvement in the design, production, and operation of systems by exposing problems before they become a reality. The overall focus is to enable city authorities to break the silos and have access to more profound knowledge and real-time situational insights for continuous learning, and to make better informed decisions in the best interest of all their citizens. In the case study of Herrenberg the clarity and openness of digital twin technology was proven to generate significant benefits as a planning tool, as it was easily communicated to and understood by the local population. Such a useful tool facilitated the precise explanation of the consequences and repercussions of strategies, policies, and decision-making while allowing people to understand planning more succinctly. This had the advantage of improving communications and interactions between government officials and the local population around issues such as urban planning and design.

In Singapore, using open data systems as part of the digital twin, planning bodies mobilised 'crowd wisdom' to include stakeholders in the decision-making process in urban planning. This acted as a convenient forum for residents to visualise upgrades to the built environment which enabled them to provide the related agencies with timely feedback. Singapore's digital twin also allowed geovisualisation, analytical tools, and 3D semiconductor information to provide a virtual yet realistic platform for connecting and creating awareness of the factors and services that enrich their communities.

12.5 Optimisation of Urban Planning and City Science

Digital twin-related technologies are maturing to deliver intelligent solutions for urban planning and city science. They can be used to involve citizens in city planning through the idea of integrating physical objects with their digital counterparts. A smart city concept is one that can facilitate more human–infrastructure–technology connections and therein, through data analytics framework technologies, create the real-time intersection of realism and virtual realities. In addition, such integrated concept models can be developed to allow an unparalleled degree of precision for urban planning, project implementation, and operations (Khajavi *et al.*, 2019). In this way, they allow simulation and testing of plans before they are implemented, to expose problems before they become a reality while managing urban issues in a more systematic and efficient way, from strategic planning to land-use optimisation (Memoori, 2020). Furthermore, such virtual technologies can help us manage demands on transport infrastructure, emissions, increasing energy use, and other challenges in urban areas more effectively to address the ever-growing challenges around environmental sustainability (IET, 2019). These models can expose the interplay between different factors and variables. An example is the relationship and interplay between transport and energy which can improve understanding and allow more informed decision-making among city planners, designers, and operators. On a large scale, this will allow a deeper evaluation of cities and facilitate a better monitoring of their current and future operation and performance (IET, 2019). The rich data generated can inform strategies around energy efficiency initiatives and future maintenance requirements by allowing us to understand how the physical twin performs in the real world (Madni *et al.*, 2019). Furthermore, an artificial intelligence (AI)-enabled digital twin could also provide the necessary catalyst to drive strategies around car-sharing, space, storage, and equipment. In this way it can build systems that track and reflect our urban patterns where we can learn about the behaviours and desires of the population (IET, 2019).

12.6 Monitoring and Control of Scenarios in Real Time

Digital twin datasets could be used to monitor and test scenarios and constraints, train personnel, and boost the performance of any number of adaptable services, such as remote operations, through simulations in artificial reality and virtual reality-driven digital environments (IET, 2019). While the significance of simulations and tests is not refutable in the first phase, in the operational phase, the potential for real-time data availability opens up new avenues for tracking and optimising operations during a product's life cycle. Such technologies help us to monitor system performance, for example, to understand how modifications are being made, and to gain a deeper understanding of the operating environment (Madni *et al.*, 2019). In addition, they may help identify trends for improving operations, optimising asset maintenance, and monitoring output remotely. This could enable project teams to undertake digital simulations on construction sequencing and logistics, familiarising the workforce with the necessary tasks and reducing costly reworking (IET, 2019). Digital twins also enable building operators to gain new insights, optimise workflows, and remotely monitor processes in smart buildings (Castaldini, 2019). Furthermore, they can monitor relationships between the real and virtual worlds. Through virtually testing a design concept in production and operational scenarios, it is possible to simulate the constructability and intended functional performance of the built environment to test whether the design meets all the requirements. In doing so, design and construction will recognise design and quality flaws, and develop solutions through collaboration. Thus, they can identify and predict possible virtual space problems before they happen in physical space. This can be made possible through using feedback and tracking mechanisms and has the benefit of informing maintenance planning, identifying possible risks, and allowing troubleshooting.

With the advent of drones, robotics, and artificial intelligence (AI)-based machine vision, inspection activities can be streamlined into a living digital twin, enabling experts to conduct inspections remotely, massively improving productivity and maximising awareness of scarce resources.

12.7   Scenario Planning and Risk Assessments

A digital twin is a data resource that can enhance the design of a new asset or understand the existing asset condition, verify the situation as it has been built, run real-time 'what if' models and scenarios, and provide a digital preview for upcoming work (IET, 2019). 'Digital siblings' can be viewed as copies of digital twins, and thereby of physical assets too, that do not need to run in real ime but can be used to check hypothetical 'what if' scenarios by considering and evaluating threats. They enable optimisation of asset performance and operational and occupational data can be tracked and analysed in real time, offering useful scenario insights of the risks involved in the use and output of the asset. Digital siblings provide the opportunity to answer questions, such as: Where are the highest risk elements of maintenance? In addition, they can evaluate such situations as: If I change X, how does it affect Y? This can substantially reduce the errors and discontinuities found in more conventional information management approaches (IET, 2019).

12.8   Predictive Analytics and Scheduling

A digital twin can act as a validation model framework with data from the real world. Data about the operating environment and the system's interactions with that environment can be integrated into the digital twin to validate its models and to make comparisons and predictions (Madni *et al.*, 2019). Accordingly, this can predict virtually everything that will happen in the physical world (Iberdrola, 2020). The recent global COVID-19 pandemic supports digital twin-market growth. For example, the researchers at the Biocomplexity Institute at the University of Virginia have built a digital twin simulation framework that can help state and local governments better predict the spread of the COVID-19 pandemic and the effects of that spread (Research and Markets, 2020). This will help policymakers recognise the widespread effects of coronavirus policies based on the analysis of broad datasets. Such technology can also provide health support for plant and equipment, using analytics and providing real-time monitoring and tracking of physical assets (Research and Markets, 2020). Furthermore, the technology is designed to represent the physical twin's structure, efficiency, condition, and unique characteristics, such as malfunctions it has experienced, and a history of maintenance and repair. A digital twin represents the age of the physical system by integrating physical system operating and maintenance data into its models and simulations. In this way, it helps in deciding when to schedule preventive maintenance based on knowledge of the maintenance history and device activity (Madni *et al*, 2019). The importance of linking digital models and simulations with live input to provide better design and control has unlimited applications and advantages; one that opens doors for better operations and maintenance, offering greater predictability, enabling more inclusive designs, and achieving more sustainable strategies. Digital twins can track assets and operations continuously and detect abnormal behaviour, allowing human operators to respond quickly and minimise downtimes using machine learning to manage predictive maintenance. The technology will predict maintenance activities and incidents through data-driven decision-making, Internet of things (IoT) sensors, and artificial intelligence (AI) or machine learning, which in turn can help manage unforeseen disruptions and eventually reduce construction costs, streamlining expenditure over the operational life of the asset (Madni *et al.*, 2019). Cost reduction is a significant benefit of digital twins; by helping to anticipate and prevent unexpected costs, they help facilities run more effectively, and by detecting device inefficiencies and better predicting when new parts and improvements are required they help to avoid unexpected costs. One other advantage is that they can provide a live or near real-time model of inventory and logistics by enabling automated resupply, scheduling according to demand, intersecting with an intelligent transport network linked to storage and parking facilities, and negotiating paths to and from construction sites. This can provide a greenlight ride for building traffic, thus reducing congestion and air pollution, as well as enabling quicker and more efficient distribution of materials (IET, 2019).

12.9 More Effective and Informed Support System for Decision-Making

The digital twin is the trustworthy data collector, offering both knowledge of the current state as well as the measures required to improve it. It contains a mechanism which incorporates modern construction and facilities management (FM) technologies with the Internet of things (IoT) to generate asset management systems that are not only integrated, but also capable of interacting with, analysing, and using data to push smarter and more informed action back into the physical realm. This may range from forecasting more accurately and reducing waste to proactively managing more complex thresholds for usage, such as monitoring air quality, identifying low-quality spaces, and recognising and regulating habits to improve the outcome (IET, 2019). A digital twin aims to transform decision-making and investment across a wide variety of stakeholders, from urban planners to individual owners of buildings (Arup, 2019). In addition, it provides more efficient asset planning, project execution, and asset operations by continuously incorporating data and information across the asset life cycle to achieve performance and productivity benefits in the short and long term (IET, 2019). In this way it helps stakeholders to understand how the physical twin performs in the real world, and how it can be expected to perform in the future with timely maintenance (Madni *et al.*, 2019).

With the advent of the digital twin, businesses can also gain substantial value for a new product in terms of speed to market, improved operations, reduced defects, and new business models emerging to boost revenues. A digital twin allows businesses to solve physical challenges more effectively by identifying problems and issues early, predicting results to a much higher degree of accuracy. This allows the users to develop and construct more appropriate and effective corrective measures to address adversities. Through this kind of smart architecture design, enterprises will understand value and profit iteratively and more rapidly than ever before. A digital twin will also enable project teams to make use of rapid, inexpensive development and testing of new concepts and designs, mainly from a user experience perspective. This can include taking the weather, energy, human interactions, lighting, and friction into account. For example, digital transportation hub twins boost passenger experience by recognising peak hours and providing a better understanding of human traffic, resulting in reduced congestion on networks. The digital twin, as a platform for data collection, interpretation, and information, can be used to identify the best climate change responses to more severe weather events, therefore, enhancing situational awareness capabilities to react to events leading to improved decision-making. For example, but not limited to, creating adapting environments by growing trees in upper catchment areas or proactively managing water demand to reduce the impact of drought (IET, 2019).

12.10 Better Synergies in Intra- and Inter-Team Collaboration

A digital twin will allow information and data flow, enhance collaboration across the supply chain, reduce silos, and increase understanding of existing built asset projects. This can improve current performance, remove constraints, and provide much needed opportunities for collaborative improvement. It can foster traceability of information between the stages of the life cycle of a built asset through digital thread connectivity (Madni *et al.*, 2019). Furthermore, it can aid in asset management by keeping models, inventory records, schedules, procedures, historical data, and additional equipment (comprising manuals to inspection data), enabling improved productivity and collaboration during an asset life cycle. This is particularly important for quality assurance across an asset's life cycle and vital information about the built asset can be preserved, collaboratively shared, evaluated, and kept current. Such information can be readily obtained and used to help with efficient project implementation and decision-making (IET, 2019). One example would be a digital twin model of a physical road network, that allows inspectors to log data including water leakage, road repairs, the underlying infrastructure, and photo inspection. With the maturity of the digital twin, it will refine the network over time, responding to various situations to enable better planning and service decision-making (Arup, 2019). This fosters effective communication between teams facilitating better use of their time to strengthen synergies and collaboration while contributing to improved efficiency. Readily accessible real-time information in conjunction with automated reporting can help to keep stakeholders well-informed and thus boost transparency.

12.11   Optimisation of Asset Performance and Sustainability

Design teams can use a digital twin to improve the performance of future buildings. For example, creating a sensor network for a building facade integrated into this technology makes it possible for building designers and architects to enhance a building's performance during modifications and renovations, and to plan its future adaptation and maintenance. In this way, a digital twin can leverage information on how the facade or other building component deal with environmental stresses such as extremes of temperature, sunlight, wind, and snow. An example of such technology has been used by the University of Salford in the UK, as part of its Energy House research. This Energy House has allowed the university to theoretically develop a platform that supports energy efficiency in building fabric design, lighting, ventilation, and cooling. Built environment experts can also use sensors and actuators integrated into a digital twin to understand better how people use the space they work and live in. It can allow analysis of energy use across various scenarios by replicating their assets and their energy profile. This helps owners to give building occupants more control over their workspaces and environmental conditions, thereby increasing their comfort levels while also finding ways of reducing energy consumption. Energy is consumed by the assets and attempts to increase energy performance are a focus of the management of the related operational costs and environmental effects.

The digital twin provides a living outline of the future of smart buildings (Adjacent Digital Politics Ltd, 2020). They enable a connected building system in smart buildings by leveraging integrated technology such as device and sensor technology, the Internet of things (IoT), big data, and machine learning. In addition, they support smart buildings in achieving optimum performance levels and help to make them energy efficient. In this way, building users' experiences are tailored to their individual preferences and real-time data is collected on the building's efficiency. In turn, this will improve occupant interaction and create more appealing and desirable places to work and live (UnWork Ltd, 2017). Another use of the technology revolves around the creation of a more circular economy by guiding material reuse in built assets and equipment through artificial intelligence (AI) (IET, 2019). The digital twin can be used to track components, ensuring that the components are reused, recycled, and repurposed at the end of their lives. This type of technology can be fully accessible to others, enabling spares to be tracked efficiently and creating a realistic capture of how the resources are used. Artificial intelligence (AI) has integrated where resources are not collected, consumed, and disposed of linearly, but are effectively recycled.

12.12 Greater Efficiency in Safety

Digital twins can be configured through artificial intelligence (AI) to monitor air quality and promote health and safety on sites, operational built assets, and the urban environment. In this way, individuals can get real-time monitoring and warnings, including updates of dangers, and guidance for responding to emergencies (IET, 2019). Potential advantages in this regard can ensue from better health and wellness to enhanced air quality in our dense urban built environments. By focusing on providing results that individuals want, the technology can help control security operations, enhance the distribution of resources, and inform responses in emergency cases in urban buildings and environments (IET, 2019). It can also prevent serious injuries by tracking assets to predict potential failures (Savian, 2019).

12.13 The Ecosystem of Connected Networks, Portfolios, and Sectors

Digital twinning can also be conceptualised as mapping a physical asset to a digital network using sensor data, hooking up Internet of things (IoT) endpoints on physical assets to feed, and evaluating their performance, condition, and status in real time. The convergence between the physical and digital built environment matures, using smart, stable connected networks. This can generate a new value proposition where high-performance built assets enable a new north star of optimised full-life asset efficiency, not just for individual projects, but increasingly across portfolios, networks, and entire sectors. This invisible connectivity, combined with data analytics, can reform operational efficiency levels. It also allows the redesign of business models where additional insights and predictive data models can affect a seismic shift in traditional ways of working.

12.14 Summary

Digital twin technologies represent a new opportunity for the built environment and to demonstrate this notion, two case studies for the use of digital twin technologies have been explained in this chapter. The first case study, related to Herrenberg in Germany, which was not only vulnerable to high levels of traffic but also to carbon and noise emissions. To address these problems the town developed a pilot digital twin project which they branded as their 'Integrated Mobility Plan 2030'. They developed this project using 3D visualisation technology, which has already proved useful in promoting a collaborative urban environment and better quality of life for its population. The model they instigated was predicated on conducting simulations of urban mobility and air flows. This gained a better understanding of the quantity and distribution of pollution and its relationship with the urban grid, morphology, topography, and geometry. The second case study related to Singapore where 'Virtual Singapore', a city-state digital twin and collaborative data platform, has been proven to enhance planning and decision-making and has found ways to tackle urban challenges in real time to improve the standard of living. This digital twin was designed to operate on Internet of things (IoT) sensors, big data, and cloud computing, in conjunction with 3D models, geospatial datasets, and building information modelling (BIM).

This chapter of the book has stressed that for digital twin technologies to be successful they must provide determinable insights for the built environment by enhancing live capabilities. The 'Gemini Principles', arguably the cornerstone of digital twins, outline that such technologies must be trustworthy while enabling security, openness, and quality of information. Furthermore, the related technologies are constantly maturing to deliver intelligent solutions for urban planning and developing smart cities which can facilitate more human–infrastructure–technology connections. Such integrated concept models can then be further developed to allow an unparalleled degree of precision for improved urban planning, project implementation, and operations. In this way, they allow simulation and testing of plans before they are implemented, to expose problems before they become a reality, while managing urban issues in a more systematic and efficient way, from strategic planning to land-use optimisation.

Digital twin datasets could also be used to monitor and test scenarios and constraints, train personnel, and boost the performance of any number of adaptable services. Furthermore, they can monitor relationships between the real and virtual worlds. For instance, through virtually testing a design concept in production and operational scenarios, it is possible to simulate the constructability and intended functional performance of the built environment to test whether the design meets all the requirements. This opens a wealth of opportunities and potential applications which could include identifying design flaws before construction works start and testing the energy performance of certain architectural and engineering concepts. The value proposition of such applications relates to checking hypothetical 'what if' scenarios and considering and evaluating threats.

Predictive analytics and scheduling are another potential use of digital twin technologies as they can act as a validation model framework with data from the real world, creating a model that can predict virtually everything that might happen in the physical world. The Biocomplexity Institute at the University of Virginia, as an example of this application, built a digital twin simulation framework that can help state and local governments better predict the spread of any future epidemic. Such technology can also provide health support for plant and equipment, using analytics and providing real-time monitoring and tracking of physical assets, efficiency, condition, and their unique characteristics, such as malfunctions they have experienced and a history of their maintenance and repair.

In addition to the above uses and benefits, effective and informed support system for decision-making can be supported by digital twins as they provide more efficient and accurate asset planning, project execution, and asset operational data. This richer and more reliable information across the asset life cycle can achieve performance and productivity improvements in the short and long term for many different organisations. Furthermore, a digital twin will allow information and data flow, enhance collaboration across the supply chain, reduce silos, and increase understanding of existing built asset projects. This can improve the current performance of project teams, remove constraints, and provide much needed opportunities for collaborative improvement and partnering. In addition, readily accessible real-time information, in conjunction with automated reporting, can help to keep stakeholders well-informed and thus boost transparency. Furthermore, design teams can use a digital twin to improve the performance of future buildings. In this way, designers can leverage information on how facades or other building components deal with environmental stresses such as extremes in temperature, sunlight, wind, and snow. An example of such technology has been used by the University of Salford in the UK and articulated in this chapter. Digital twins can be configured through artificial intelligence (AI) to monitor air quality and promote health and safety on sites, operational built assets, and the urban environment. In this way, individuals can get real-time monitoring and warnings, including updates of dangers, and guidance for responding to emergencies.

Finally, the technology can also be conceptualised as mapping a physical asset to a digital network using sensor data, hooking up IoT endpoints on physical assets to feed, and evaluating their performance, condition, and status in real time. This has the unique benefit of generating a new value proposition where high-performance built assets enable a new north star of optimised full-life asset efficiency, not just for individual projects, but increasingly across portfolios, networks, and entire sectors.

References

Adjacent Digital Politics Ltd (2020). Digital twin creates a blueprint for future smart buildings. https://www.pbctoday.co.uk/news/bim-news/digital-twin-smart-building/73253/ (accessed 3 July 2020).

Arup (2019). Digital Twin: Towards a Meaningful Framework. London: Arup.

Castaldini, F. (2019). How digital twin technology is central to smart buildings. *Facility Executive*. https://facilityexecutive.com/2019/02/how-digital-twin-technology-is-central-to-smart-buildings/ (accessed 3 July 2020).

Iberdrola (2020). Gemelos digitales: claves en la Cuarta Revolucion Industrial (Digital twins: Keys to the Fourth Industrial Revolution). https://www.iberdrola.com/innovation/digital- twin (accessed 17 July 2020).

IET (2019). Digital Twins for the Built Environment. London: The Institution of Engineering and Technology (IET).

Khajavi, S.H., Motlagh, N.H., Jaribion, A., *et al.* (2019). Digital twin: Vision, benefits, boundaries, and creation for buildings. *IEEE Access* 7: 147407–147419.

Madni, A.M., Madni, C.C. and Lucero, S.D. (2019). Leveraging digital twin technology in model-based systems engineering. *MDPI* 7(1): 1–13

Memoori (2020). BIM and GIS Combine to Advance the Digital Twin for Smarter Cities. Stockholm: Memoori Research.

Research and Markets (2020). Global Digital Twin Market (2020 to 2035): Opportunity and Trend Analysis. Dublin: Research and Markets Press.

Savian, C. (2019). Potential to use BIM data in digital twins is being overlooked. *BIMPlus*.

UnWork Ltd (2017). Smart Workin:Smart Buildings and the Future of Work. Kingston upon Thames: Unwired Ventures Ltd.

13

Digital Twin Enablers for Collaboration and the Risks and Barriers to Adoption of Digital Twins

Technology is a useful servant but a dangerous master.

Christian Lous Lange, Historian

13.1 Introduction

This chapter of the book looks at enabling technologies for urban digital twins and is based on the MSc research of Alex Mbabu. It explains the role and importance of the following aspects:

- building information modelling (BIM)
- the Internet of things (IoT)
- big data
- cloud computing and data analytics
- 3D and 5D modelling and high-defintion simulations
- artificial intelligence (AI)
- digital twin ecosystems
- smart buildings
- smart cities.

In addition to the above, the chapter covers the current state of adoption and development of digital twins across the world. The digital twin market and uptake outlook and the importance of this to the global economy is then analysed. In addition, some emerging market case studies will be referred to, alongside the successful outcomes that these have generated, and the challenging plans for future expansion and development. Following on from this, the digital twin information framework is discussed, alongside the Digital Twin Hub initiated by the Centre for Digital Built Britain (CDBB) as a platform for organisations and researchers who wish to improve governance around digital technology for the built environment.

The chapter then introduces the various issues that need to be considered for the adoption of digital twins, considering the complexity of the technology that is involved in their

The Smart Estate, First Edition. Edited by Jason Challender/Henry Oti.
© 2024 John Wiley & Sons, Ltd. Published 2024 by John Wiley & Sons, Ltd.

composition. In this regard, the technological challenges associated with addressing some of these issues will be articulated including the following:

- spatial–temporal sensor data resolution
- connectivity latency
- broad data volumes
- high data generation rate
- wide data variety
- high data veracity
- fast archival retrieval and online data processing.

Following this, the chapter then looks at the specific risks and barriers to development and implementation, including:

- insufficient business case and evidenced case studies
- complexity in data
- slow industry uptake in BIM.
- multidimension fragmentation
- incompatibility in the data language
- incompatibility in modelling social, economic, and environmental datasets
- data ownership, privacy, and security

Finally, conclusions and recommendations are identified and discussed, which include the best ways to introduce digital twins for the urban built environment. These cover the potential of smart cities, which could herald the adoption of city-scale digital twins to solve current global urbanisation challenges.

13.2   Enabling Technologies for the Urban Digital Twin

13.2.1   Building Information Modelling (BIM)

Digital twins can be seen as a natural evolution of building information modelling (BIM), which is already beginning to reflect the built environment digitally (BSI Group, 2018). BIM is a descriptive term for the advanced, collaborative, and information-centred process used to drive built environment design, construction, and operations. As a revolutionary technology, it optimises the construction industry's conventional way of operating, by harnessing early collaboration to increase efficiency from the design stage to the construction stage with the greatest advantages in the operational phase of the asset. BIM is a value-generating collaborative process during a built asset life cycle, focused on the creation, compilation, and exchange of shared 3D models and the integration of intelligent and structured data.

A BIM model forms a core subset and enabler of a digital twin, as illustrated in Figure 13.1. The BIM model is constituted of persistent data, collaboratively gathered, and updated information from key phases of a project. The model is a finely tuned tool for providing more accurate information on the phases of a building's life in design, collaboration, visualisation, costing, and construction sequencing. The primary function of BIM is to design and construct a building and to provide a digital record of a completed project after completion.

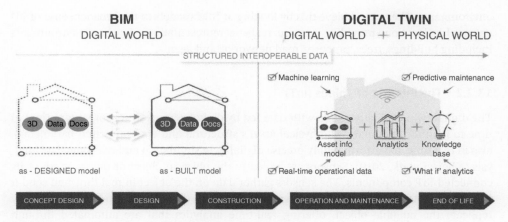

Figure 13.1 *The relationship between BIM and a digital twin.*

BIM should be regarded as a core enabler of the progress of digital twins for the built environment. The primary role of BIM is to design and construct an asset collaboratively and to create a digital record forming the asset information model (AIM) upon completion of a finished project. This is useful in the operational phase of the built asset and continuous improvement of the model provides background for the digital twin. The digital twin harnesses the AIM and links it to the physical built asset using the Internet of things (IoT) and a geographical information system (GIS) to provide a digital context. Connected devices and sensors are attached to the physical asset to enable real-time operational data collection. Such devices provide feedback to the AIM to integrate the operational and digital twin data thus providing real-time analytics of the physical asset. This forms a basis for a common interoperable knowledge base on the cloud, useful in the operational performance of the built asset through aspects such as predictive maintenance and 'what if' analysis test cases.

The digital twin is designed to monitor and improve the operational performance of a physical asset and to allow predictive maintenance (Khajavi *et al.*, 2019). BIM is not designed to operate with real-time data and is mostly used to design, build, and maintain tasks and interoperability that do not inherently require real-time capabilities. It is, however, a strategic facilitator for product life cycle management (PLM) for both buildings and infrastructure assets. PLM was a central focus of the introduction of the digital twin concept (Grieves, 2014) and is the process of managing a product's entire life cycle from conception, through design and production, to service and disposal. It connects people, data, processes, and systems and provides an information backbone for organisations and their extended enterprise (Javvadi, 2011). A fusion of BIM into the digital twin can promote the PLM of built assets by enabling product function analysis, performance prediction, product monitoring, ergonomics analysis, layout planning, prediction of the status of equipment, process analysis, operation optimisation, and the forecast of maintenance (Zheng *et al.*, 2019).

Building information modelling (BIM) is a rich dataset for built assets and its integration with GIS helps bring more efficient project delivery. Integrating the two systems can add more advantages to datasets including a combination of large-scale and small-scale built environments. They can achieve this by looking at BIM models in the broader sense of 3D geographic location, providing a more realistic representation of urban environments including buildings, trees, property, road networks, and agents.

13.2.2 The Internet of Things (IoT)

The digital twin explicitly works with data fed by digital devices or sensor systems in real time to monitor and analyse a physical asset's structural and environmental parameters, also in real time, to perform highly precise digital twin simulation and real-time data analysis (Khajavi *et al.*, 2019). Sensors are added to the physical object or one or more of its connected IoT components. The sensors gather data on the object in real time and send it to a cloud-hosted system for processing of the data. This allows the digital twin to digitally replicate the tangible object, offering real-time analytics that are automated through machine learning. In this way, it detects trend behaviours and probabilities in built assets for potential project performance improvements or well-informed decision-making. In addition, it offers insights into life-cycle operational functionality, while predicting any potential problems with regard to how the asset will change or behave in the future (Dentons, 2020).

Linking digital twins with the IoT provides the data required to understand how the physical counterpart conducts itself and interacts in its operational environment (Madni *et al.*, 2019). The integration of IoT and digital twins enhances preventive maintenance, and artificial intelligence (AI)-based physical system and operational process optimisation. The IoT transmits performance, maintenance, and safety data, and other data, from the physical twin to the digital twin, serving as a link between the physical and virtual worlds. The IoT facilitates predictive modelling by transmitting multisensor information to the digital twin (Madni *et al.*, 2019). The integration of the digital twin and the IoT makes it possible for an organisation to gain insight into how consumers use products. These insights will allow customers to optimise the schedule of maintenance and use of resources, proactively anticipate possible product failures, and reduce system downtimes.

13.2.3 Big Data

Big data refers to vast volumes of heterogeneous, multisource data defined by the 5 Vs, namely: (high) volume, variety, velocity, veracity, and value. Big data analytics offer a modern way of understanding the physical realm. A vast amount of data is generated during the operation of a digital twin and to retrieve valuable raw data and information, advanced data analytics and fusion technologies are required. By integrating big data with developments in AI and machine learning prospects in digital twins can be enhanced.

Twin data is an essential digital twin enabler. It addresses multitime, multidimensional, multisource, and heterogeneous data obtained from physical beings. Virtual models generate some simulation data while specific data is obtained from systems, defining the invocation and execution of the service. Some data is knowledge which is produced or extracted from existing sources by industry professionals.

13.2.4 Cloud Computing and Data Analytics

Cloud computing and data analytics, integrated into a digital twin, offer insights into assets and their performance, enabling users to take timely and well-informed action, and promoting feedback mechanisms that lead to product and process improvements. As the sensors continue to proliferate, edge computing is another significant technology gaining traction as an advancement to cloud computing. It involves processing data on a network's periphery. At a time when more and more of our data is being processed in the cloud, the prospect of continuous feedback loops seems daunting, but edge computing can mitigate these problems by storing data at or near the source. The next generation of autonomous, driverless vehicles are prime candidates for both gains from edge computing and 5G networking, which together would promote instant reactivity in an ever-changing built environment.

Through linking objects to a cloud-based network that processes the collected data, the performance of entities in the physical world can be used to evaluate virtual model performance. Digital twins create efficiencies by optimising processes and workflows by interacting with virtual objects and systems to enhance asset management proactively. In this way, they can provide decision support to users (Madni *et al.*, 2019). Furthermore, enabled by remote assistance technology, they can alert users of any potential malfunction, incident, or anomaly in their service. Such a concept is aimed at addressing outdated methods for troubleshooting, enabling operators to instantly fix the issue at hand. In this way, the digital twin can operate autonomously by being able to evaluate a scenario, formulate tailored solutions, and bring them into action (Iberdrola, 2020).

13.2.5 3D and 5G Modelling and High-Definition Simulations

3D modelling is the first step towards digital twin modelling and the method of transforming the surface of an object into a graphical model for a digital twin. The models can be built either by a 3D scan of the object or by specialised computer-aided design (CAD) or BIM software, and finally described in terms of geometries. 3D modelling is a key enabler in developing a graphical representation ofor the digital twin. It attaches experimental modelling to test the digital twin model, through high-definition simulation. This is performed using a distributed model linked to physical objects, equipped with sensors, and simulation-based support systems to facilitate real-time decision- making.

The digital twin case study of Herrenberg, Germany, was produced using a Faro 3D laser, which enabled the incorporation of several datasets into the 3D model, allowing it to conduct a high-definition simulation of urban mobility and air flows. Such simulation tests are carried out using a distributed model, using physical assets fitted with sensors and support systems facilitating real-time stakeholder decisions. For example, high-definition simulation tests in Singapore enabled users and city officials to run virtual test-bedding simulations of everything from population growth to public events to natural disasters and other emergencies. Conversely, the Herrenberg digital twin allowed the public and stakeholders to gain a deeper understanding of potential approaches to urban problems that require collective decision-making. 5G is a significant enabler in this case study since ultra-low latency is essential but does rely on data from sensors being collected continuously and accurately to create an accurate digital twin. One of the benefits of 5G is that it removes the likelihood of missing the appropriate data point describing the anomaly or feeding incorrect data into the analytics programme. This prevents the condition from being misdiagnosed and alternative solutions, such as wi-fi or long-term evolution (LTE) connectivity, do not have the same level of coverage and service quality.

5G is gaining importance, and its integration into digital twins will lead to increasingly large datasets processed at much faster speeds. For this reason, it is a step-change in the capacity of data transmission and can introduce very high carrier frequencies with exponentially increased bandwidth. In addition, 5G can map, monitor, route, and optimise information flows around the world and can enhance real-time visibility in locations and conditions. Furthermore, corrective forces using 5G would be able to take corrective measures without human intervention by controlling product changes, and changing procedures and steps on the physical objects.

13.2.6   Artificial Intelligence (AI)

Artificial Intelligence (AI) is the broad concept of machines designed to perform tasks in a way that we would find 'smart.' In contrast, machine learning is a current implementation of AI focused on the premise that we should be able to provide machines with access to data and let them learn for themselves. Machine learning entails any algorithm applied to a data stream to discover patterns for a particular application and can automate complex analytical tasks. Machine learning can analyse real-time data, modify actions with minimal supervisory needs, and increase the probability of desired outcomes (Madni *et al.*, 2019).

Digital twin technology includes continually evolving AI which uses supervised and unsupervised learning algorithms on twin and sensor-based data. It powers the virtual model of the physical object with the capability to comprehend changes in the physical entity's status through sensing data, analysing, predicting, and estimating. The physical entity responds to adjustments based on the optimised scheme retrieved from the digital twin, continuously relying on real-time data.

13.2.7   Digital Twin Ecosystems

The transformative potential of urban digital twins lies in connecting them from a single digital twin to an ecosystem of linked digital twins, to provide more data in a broader context. The Gemini Principles, referred to previously in the book, outline that a digital twin must function effectively, based on a standard connected environment, and must be able to adapt as technology evolves. For this reason, the digital twin connections rely on federating existing and planned interconnected built assets. The ecosystem framework can be applied not only to the public built environment at an urban scale up to the state level, but also the private built environment. Accordingly, some of the many challenges that lay in urban environments also apply in privately built estates.

Urban built environments and states have so much data that they are unable to analyse it correctly and sometimes crisis situations reveal that they lack the data they need. A digital twin could be regarded as a key to resolving this challenge, progressing an urban-scale concept to state or national digital twin level. Urban-scale and state digital twins are both connected through digital twin ecosystems with a distinguished difference in the level of operation. However, both have the potential not only to mirror but also to help manage the ecosystem.

13.2.8 Smart Buildings

Smart buildings are an excellent example of applications that benefit from digital twin machine learning capabilitie. The use of machine learning in a digital twin includes the supervised learning of operator or user preferences and involves setting up priorities in a simulation-based, controlled test-bed. This can be achieved through supervised learning of objects and patterns using clustering techniques in virtual and real-world environments. It can also entail improving environmental systems and learning in unpredictable situations and operational environments which are only partly measurable (Madni *et al.*, 2019).

13.2.9 Smart Cities

Digital twin technology is a game changer technology for smart cities. Urban-scale digital twins provide a platform for smart cities where assets, buildings, and services can interact with one another, turning physical assets from static structures into connected ecosystems. The urban digital twin is a virtual representation of an instrumented, interconnected, and intelligent urban area. Instrumented refers to collecting and integrating live real-world data using cameras, sensors, monitors, personal computers, and other associated devices. They are interconnected by federating digital twin data into a central life cycle repository, such as a common data framework, that enables this information to be shared between the various city stakeholders and services. In contrast, digital twin intelligence refers to the use of advanced analytics, modelling, optimiiation, and visualisation techniques for better insights.

13.3 The Current State of Adoption and Development of Digital Twins

13.3.1 The Digital Twin Market Outlook

The global digital twin market was valued at US$3.8billion in 2019 and is expected to be US$35.8 billion by 2025 (IET, 2019), reaching US$115.1 billion by 2035 (Research and Markets, 2020), which represents a huge increase. The concept has risen to prominence and is now being used in a variety of fields. Digital twins are transformational as they enable businesses to optimise or change and augment their business models. Market growth is fuelled by the growth in Internet of Things (IoT) connected devices. With the availability of inexpensive IoT sensors, technology is now available to do more things and is becoming more affordable. The advent of 5G has led to ultrafast speeds, greater capability to accommodate large device densities, improved processing power, and more massive datasets for digital twins. Furthermore, the growing demand for process optimisation, performance monitoring, and product and system conditions has contributed to the growth of the digital twin market. In turn, this has contributed to the improved quality and increased capabilities of digital twins as they have become more accessible across all sizes of organisations.

The built environment is yet to catch up with other sectors in the use of digital twins, with only 5% of the built environment having started the implementation of digital twins and less than 1% of assets having one in operation (IET, 2019). Urban-scale challenges, including the COVID-19 pandemic, rising global energy prices, and the increasing cost of living, have continued to enable the digital twin market to expand. This can be explained from the perspective that digital twins have played a major part in tackling these problems. In this regard, the COVID-19 pandemic forced industry and government toward a greater focus on digital technologies as a way of improving collective health and well-being. For instance, research teams at the University of Virginia's Biocomplexity Institute developed a digital twin modelling tool that helped local and state governments predict the spread and severity of the infection. This helped policymakers understand the common impacts of coronavirus policies based on the review of broad data sets.

13.3.2 Global Digital Twin Uptake Outlook

Data-driven decision-making has led to greater efficiencies in designing, constructing, and operating our built environment, and those services that it provides. Accordingly, digital twin technologies are being harnessed as an evolution of building information modelling (BIM) in an increasing proportion of development projects across the globe. An example is SenSat, a UK-based data capture and digital twin software firm, who were appointed to model the path of the planned High Speed 2 (HS2) railway line from London to the north west of England, generating some 18 billion data points. This technology was designed to assist stakeholders in tracking the progress of the project, to achieve greater efficiencies, and to ensure smoother workflows, which were deemed essential given the significant cost overruns of the project. Other urban digital twin projects in Europe have included Rotterdam and Amsterdam, where delivering better operations, such as energy efficiency, smart parking, intelligent mobility, and better traffic flows, have hugely benefitted their smart city credentials. Other examples have included the Rennes Metropole in France where digital twins have been harnessed in many ways for urban development, such as sunlight simulation, noise modelling, and tree shadow effects on buildings.

Emerging markets in Asia-Pacific are taking the lead in embracing digital twins in the design, construction, and operations of new urban set-ups and existing built environments. The case study of Singapore is the torch-bearer for digital twins. At the same time, in China, Shanghai Railway Engineering harnessed digital twin technology to design, build, and operate Beihu Sewerage Plant, the largest sewerage plant to be built in Asia, reaping significant benefits such as cost and schedule savings. Shanghai, the largest city in China, is also in the process of developing its digital twin which could soon be able to optimise the built environment and solve some of the city's most significant urbanisation challenges. In addition, thee state government of Andhra Pradesh, India, is in the process of developing Amaravati, the first whole new smart city, out of a digital twin which aims at revolutionising development, planning, operations, and citizen participation across its new state capital. The Association of Southeast Asian Nations (ASEAN) has also set up a pilot plan to create a network of digitally twinned smart cities which will include Jakarta, Indonesia, and Cauayan City, Philippines, in addition to Singapore. The goal is to use the shared resources and capabilities of the participating cities to work together on solutions to critical urban challenges.

13.3.3 Digital Twin Information Framework

We are still early into the digital twin age and the pathway from creating an urban digital twin to a national digital twin is still not explicit in the UK. Notwithstanding this challenge, the research into digital twins continues to be significant. The Digital Framework Task Group (DFGT) maps interaction and interoperability tools, to promote and develop the capabilities of a fully integrated UK digital twin by the year 2050. Furthermore, the Digital Twin Hub, initiated by the Centre for Digital Built Britain (CDBB) and now under the wing of the Connected Places Catapult, is a platform for organisations and researchers who wish to improve governance around digital technology for the built environment. The CDBB focused on providing an understanding of how emerging digital technology could transform the built environment. It enabled this through establishing information management frameworks for the built environment, raising awareness, and implementing BIM and digital twins in the UK and globally. The ultimate objective is to improve the performance of buildings and infrastructure, and to increase efficiency, productivity, and sustainability, thereby improving the quality of life for all.

The transformative potential of digital twins lies in linking them together and providing greater insight into the broader context. The CDBB vision for the national digital twin was as an ecosystem of conjoined digital twins, which is formed with a shared vision and values. The CDBB envisaged it as a shared national resource enabling secure, resilient data sharing across the built environment, and known as 'the Commons.' The goal was to create a single version of truth for assets in which all data can be accessed and interpreted during the design–build–operation life cycle.

13.4 Risks and Barriers to Adoption of Digital Twins

13.4.1 Introduction to the Risks and Barriers

There is caution about using digital twins in the built environment related to ambitious expectations of economic returns and advancements based on existing case studies, even though there is little evidence that the investments will yield safe returns. A digital twin needs significantly more initial investment compared to other business ventures of a similar scale and value. Costs can vary depending on the degree of complexity, time, and effort that needs to be invested to create a virtual representation of the system. The cost of creating a digital twin is a function of the number of components in the system and the component interfaces and dependencies. It also is very dependent on the sophistication of the algorithms used to execute particular functions, and the skill and know-how required to construct the digital twin (Madni *et al.*, 2019). Owing to the large sums of financial investment involved, wherever possible, it is preferable to design the digital twin architecture for reuse which will reduce the costs for further application and thus increase its value for money.

The outcomes from the digital twin technology rely on a two-way, real-time connection between the physical asset and its digital twin to create physical realism with no compromises. However, dealing with such complex systems introduces challenges associated with ensuring spatial–temporal sensor data resolution, connectivity latency, broad data volumes, high data generation rates, wide data variety, high data veracity, fast archive retrieval, and online data processing. In addition, digital twins must be maintainable, trackable, reproducible, flexible, and as human-centred as possible (Dentons, 2020). Another challenge is posed as the physical asset evolves over time; a corresponding evolution of the digital twin is required while maintaining its backward compatibility aspect. For this reason, digital twins need to maintain a representative state of the physical object with the ability to absorb a wide range of data at various times and levels, and to adapt the underlying data model across their existence.

Digital twins represent physical assets which require a high degree of safety and security. Consequently, the decisions taken based on digital twin information will need to be made more openly, transparently, and be more interpretable. Given that the Internet of things (IoT) and cloud computing can help businesses improve their services and processes in leveraging digital twin technologies, the increasing adoption of these technologies is especially useful for the global market. However, the IoT and cloud networks are vulnerable to cybercrimes and risks to data protection would curb market growth. Current security protocols, data encryption, data validation and authentication, access rights (including simple user definitions), lease privilege principles, mitigation of known device vulnerabilities, and regular security audits are some of the most critical security measures to be considered in a digital twin (IMA, 2019).

Digital twins must be interpretable and indistinguishable from the physical asset by end-users so that the process becomes smoother and more intuitive. Information volume and flows also need to be structured effectively with the opportunity to make improvements, to ensure that problems are addressed and that there is no potential misuse. This sometimes calls for cross-working between teams to redefine major digital twin outcomes and secure changes in decisions.

Another challenge for the digital twin is the development of a common language with specific domain knowledge for diverse participants. The ability to implement digital twins, sharing information across various industries and connecting them into an ecosystem, also poses the challenge of developing and using a standard language and framework across sectors (Dentons, 2020). Other potential issues include whether the digital twin can be built fast enough and how to manage old physical systems when very few people are qualified to undertake these tasks. Several companies are still dependent on 2D drawings and yet to adopt building information modelling (BIM), particularly the small- and medium-sized ones. If these organisations do not gain adequate expertise, they are at risk of losing their customer base to their competitors which can also hamper market growth. New skills and talents need to be brought in, new infrastructure for training created, and cultures require change. The evolving requirements and software licensing frameworks are making mostly small- and medium-sized companies uncomfortable when it comes to choosing paths for their digital twin ambitions. The digital twin has tremendous potential for the urban built environment, but certain risks and challenges must be tackled to achieve this value. This section analyses the risks and challenges of adopting digital twins for our urban built environment.

13.4.2 Insufficient Business Case and Evidenced Case Studies

There is little evidence in case studies of the benefits of digital twins and they are assumed to need more significant initial investment in technology and skill. Accordingly, some sections of the built environment are reluctant to adopt the technology with insufficient evidence of the return on investment (ROI). Furthermore, the framework for creating a digital twin at the urban–national level is still not clear from the evidence to date. The UK has taken steps to support digital twins in the built environment while developing the information management framework initiated by the Centre for Digital Built Britain (CDBB). However, more evidenced research is expected to be gathered to create an information framework to govern, leverage, and regulate the power of digital twins.

13.4.3 Complexity in Data

Determining the optimum level of detail is a challenge when initiating the digital twin of a built asset. At the same time, an excessively simplistic model may not deliver the value that the digital twin pledges. Furthermore, taking an approach that is too fast and wide-ranging can guarantee loss due to the complexity of millions of sensors and the signals produced by them adversely affecting the quality of information. Scaling up is another challenge for digital twins due to the need for more data, higher resolutions, larger data stores, and more computing resources. This presents a complex challenge in ensuring spatial–temporal sensor data resolution, the latency of connectivity, broad data volumes, high data generation rates, wide data variety, high data veracity, and fast archive retrieval and online data processing.

13.4.4 Slow Industry Uptake in BIM

The construction and engineering industries are still seeking a common understanding of BIM level 2. This predicament, and other challenges with BIM, leave us uncertain if these industries are ready to progress to digital twins. The technology remains skill- and cost-prohibitive, especially for small projects. Skill shortages also serve as an obstacle to the widespread adoption of digital twins and the evolving requirements and software licencing frameworks make it cost-prohibitive for small- and medium-sized enterprises.

13.4.5 Multidimension Fragmentation

Enablers to digital twins according to the 'Gemini Principles' are openness and live capabilities. Open platforms reflect significant benefits in allowing collaboration and access to data, as discussed earlier in this chapter. However, urban-scale connectivity requires open data systems and an interoperable database for data sharing which is sometimes a challenge. The built environment and government departments are still yet to break the silos to create better collaboration and information exchange. Multidimension fragmentation exists between sectors and systems and thus data sharing poses real problems in realising connected digital twins.

13.4.6 Incompatibility in the Data Language

As a physical asset evolves in life, a corresponding evolution of the digital twin is important while retaining the physical object's representative state, as well as predicting future scenarios. Due to digital twin advancements across the built environment, the linking of historical data comes at a high cost, and with many challenges. Organisations wishing to incorporate digital twins into their asset management have non-current models and outdated systems which use data language incompatable with digital twin technologies. Multiple data formats exist between assets and industries and the appropriate level of data connectivity remains an obstacle. The ability to deploy digital twins and exchange information across different sectors and assets, and link them into an ecosystem, also raises the challenge of creating and using a common language and framework across diverse assets and systems. The consistency validation of digital twins presents another problem, in that they must validate several models coming from different assets and sectors.

13.4.7 Incompatibility in Modelling Social, Economic, and Environmental Datasets

Urban digital twins provide the opportunity to check a series of problems and possible solutions, and to assess their effects using real-life scenarios. However, there is a challenge in that some human factors cannot be replicated in digital twins, such as history, interpersonal relationships, happiness, and joy. The limitation to the Herrenberg, Germany, digital twin project was that not enough real-life social, economic, and environmental data was integrated within it. This caused issues around consistency with the real world, and a deficit of precise data for tackling complex issues.

13.4.8 Data Ownership, Privacy, and Security

The rise of digital twins in transforming diverse sectors and market segments, offers vast opportunities and efficiencies but increases their vulnerability to attacks on security and privacy. Security and privacy are essential for those who run and interact with digital twins. With the advancement in the technology, and particularly connectivity, there is an increase in the potential for cyber-threats and data protection risks. In addition to the risks of security and data privacy, digital twins lack clarity on the ownership of data. The limitations to the Singapore digital twin project were found to be security and data privacy vulnerabilities that could be exploited by prospective terrorist plotters. The government of Singapore asserts that it has measures to protect against such problems, and their digital twin is limited to computers not connected to the worldwide network, referred to as 'Internet isolation'. The issues of data privacy have become more complicated in Singapore when deciding on the quantity and quality of data that will be available to persons using the digital twin.

13.5 Conclusions and Recommendations

The global digital twin market continues to grow at a fast rate and the rapid pace of digital innovation has forced dramatic business transformation in almost every sector. This has brought with it wide-ranging strategic changes for many organisations leading to the development of focus areas that harness the potential of the digital twin; for example, product quality management, real-time tracking, education, production systems, autonomous mobility, smart grids, energy efficiency, and healthcare services. The power of digital twins and data is thus increasingly helping organisations monitor, manage, control, predict, and prescribe the environments in which they operate in.

The use of digital twins for the built environment is just beginning, and for this reason needs to catch up with other industries. The adoption of digital twins for the urban built environment is currently being fuelled by their ability to solve significant urban-scale challenges such as netzero carbon targets for environmental sustainability. Building information modelling (BIM) is already beginning to reflect the built environment digitally, and it is currently driving greater efficiencies in urban planning and policy, design, construction, and the operation of our built environment and its services. This improvement in technology is encouraging a new era of digital twins, resulting in better managed product life cycle management (PLM) systems over the entire asset life cycle, matched to live data. Although digital twins are in their infancy, with an array of challenges to contend with, they still present an array of potential opportunities and benefits for the urban built environment.

Digital twins push us to concentrate on the entire asset life cycle, helping us to see beyond the apparent importance of physical assets and instead to consider the real value of digital assets. Technologies and solutions that accelerate the growth of digital twins include, among others, 3D modelling, experimental modelling, high-definition simulators, twin and big data, artificial intelligence (AI), cyber–physical systems, and the Internet of things (IoT). Factors such as increased use of connected devices or sensors, remote assistance technology across assets, increased adoption of cloud platforms, and the emergence of high-speed networking technologies such as 5G are accelerating the adoption of digital twins for the urban built environment.

Digital twins for the built environment are a vital contributor to the joint strategy for government and industry in the UK, Construction 25, in terms of improved quality of life. They have many benefits during an asset's life cycle and can address questions in real time that could not be answered before. In addition, they can deliver longer-lasting value creation, improved asset performance, and real-time insights into current urbanisation and sustainability challenges. The era of smart cities is only just starting with the adoption of city-scale digital twins to solve current urbanisation challenges. Digital twins can contribute greatly to this agenda and promote many successful outcomes. These include data-driven collaborative urban modelling, planning and development for the public good, zero-carbon goals for healthy and sustainable urban built environments, automated built asset operations, real-time monitoring, and control of urban infrastructure and services. Other positive digital outcomes that could be generated include connectivity between diverse assets and industries, improved energy environments, scenario risk and compliance assessments, improved safety, scheduled maintenance, and planning, increased efficiency, higher accuracy, reduced life cycle costs, and pandemic-resilience in urban built environments.

Digital twins have enormous potential benefits for the urban built environment but still possess some risks and barriers to their adoption. For instance, there is limited evidence from case studies on the value and benefits of digital twins and it is believed that they require significant and potentially unaffordable initial investment in technology and skills. Some parts of the built environment are therefore hesitant to embrace the technology with inadequate proof of return on investment (ROI). Accordingly, this hesitancy to embrace the technology is contributing to low uptake in the estates, construction, and engineering sectors. In addition, digital twins pose a complexity challenge in the management of the increasing quantity, velocity, and variety of data flows. For this reason, they remain skill- and cost-prohibitive, especially for small projects and those organisations yet to adopt BIM level 2. Data sharing always comes with challenges in realising connected digital twins with existing multisector and discipline fragmentation. Uncertainty remains around the compatibility of historical asset data and multiple data formats across a diverse range of assets. In addition, digital twins are unable to mirror deeply human factors, related to history, interpersonal relationships, happiness, and joy, to achieve consistency with the real world. A further challenge for their adoption lies in the premise that they lack clarity on ownership, management, and the regulation of data, which increases their vulnerability to cyber-threats and data protection risks.

Notwithstanding the above challenges, digital twins are increasingly becoming a major contributor to the digital built environment. They are facilitating digital transformation in systems, processes, records, and workflows through the usage of big data, cloud computing, and AI technologies to allow collaboration between projects, digital threads, and stakeholders. The technology allows urban built environments to become healthy and sustainable and, through the incorporation of analytics, facilitates the improved performance of physical assets. These provide value in transforming cities and towns to address urbanisation and sustainability challenges as demonstrated through the two case studies discussed in this chapter. Perhaps the best way to introduce digital twins for the urban built environment is through target value design. By adopting this approach, it facilitates a collaborative, partnering mentality with co-located project participants working together to create designs that provide the building owners with whole-life value. The life-cycle operations and cost should consequently form the guidelines for the design of any digital twin. In this way, they can enhance predictability in life-cycle costing and physical asset operational functionalities. Accordingly, cost reduction is a significant benefit of digital twins, by helping to anticipate and prevent unexpected costs, and allowing facilities to operate more effectively by detecting inefficiencies and better predicting future maintenance to avoid unforeseen costs. Given the savings and value they can generate in this regard, they should be recognised on the balance sheet. Therefore, the ROI) could be calculated by measuring the costs of producing the digital twin against the savings created over the lifetime of an asset.

Development of knowledge centres is needed to facilitate a full awareness of the capabilities of technology in the built environment. These centres could focus on aspects such as collaboration, future-ready skills, and government policy, contributing to the digital twin ecosystem. In addition, there is a need for change management to include sharing knowledge, overcoming barriers, and understanding the value and impact of digital technology from an asset and ecosystem life cycle perspective. For this reason, the digital twin for the built environment will require new skills and competences, possibly related to scientific analytics. Digital twin technology automation capabilities have the power to reduce some of the existing jobs in the built environment. Accordingly, this reinforces the need for developing new skills and upskilling which will facilitate the embracement of the emerging technology for the built environment.

Industry sectors need to appreciate the value of collaboration and the holistic benefits of digital twin ecosystems as, working together, they will enable parties to develop innovative ideas and forge new ways of working. In the UK, the Centre for Digital Built Britain (CDBB) formed a partnership between government, industry, and academia. There is a need for community engagement to educate people and forge a clear understanding of the value of digital technologies in the built environment. This could have the goal of improving people's capability and capacity to adopt digital twins in their daily working lives. Furthermore, full engagement across different industries and sectors would draw more insights and connectivity across the ecosystem, and therein create policy frameworks and standards for digital technologies. For this reason, an information management framework is of critical importance. This should set a clear roadmap for the introduction of digital twins, covering their regulatory framework, management, curation, vision, and the strategic steps for implementation. The information framework should also work towards guiding standards on data complexity and the adoption of a common data language to foster metadata interoperability in connecting diverse digital twins. These standards can range from the data storage file format to the specifics of how data can be compressed and security standards maintained across different geographical areas. The 'Gemini Principles' previously referred to in the book specify that digital twins must be as secure and as open as possible. Consequently, running connected digital twins requires trusted and resilient data sharing mechanisms. Furthermore, the need for their adoption on a national scale by governments or urban-scale local authorities, requires open data infrastructures to be dependable, transparent, user-friendly, agile with fast updating capabilities, and the IoTs enabled in real-time, to make the data as accessible as possible.

The practice of digital twins must be safe and secure in order to achieve trust. Accordingly, the secure integration of the whole ecosystem and the supply chain is essential, as all stakeholders need to be part of the process for interoperability of the digital twin. These stakeholders must ensure that information is safe and secure across the entire digital twin assembly process leading to its incorporation into the asset life cycle. Security must therefore serve as an embedded enabler using applications for encryption, authentication, language conformance, and threat detection, and with the required security policies in place to build and maintain digital confidence. The data security strategy must follow current information security standards set out on ISO 19650-5:2020; a security-minded and risk-based approach to information management for the built environment. This framework is designed to help users understand key vulnerability issues and instal the necessary controls needed to manage potential risks, such as sophisticated cyber–physical malware, in a combined physical and digital environment. Furthermore, it should encourage collaborative work and information interoperability through a wide range of independent entities in the built environment sector. Consistent technology and policy updates to data security strategies are also critical in keeping organisations one step ahead of cybercriminals by securing multiple assets and process endpoints.

13.6 Summary

Digital twins can be seen as a natural evolution of building information mModelling (BIM) where persistent data is collaboratively gathered, and information is updated at key phases of a project. They are designed to monitor and improve the operational performance of a physical asset and to allow predictive maintenance. The primary function of BIM is to design and construct a building and to provide a digital record of a completed project after completion. For this reason, BIM's role is to design and construct an asset collaboratively and to create a digital record forming the Asset Information Model (AIM) of a finished project. This is useful in the operational phase of the built asset and continuous improvement of the model provides background for the digital twin. BIM is a strategic facilitator for product life cycle management (PLM) for both buildings and infrastructure assets. For this reason, a fusion of BIM into the digital twin can promote the PLM of built assets by enabling product function analysis, performance prediction, product monitoring, ergonomics analysis, layout planning, prediction of the status of equipment, process analysis, operation optimisation, and the forecast of maintenance.

The digital twin explicitly works with data fed by digital devices or sensor systems in real time to monitor and analyse a physical asset's structural and environmental parameters, also in real time, to perform highly precise digital twin simulation and real-time data analysis. The sensors gather data on the object in real time and send it to a cloud-hosted system for processing of the data. This allows the digital twin to digitally replicate the tangible object, which offers insights into the asset and its performance, enabling users to take timely and well-informed action while promoting feedback mechanisms that lead to product and process improvements. Through linking objects to a cloud-based network that processes the collected data, the performance of entities in the physical world can be used to evaluate virtual model performance. 3D is the first step towards digital twin modelling and the method of transforming the surface of an object into the graphical model of a digital twin. The models can be built either by a 3D scan of the object or by specialised computer-aided design (CAD) or BIM software, and finally described in terms of geometries. Digital twin technology includes continually evolving artificial intelligence (AI) which uses supervised and unsupervised learning algorithms on twin and sensor-based data. The transformative potential of urban digital twins lies in connecting them from a single digital twin to an ecosystem of linked digital twins, to provide more data in a broader context. Smart buildings are excellent examples of applications that benefit from digital twin machine learning capabilities including the supervised learning of operator or user preferences and involving the set-up of priorities in a simulation-based, controlled test-bed.

Digital twin technology is a game changer technology for smart cities. Urban-scale digital twins, provide a platform for smart cities where assets, buildings, and services can interact with one another, turning physical assets from static structures into connected ecosystems. Notwithstanding this premise, the built environment is yet to catch up with other sectors in the use of digital twins, with only 5% of the built environment having started the implementation of digital twins and less than 1% of assets having one in operation. For this reason, the adoption of digital twins in the built environment globally has been covered extensively in this chapter. The narrative covered merging markets in Asia-Pacific which are taking the lead in embracing digital twins in the design, construction, and operation of new urban set-ups and existing built environments. Case study examples were given of Shanghai and Amaravati. Despite these international examples of excellence, we are still early on in the digital twin age and the pathway from creating an urban digital twin to a national digital twin is still not explicit in the UK. However, the Digital Framework Task Group (DFTG) maps interaction and interoperability tools, to promote and develop the capabilities of a fully integrated UK digital twin by the year 2050. Furthermore, the

Digital Twin Hub initiated by the Centre for Digital Built Britain (CDBB) is a platform for organisations and researchers who wish to improve governance around digital technology for the built environment.

Notwithstanding the uses and potential benefits of digital twins they are not without their challenges, barriers, and risks. For example, a digital twin needs significantly more initial investment, compared to other business ventures of a similar scale and value. In addition, there are also risks associated with dealing with such complex systems which introduce challenges including data processing and sensor data resolution. As they are representing physical assets, other challenges relate to them requiring a high degree of safety and security. Accordingly, information volume and flows also need to be structured effectively with the opportunity to make improvements, to ensure problems are addressed and that there is no potential misuse. Another challenge for the digital twin is the development of a common language with specific domain knowledge for diverse participants.

Finally, conclusions and recommendations were given in this chapter and examined the future development and use of the technology. The adoption of digital twins for the urban built environment is currently being fuelled by their ability to solve significant urban-scale challenges such as net-zero carbon targets for environmental sustainability. Furthermore, improvements in technology are encouraging a new era of digital twins, resulting in better managed product life cycle management (PLM) systems over the entire asset life cycle, matched to live data. In addition, they can contribute greatly to the smart city agenda and promote many successful outcomes. These include data-driven collaborative urban modelling, planning and development for the public good, zero-carbon goals for healthy and sustainable urban built environments, automated built asset operations, real-time monitoring, and control of urban infrastructure and services. These initiatives provide value in transforming cities and towns to address urbanisation and sustainability challenges as demonstrated through the two case studies discussed in this chapter.

References

BSI Group (2018). Digital Twins for the Built Environment. London: BSI Group.

Dentons (2020). Digital twins and the Internet of things (IoT): Utilising data. https://www.dentons.com/en/insights/alerts/2020/january/24/digital-twins-and-the-internet-of-things-utilising-data (accessed 3 July 2020).

Grieves, M. (2014). Digital Twin: Manufacturing Excellence Through Virtual Factory Replication. Digital Twin White Paper.

Iberdrola (2020). Gemelos digitales: claves en la Cuarta Revolucion Industrial (Digital twins: Keys to the Fourth Industrial Revolution). https://www.iberdrola.com/innovation/digital- twin (accessed 17 July 2020).

IET (2019). Digital Twins for the Built Environment. London: The Institution of Engineering and Technology (IET).

IMA (2019). Digital Twin Technology Benefits and Challenges. Chatsworth, CA: Identity Management Institute.

Javvadi, L. (2011). Introduction to product lifecycle management. New York: MphasiS Corporation.

Khajavi, S.H., Motlagh, N.H., Jaribion, A., *et al.* (2019). Digital twin: Vision, benefits, boundaries, and creation for buildings. *IEEE Access* 7: 147407–147419.

Madni, A.M., Madni, C.C., and Lucero, S.D. (2019). Leveraging digital twin technology in model-based systems engineering. *MDPI* 7(1): 7.

Research and Markets (2020). Global Digital Twin Market (2020 to 2035): Opportunity and Trend Analysis. Dublin: Research and Markets Press.

Zheng Y., Yang S. and Cheng, H. (2019). An application framework of digital twin and its case study. *Journal of Ambient Intelligence and Humanized Computing* 10: 1141–1153.

14

Reflections, Overview, and Implications for Future Practice and Closing Remarks

Clearly, the thing that is transforming is not the technology – it is the technology that is transforming you.

Jeanne W. Ross, MIT Sloan's Centre for information Systems and Research

14.1 Introduction

This final section summarises each chapter of the book and extrapolates the key findings and issued raised. Following on from what has been articulated and discussed, it presents some reflections, implications and recommendations for the future of collaborative working with digital information management as part of organisational smart estates strategies. Furthermore, for the built environment, it suggests the ways and means to address the inherent dilemmas and challenges that are faced along the journey to smart estates.

14.2 Summary of the Key Issues Raised throughout the Book

14.2.1 Introduction

There are many different aspects and themes relating to smart estates, especially within the context of collaborative working with digital information management. For this reason, the book's focus has become an increasingly 'hot topic' over recent years, predominantly to address some of the challenges in the sector on a national and international level. Such challenges have revolved around not only the lack of collaborative working and partnering but also the quality and availability of useful digitally enhanced information and technologies. Accordingly, *The Smart Estate: Collaborative Working with Digital Information Management* is concerned with how we make improvements and positively contribute to the estates and facilities, construction, and engineering sectors and adopt different innovative initiatives and measures in addressing some of these challenges. For this reason, the book covers collaboration and partnering philosophies working alongside digital technologies, such as building information modelling (BIM) and digital twins, for procuring more successful project outcomes. In recent years, companies have realised that they need to focus on non-financial strategies linked to these aspects alongside their economic goals. This involves investing jointly in their staff and their systems which can bolster their reputations and in turn increase their success in the marketplace. In addition, commitment to collaborative partnering and investments in digital technologies can have a positive relationship with the job satisfaction and career success of employees and provide a safe and caring environment for them to prosper. As a result, companies that have embraced these areas have found that this raised the motivation levels of employees and increased the productivity and retention of the workforce. Accordingly, the evidence would therefore suggest that collaborative working linked to investment in digital technological advancements could have far-reaching positive effects on organisational success. Notwithstanding this assertion, such positive measures are not always easy to integrate into the built environment, which is predominantly associated with fragmented, complex, and potentially confrontational practices. This can create a dilemma for the sector and is evidenced in reported case studies referenced throughout the book. The book responds to this dilemma and addresses how standards can be pragmatically applied to professional practice and provides case studies and example scenarios aligned to modern-day requirements.

The book's toolkit includes the use of case studies to look at how successes, failures, and key risks can be influenced by collaboration policies working with digital technologies. Other sections identify policies and strategies that support smart estates, including BIM and digital twins, that can assist businesses in the built environment achieve more successful outcomes. These tools are intended to assist academics, construction-related practitioners, and clients in their awareness, breadth of knowledge, and comprehension of the issues around collaborative working with digital information management. This can then be linked to development of their smart estates with the overarching aim of delivering more successful project outcomes.

Although the research was mostly undertaken in the UK, the book utilises international case studies including those from Germany, Australia and Singapore. Accordingly, the findings are likely to have best fit with the UK construction industry, albeit the overall knowledge and understanding provided by this book will have international relevance.

14.2.2   Introduction and Background to Collaborative Working and Partnering

The choice of procurement strategies on projects has long been a contentious issue within the construction industry. Government reports of the past have identified deficiencies with traditional procurement strategies, predicated on commercially orientated contracts. Such approaches have had a negative effect on project outcomes, in a lot of cases brought about by adversarial relationships and disputes.

Although there are many different definitions of partnering, it could be defined as a business relationship designed to achieve mutual objectives and benefits between contracting organisations. The definitions of partnering and collaborative working have been articulated in Chapter 2 alongside an understanding of what it means to collaborate and the ways and means to improve and support its successful practice. Early collaboration, under partnering-type contracts, minimises disputes and facilitates significant improvements in client satisfaction, cost predictability, safety, and time predictability. The benefits of collaboration have been argued to include an increase in profits brought about by sharing expertise, knowledge, ideas, innovation, and best practice, and promoting efficiencies and improvements in decision-making.

Traditional procurement strategies have achieved low client satisfaction levels, poor cost predictability, and time certainty, largely attributable to coordination difficulties associated with separation of design and construction and the greater need for teamwork. Collaborative working and partnering were introduced as a way to 'turn the tide' on procurement in the built environment. In this sense, collaborative working at an early stage between contractors and design teams has been, post-Latham, regarded as bridging the gap between design and construction to improve project outcomes. Accordingly, many have identified collaborative procurement routes, such as partnering, as a critical success factor on construction projects. It has also been suggested that collaborative working would reduce the negative aspects of construction procurement, minimising conflicts and disputes through increased cooperation, and developing relationships built on trust.

Notwithstanding the perceived benefits that increased partnering and collaborative working practices could bring to the UK construction industry, these alternative procurement methods are still relatively rare. This could possibly emanate from client perceptions that open and competitive procurement systems, that truly market test prices, are the only way to assure stakeholders of the lowest possible initial capital cost.

The degree of trust between key members of teams has been identified as a critical factor in shaping relationships between all project team participants, as well as a key influence on project outcomes. To enable the communication and sharing of knowledge necessary for fully integrated practice, trust between supply chain members, from clients to the smallest SMEs, is a fundamental requirement. Academics have long considered the origins and make up of trust in an attempt to understand its meaning. From a social sciences perspective, its origins may emerge from a series of beneficial exchanges between two parties, where relationships are built up on cooperation and collaboration. Trust is considered to be a 'bonding agent' between collaborating partners and an 'essential foundation for creating relational exchange'. In addition, levels of trust can grow if acts of trust can be reciprocated but the risks of non-reciprocation can be high, especially at the early stages of a new relationship. Furthermore, expectations of trust, when broken, can have emotional consequences with parties feeling violated and can signal that relationships have become damaged. In such cases, this can change the dynamics of trust between parties and in extreme cases can lead to its complete collapse.

The project-based nature of much construction work can be seen as a fundamental barrier to the development of trust in practice, where relationships are often perceived to be short-term, and true collaborative working practices struggle to emerge. Finally, the quality of collaboration can be reinforced or weakened, depending on the behaviour, approaches, and attitudes of organisations and individual participants.

14.2.3 The Importance of Trust, Collaboration, and Partnering for the Built Environment

Chapter 3 of this book is largely based on the research study by Challender (2017) which focused on trust in collaborative construction procurement strategies.

The construction industry has in the past been characterised by complex processes and exchanges of information, and some believe that they can lead to the emergence of opportunistic behaviours. The benefits of trust within a capitalist economy should allow for greater cooperation without exertion of power and, from a transaction cost economics perspective, reduce opportunism. The development of trust in the built environment could be a potential means of reducing opportunism, while encouraging greater cooperation to improve project outcomes. The perceived benefits of trust have, however, attracted their critics in some instances. Notwithstanding this premise, some have debated whether such reliance on trust is appropriate where large sums of money are involved, and opportunism could emerge.

To encourage trust-building, it is important for project teams to communicate well and operate within an environment leading to 'an upward cycle of trust'. Increased trust in partnering can encourage greater scope for cooperation, teamwork, and collaboration, and it can lessen the need for excessive monitoring and formal control mechanisms. Notwithstanding the support for trust in collaboration and partnering, some professional practitioners still remain suspicious of the realisable benefits. This has emanated from experiences where traditional commercial positions have re-emerged, through claims and disputes, causing parties to retreat back to adversarial contractual positions. Possibly, this could explain why trust appears to be a stranger in construction contracting where confrontation remains the prevalent environment. One contributory factor for such lack of understanding may come from trust receiving only limited attention in construction project management.

In consideration of what can encourage trust, research by Challender (2017) found that there are many wide-ranging sources or attributes of trust. Either positively or negatively, confidence, teamwork, and the personalities of individual team members were all found to be important trust-building attributes in partnering. In the research study, professional practitioners outlined their opinions on many different trust-building mechanisms to increase trust in partnering arrangements. These included measures to increase fairness of contract terms, the existence of a dispute resolution process which could address the abuse of power, and deployment of market leverage scenarios.

It is generally accepted in the construction and engineering industries that partnering and collaborative working can facilitate the early integration of main contractors and subcontractors into the wider project team. This can bring many benefits for projects by having their expertise and familiarisation embedded at earlier stages of the design development. Furthermore, collaborative processes in partnering arrangements can potentially provide more effective open book mechanisms for developing final contract sums with contractors, ensuring that tendering processes are fully transparent, fair, and appropriate, in most cases. Specialist input and value-engineered solutions at preliminary design stages, possibly enabled by early integration of contractors, could shorten pre-tender periods while enhancing quality control and giving greater client satisfaction. In addition, partnering could be more successful than traditional procurement routes, where health and safety issues on projects represent greater risks to programme and quality.

The suitability of partnering and collaborative working may be affected by the different types of building project, especially in terms of complexity and specialism. Partnering is generally regarded as being best suited to large or complex projects where, in the early stages especially, the expertise of contractors in value engineering and project logistics would be extremely beneficial. The duration of projects may also have some influence over the success of partnering in practice. For instance, shorter projects do not facilitate enough time to build strong working relationships and for partners to become familiar with each other's ways of working.

The research study by Challender (2017) suggested that having the right contractor on board is more crucial in partnering arrangements than in traditional procurement. A possible reason for this may be the greater sense of teamwork and shared philosophies required in partnering. In more traditional procurement routes, the contractor selection process is still important in terms of evaluating expertise, experience, and specialism.

A 'culture' of trust allows projects to move forward effectively and creates an environment where problems can be shared and therefore solved more easily. Trust generated from previous relationships and dealings between individuals at senior levels is regarded as critical in the cascading of trust throughout organisations, and between those currently operating partnering arrangements. Not surprisingly at an operational level, 'human' attributes such as integrity, honesty, consistency, reliability, and competency are regarded as important in facilitating trust and good collaborative working. The research study by Challender (2017) clearly highlights barriers to successful implementation of partnering including factors related to fairness, cooperation, and sharing information. Perhaps BIM as a management tool, in encouraging greater collaboration, could assist in changing the culture of the UK construction industry and facilitate integration across the whole supply chain to address perceived deficiencies.

14.2.4 Analysis for the Lack of Collaborative Working and Partnering in the Built Environment

Over recent years, organisations have largely focused on increasing partnering strategies for collaborative procurement of major capital projects. Such initiatives have often been heralded as vehicles to obtain best value, improve levels of quality, and optimise service delivery, as has been articulated in the earlier chapters of this book. Notwithstanding this premise, such approaches have attracted their critics. There remains evidence of low levels of client satisfaction, owing mostly to poor cost and time predictability, which have in turn been attributed to a low level of trust in practice. Views have been presented in Chapter 4 that partnering practices within the UK construction industry have failed to realise the full extent of benefits and positive effects that have been experienced in other sectors such as manufacturing. In addition, there is a wide-ranging consensus that potential barriers in the construction industry could have hindered successful partnering: these barriers include fear of the unknown, perceived loss of control, uncertainty, and the lack of understanding of how to change the way one works. Within the context of these potential barriers, there have been reports that some advocates of partnering may be displaying acted behaviours to collaborative working but ultimately behaving consistently with their true beliefs, which only 'pay lip service' to partnering.

A lack of trust has emerged from the highly competitive nature of the UK construction industry, where commercial considerations and opportunities have prevailed over partnering philosophies. Despite authoritative calls for such partnering practices there has been a growing trend over recent years for organisations to move back to traditional procurement routes. There have been reports that clients may be feeling the only way to assure themselves that they are not paying too much is to market test their projects in a highly competitive environment. Organisations have been feeling vulnerable to partnering and reluctant to take unnecessary perceived risks. Furthermore, the 'one-off' and short-term, project-based nature of the construction industry has hindered the development of trust through good working relationships and repeat business.

When partnering is used, there may on occasion be an abuse of power by clients toward main contractors, or main contractors toward their supply chain – that is to 'squeeze too hard'. In times of austerity and during the COVID-19 pandemic, the desire to squeeze became a necessity, challenging the benefits of the partnering relationship. Indeed, one of the most prolific barriers to increased collaboration could be psychological whereby clients seek to prolong strategies associated with market leverage and power to disadvantage their 'partners'. The concept of integrated teams and partnering has been tainted in the past by inequitable working arrangements. This can result in giving little or no benefit to partnered organisations and, in some cases, anecdotal evidence has been presented of organisations that have suffered financially. In addition, any exploitation through partnering frameworks may increase the risk of this procurement option, reducing its attractiveness and contributing to a reduction in willing partners.

When the economic climate puts financial strain on many construction organisations, the management of cash flow and financial accounting becomes ever more focused and short-term commercial interests override the principles and perceived benefits of partnering. Suspicion of realisable benefits has emerged from previous research (Challender *et al.*, 2014). For example, cost savings for clients from collaborative working are perceived by some as being exaggerated over time. Other reports have revealed negative experiences in sharing information and prompt payment initiatives, leading to organisational mistrust.

In times of austerity, such as experienced in the UK during the recession of 2008–2012 or the economic uncertainty brought about by the COVID-19 pandemic, job security and 'playing safe' in times of austerity or uncertainty may therefore override the adoption of collaborative working practices. Furthermore, there is sometimes reluctance from organisations and individuals to expend time and resources in developing collaborative relationships, especially when affordability is an issue. Finally, to overcome some of these issues, professional development, education and training, operational and cultural change, and commitment are considered vital for future continual improvement in partnering practices.

14.2.5 Potential Risks, Problems, and Barriers for Collaborative Working in Estates and the Built Environment

Despite the benefits of collaborative working practices, identified in the earlier chapters of the book, these practices have attracted criticism. There is evidence to suggest that there can be barriers to the adoption of partnering and that practices may be difficult to integrate within a traditionally adversarial environment. Another contentious factor is whether the fractious nature of the UK construction industry, based largely on 'one-off' projects, facilitates the right environment and conditions for trust to prosper.

The quality of collaboration can be reinforced or weakened depending on behaviour, where relationships are perceived to be short-term and true collaborative working practices struggle to emerge. Other problems for partnering could occur on occasions where an abuse of power has occurred, with buyers' dictating to 'sellers' the terms of their employment and what is required of them. In fact, there are many potential adversities for partnering and collaborative working, including:

- poor compatibility of systems, processes, and procedures;
- poor technology interfaces;
- reluctance of organisations or individuals to share expertise and knowledge;
- supply chain inadequacies;
- non-supportive senior management;
- weak knowledge bases;
- high start-up costs;
- rigid organisational hierarchies;
- mismatch in organisational cultures; and
- conflicts in styles of leadership.

Where trust becomes an issue for project teams, or where they believe there is an imbalance of power, some parties may feel that there is a loss of control which can act as a barrier to collaborative working. In such cases, there is a concern that sharing of knowledge results in loss of knowledge, adding to a more general uncertainty. In times of economic uncertainty, which existed in the early stages of the COVID-19 pandemic, the desire to 'squeeze' became a necessity for some organisations which challenged the benefits of the partnering relationship. Cases emerged of employers trying to renegotiate contract terms with their supply chains to their commercial advantage.

For the above reasons, there is evidence that partnering and collaborative working is met with scepticism by some practitioners. Suspicion of realisable benefits has emerged in some circles; for example, cost savings for clients from collaborative working are perceived to have become exaggerated over time. The perceived lack of financial benefits or incentives to move toward collaborative practices has grown in influence over the years.

For collaborative practices to succeed, a cultural shift is required and BIM has been put forward as the necessary catalyst.

14.2.6 Collaborative Working with Digital Information Management in Estates and Construction

In Chapter 6, the importance of collaborative digital information management is established in the context of the built environment as a sector that is knowledge management dependent. Collaborative digital information management is central to acquiring, processing, and exploiting information that is valuable to businesses and establishments across various sectors. Digital information management scope can vary but generally encompasses some or all of the nine aspects of creation, representation, organisation, maintenance, visualisation, reuse, sharing, communication, and disposal. Depending on the organisation, the workflow for each of these aspects may vary within an organisation or across organisations. Also, processes have improved over time based on the technologies available to aid inherent tasks. This book adopts the definition of digital information management as 'the process by which an organisation collects, structures, stores, uses and shares its data to perform its core business across asset lifecycle activities'. The process described by this definition is built on the advances made in information technology (IT) with origins in the inventions of early hardware like giant calculators to the EDVAC and the launching of the World Wide Web. At centre stage of the development of digital information are the target requirements to meet. Although requirements may vary, stakeholders' needs are key in driving the requirement analysis process of digital applications. The fit-for-purpose factors identified in this book include generality, formality, flexibility, ease-of-use, scalability, and time-efficiency. Chapter 6 concludes by examining trends in digital information management looking at collaboration hubs of various common data environment tools and identifying BIM, artificial intelligence (AI), machine learning, and digital twinning as some of the trending innovations.

14.2.7 Technologies for Collaborative Digital Information Management in Estates and Construction

Having examined emerging digital technology innovations in Chapter 6, Chapter 7 focused on reviewing applications in FM and estates. As a result of the peculiar nature of tasks in FM, there is a need to align with job routines in this area of the built environment. Chapter 7 established that there are variations in the way applications are implemented in estates. Based on the vision of future cities, liveability, sustainability, resilience, and affordability are identified as the essential pillars. These pillars are enabled by the five main interlinked factors: digitalisation and innovation; talent and knowledge; a value-proof business case; stakeholder engagement; and a regulatory framework. Among the five, digitalisation and innovation aligns with the theme of this book and covers aspects of smart data-driven systems and autonomous building developments that can dynamically respond to stimuli. Another essential aspect is the achievement of interconnected systems of buildings, taking advantage of technologies such as the Internet of things (IoT), to improve efficiencies and balance energy consumption as well as other performance measures. Chapter 7 also highlights the risks that come with digital transformation, and it is imperative that cybersecurity is put in place at all levels of digital infrastructure in an operation.

There is a consensus in the literature that levels of research and evidence from case studies regarding digital information management in FM is scarce compared to the design and construction phases of the asset life cycle. However, the extent of the uptake of innovative digital technology is evident in the degree of diffusion inherent in the sector. Such diffusion should encompass FM policies on integrating digital technology provisions, the levels of digital literacy, and championing transformation based on an organisational top-down approach. Also, embedding processes that embrace digital technologies in daily operations and as a route of professional development are key defining factors of the level of diffusion. The two core areas of FM, hard services and soft services, have different levels of diffusion in digital transformation due to their disparate associated functions and tasks. By nature in FM hard services, mechanical, electrical, and fabric maintenance are highly instrument/gadget reliant and have a greater tendency for adopting trends in digital information management. However, aspects of FM soft services, such as help desk applications, are moving up the ladder in their level of digital sophistication. Whether FM hard or soft services, the rudimentary elements of perceived usefulness, perceived ease-of-use, attitude toward use, behavioural intention to use, and behavioural change in system usage, as identified in the Technology Acceptance Model (TAM) constitute key influential factors.

14.2.8 Infrastructures for Collaborative Digital Information Management for Estates

In Chapter 8, digital transformation infrastructure designed to cope with data variety, volume, and velocity was examined. The review of individualised and localised systems in the Chapter 7 established the background for discussing services such as the Internet, communication satellites, wi-fi, data centres, cloud computing, and the IoT. Four key trends characterising information infrastructure in recent times are socialism, mobility, analytics, and clouds, which to large extent form the foundations for B2C and B2B networks. For enterprises to continue maintaining their relevance and competitive edge, they must possess leadership and digital capabilities along the lines of these key trends. Aspects of digital capability entail establishing strategic areas and processes so that digital transformation can be harnessed in FM and estates. Well-functioning processes in FM are key to maintaining an efficient workplace. The main areas with defined processes discussed in Chapter 8 include FM in relation to buildings, people, services, and resources; asset management of buildings, plant, and equipment; property and space management; flexible workspace and hot-desk management; flexible resource management; and environmental management and control.

Further aspects and tools for data acquisition aiding digital transformation are examined with the acknowledgement that the level of dependency on IT hardware across economic sectors including the built environment, is ever-increasing. The implication is that established digital systems will require constant improvement and refinement for better efficiencies. In the project life cycle, COBie data has been widely recognised as a standard format for producing and transferring information from the earlier stages of design and construction to the asset operation stage. Such information is vital for the reactive and planned asset maintenance regimes. Another important aspect extensively discussed in Chapter 8 are systems relating to energy consumption in buildings with a focus on building management systems (BMS). Some of the technologies covered amongst existing systems include Autodesk Green Building Studio, DOE-2, eQUEST, BEopt, Artra (Trimble), Onuma Planning Systems, Autodesk Project Dasher and QFM. A recount of best practice cases of using computer-aided facilities management (CAFM) implemented in estates wraps up Chapter 8 and sets the stage for Chapter 9, dedicated to examining associated actors in estates.

14.2.9 Actors in Digital Information Management for Estates

In Chapter 9, key actors in digital information management and transformation were examined together with the roles of professional institutions in digital information management in estates. Since digital information management is still developing in FM and estates, it was crucial to look at the emerging roles in this area of the built environment.

The commonly identified roles in the job market of the 2020s include digital director/lead, digital manager, or digital coordinator of the area of activity concerned. These roles can relate to areas of activity such as library services, marketing, music, or construction/built environment. Many tasks on these roles relate to benchmarking, monitoring achievements, and evaluating performance. On a more general basis, Chapter 9 identified the existence of some levels of confusion in the responsibilities and functions of roles in digital information management. However, a suggested hierarchy is that digital managers oversee coordinators who may in turn direct modellers, technicians, or specialists. Slight variations exist in such relationships in different establishments which are typically tailored according to the organisational functions. In any case, the crucial point is the adoption of arrangements that are most suitable for meeting organisational objectives.

The chapter also examined professional institutions as essential supporting resources for actors in estates as in the same way as other professional bodies in the built environment. The historical context of professional bodies in FM traces its origin to the 1960s in the USA. Professional bodies have seen different phases of development and refinement to reach their contemporary states. There have been mergers and change of names, and redefining of areas of operation as evident with UK's IWFM, all with the view to improve operation efficiencies and effectiveness. There is a clear recognition of the prowess and awareness of possibilities with digital information management in professional bodies covering FM. However, a clearer definition of standard roles and hierarchy will be useful. Some roles identified and discussed included asset data exploitation technician, data quality controller in CAFM, document controller and energy solutions manager with employers from the public and private sectors alike. What is clear from Chapter 9 is that roles are still developing and early definitions by professional institutions will help with standardisations for general adoption.

14.2.10 The Role of Digital Technology in Healthcare Facilities Management

Facilities management (FM) refers to the management of operation and maintenance activities that ensure end-users receive the services for which a facility was designed. A facility's FM cost is estimated at approximately 71% of its total life-cycle cost over a 40-year period. There are 11 core competencies for FM:

- communications
- emergency preparedness and business continuity
- environmental stewardship and sustainability
- finance and business
- human factors
- leadership and strategy
- operation and maintenance
- project management
- quality
- real estate and property management
- technology.

Conversely, knowledge management is regarded as creating and utilising knowledge within an organisation to foster innovation, develop new skills, and create a positive work environment, and has become the essential component of innovation in an organisation to improve performance and solve problems. It aids in developing platforms and processes for sharing tacit knowledge. The challenge of healthcare knowledge management is integrating multisource and multiformat healthcare information into a coherent knowledge base that can be used to provide day-to-day service. This is a critical issue that should concern all stakeholders in the broader health ecosystem. To address these issues, some governments have emphasised the need to revolutionise the FM sector by increasing the adoption of digital technologies.

Digital technologies can be described as scientific or engineering knowledge that deals with the establishment and application of computerised or digital devices, methods or systems that can improve the immediacy, accuracy, and flexibility of communication. Advanced digital technology is a source of numerous solutions that can facilitate the acquisition, processing, redundancy, and compression of information about used buildings, making it easier to develop cause-and-effect models, draw conclusions, and make forecasts. Systems that have long been used for FM purposes, such as CAFM, computerised maintenance management systems (CMMS), building automation systems (BAS), or electronic document management systems (EDMS), have been proven helpful in practice, despite a lack of interoperability limiting their functionality. They function appropriately as separate systems but cannot communicate because there is no platform for information exchange. As a result, time dedicated to FM actions is inefficiently managed, including the integration of critical information, which can result in both time and financial losses. The provision of healthcare FM services, which are considered non-core services in healthcare organisations, has emerged as a critical service in delivering effective inpatient care and running productive healthcare. To assist these services, both technologies and the physical environment are critical in bringing about the changes needed in healthcare. For instance, technology and social changes have altered how facilities are managed, and many tasks previously performed by hand are now done automatically. Such automation in healthcare can bring about many beneficial outcomes including improvements to patient comfort and safety and greater efficiency in estates management.

Even though technology is now rapidly evolving, the FM profession is relatively risk-averse which might explain why the rate of technological change has been relatively slow. In addition, enacting such changes can bring uncertainties which is challenging for those in charge of healthcare FM. Notwithstanding this premise, FM has extensive information requirements and to effectively manage this, the use of innovative digital technologies and tools such as BIM has proved useful. In addition, such technologies have provided greater data-processing capabilities applicable at all stages of the life cycle of built assets. This has helped estates personnel to gain a better understanding of the body of knowledge, procedures, and processes related to the management of infrastructural assets.

Healthcare facilities continue to face a variety of challenges, including non-functioning medical equipment, inadequate planning, inappropriate procurement, poorly organised and managed healthcare technical services and skilled personnel shortages. Consequently, both technology and real estate are essential for the modification of healthcare organisations and have emerged as critical resources in delivering effective inpatient care and running productive healthcare facilities. For this reason, there is a future need for the healthcare sector to constantly change, with evolving technology and advances in patient care driving demands for the quick delivery of state-of-the-art facilities. Accordingly, healthcare services need to undergo a technological transformation to improve functions such as facilities control and performance as well as to reduce costs. Despite this need for change, the architecture, engineering, and construction (AEC) sectors have yet to embrace new digital technologies. This has had the adverse effect of these industries remaining uncoordinated between offices and sites, with paper still being frequently used to manage processes and deliverables, such as design drawings and daily management. In addition, the variety of software tools and interoperability issues continue to be barriers to the adoption of digital technologies in the FM sector. Other problems are that existing technologies sometimes do not always capture and retrieve the detailed information and knowledge generated by building operation and maintenance, especially when failures arise. Such challenges may explain why there has been a slow rate of digitalisation, particularly in terms of building digital assets, expanding digital usage, and creating a highly digital workforce, compared to other sectors, such as manufacturing and distribution. To compound matters there has been relatively little research on using digital technologies in the operations and maintenance stage of the building life cycle.

Finally, there remains a need to engage advanced technology and IT tools that ensure efficient information management and integrate various actions associated with the efficient management of healthcare FM. Otherwise, this could lead to continued inefficiencies and excessive FM costs across large estates, such as those in the healthcare sector. Building information modelling (BIM) is a technology that in healthcare is attempting to 'turn the tide' in enabling new technologies to more effectively manage large estates. It acts as a reservoir for all design and construction information used by FM while BIM-enabled information systems seamlessly transfer design and construction models to FM systems. The use of BIM standards such as Industry Foundation Classes (IFC) and Construction Operations and Building Information Exchange (COBie), has been viewed as highly promising by construction and political actors to address data dematerialisation issues and maximise building information interoperability. Despite this, maintaining links between geographic information systems (GIS) and BIM applications is an ongoing issue that must be addressed on a large scale.

14.2.11 An Introduction to Smart Estates and Digital Information Management for Collaboration in the Built Environment Using Case Studies

Chapter 11 of the book has discussed the immense potential of digital twins to mitigate some of the current urbanisation-led challenges in the urban built environment. In this pursuit it has used the case study from Singapore, which is regarded as a model of good practice for transformation through digital twin technology. In this sense, digital transformation in the built environment is the practice of how technology allows the industry to develop what could not be created before; to construct new forms of building, to transform cities and towns, and to address urbanisation and sustainability challenges. Managing urban areas is now one of the twenty-first century's most significant developmental challenges. The digitalisation of the built environment is an opportunity to tackle the industry's challenges by taking advantage of the general availability of best practices from other sectors. The advent of broad deployment of emerging technologies, such as AI, sensor technology, cloud computing, open data, the IoT, and blockchain, has reinvented the way in which we can handle development and adapt to these challenges. The UK took steps towards championing the digital revolution in the built environment through policy and launched of the Centre for Digital Built Britain (CDBB). This organisation provided resources to guide the infrastructure and construction sector toward its digital transformation and also provided the framework for information management to enable stable, resilient data sharing between digital twins.

A digital twin is a cycle flow between physical and virtual realities (mirroring or twinning), where data flows from the physical to the virtual environment, and information flows between the two states. Processes in the physical state responding to the virtual state can be described as an evolving digital profile of a physical object or the process' historical and current behaviour, which helps optimise business efficiency. For this to work effectively, the digital model should be a true replica of the physical object, reproducing the physical geometries, properties, actions, and rules in a 3D geometric model. Furthermore, the digital twin must have a clear purpose for the public good, enabling value creation and performance improvement, while providing determinable insight into the built environment. In addition, the digital twin must be trustworthy while promoting security, openness, and quality of information. To allow it to function effectively, based on a standard connected environment, it must have clear ownership, governance, and regulation, and be able to adapt as technology and society evolve.

A digital twin represents open, trusted, and reliable digital representation of the elements and dynamics of a physical system or built asset, such as a building, urban network, or asset portfolio, and can be referred to as a cyber–physical system. It is embedded into multiple data points, to relay structured and big unstructured data flows from physical to virtual states. It offers the ability to incorporate analytics, including machine learning and simulation algorithms, to provide an understanding of the elements and dynamics. The digital twin idea is not a new phenomenon and has already been embedded in some current technologies, such as 3D modelling, simulation, and digital prototyping.

One should not underestimate the importance of the built environment and urbanisation on a global scale. Urban built environments such as cities and towns are engines for growth and development and are pivotal to development, significantly contributing to the gross domestic product (GDP) in both low-income and high-income countries. The built environment is also a leading source of job creation that provides job opportunities for millions of unskilled, semi-skilled, and skilled workers. To reinforce this point, the construction industry in the UK, as part of the built environment, contributes 13% of global GDP and employs approximately 7% of the global working-age population. The built environment sector is now very much a data management business, where concepts like BIM are now essential to driving information-led productivity in capital projects and programmes. Managing urban areas is now one of the twenty-first century's most significant developmental challenges. Despite this, in the UK the construction industry is underachieving when compared to the manufacturing, aerospace, and automotive industries. This may be explained by the industry being associated with outdated technologies that are incapable of meeting industry needs, leading to client dissatisfaction, inefficiencies in process and operations, deficiencies in safety, and a higher than acceptable carbon foot-print. The digitalisation of the built environment is an opportunity to tackle the industry's challenges by taking advantage of the general availability of best practices from other sectors and of advanced techniques and tools, digital workflows, and technological expertise to shift to a higher level of efficiency and to become a digital industry. A digital urban twin is a sophisticated data model that allows collaborative processes at a local and national level. City-scale digital twins aid in mapping space, people, and their activities in the physical city to a virtual city by establishing closed-loop, city-level data feed into the virtual city, as Singapore has demonstrated. These allow high degree simulation of urban plans or building operations before they are implemented, which exposes problems before they become a reality, allowing for an improved degree of efficiency and precision in a city or a building operation.

The use of digital twins in the built environment has many other applications which can bring about significant benefits for cities and their communities. These include:

- Sophisticated data models that allow collaborative processes across urban environments. Data input into a computing framework enables information to be shared between the various city services.
- Urban modelling and planning allowing governments and authorities to plan for existing and future smart urban environments.
- Better communication of plans for city development allowing communities to understand proposed plans and strategies more fully through simulation and visualisation.
- Real-time monitoring and control of urban transport infrastructure.
- Future mobility improvements that could bring to life self-driving cars or autonomous transport.
- Sustainability improvements through a journey to a competitive, decarbonised, and digitised energy environment. This includes a transition to low-carbon energy systems, renewable energy integration and storage technologies, and data analytics to measure, predict demand, and empower users.
- Scenario and risk assessments with virtual experimentation, using a 'what if' scenario or an incident status.
- Security enhancements, enabled by AI and the IoT to monitor urban security more effectively.
- Health and wellbeing improvements, enabled by the creation of healthier, sustainable, and resilient urban environments through readjusting urban spaces and infrastructure.
- Efficiency and streamlined information workflows in capital delivery, offering a dynamic, expressive real-time recording system. This can embed rich information about spaces and assets and can provide significant benefits to asset owners and users in the life cycle of built assets.
- Streamlined asset operations by harnessing data to prepare the future digital operational life of built assets.
- Building automation by integrating sensor data within complex physical systems to enable an asset to be intelligently operated with transparency.
- Predictive maintenance by continuously monitoring assets and activities, and identifying abnormal behaviour, allowing human operators to react rapidly and reduce downtime.

- Remote assistance technology to enable users to remotely monitor and control built assets, plant, and machinery.
- Research and development by creating the platforms for big data, artificial and virtual reality simulation, and innovation for a diverse range of applications.

14.2.12 The Benefits and Value of Digital Twin Technologies for Collaborative Information Management

Digital twin technologies represent a new opportunity for the built environment and to demonstrate this notion, two case studies for the use of digital twin technologies have been explained in Chapter 12. The first case study, related to Herrenberg in Germany, which was not only vulnerable to high levels of traffic but also to carbon and noise emissions. To address these problems the town developed a pilot digital twin project which they branded as their 'Integrated Mobility Plan 2030'. They developed this project using 3D visualisation technology, which has already proved useful in promoting a collaborative urban environment and better quality of life for its population. The model they instigated was predicated on conducting simulations of urban mobility and air flows. This gained a better understanding of the quantity and distribution of pollution and its relationship with the urban grid, morphology, topography, and geometry. The second case study related to Singapore where 'Virtual Singapore', a city-state digital twin and collaborative data platform, has been proven to enhance planning and decision-making and has found ways to tackle urban challenges in real time to improve the standard of living. This digital twin was designed to operate on IoT sensors, big data, and cloud computing, in conjunction with 3D models, geospatial datasets, and BIM.

Chapter 12 of the book has stressed that for digital twin technologies to be successful they must provide determinable insights for the built environment by enhancing live capabilities. The 'Gemini Principles', arguably the cornerstone of digital twins, outline that such technologies must be trustworthy while enabling security, openness, and quality of information. Furthermore, the related technologies are constantly maturing to deliver intelligent solutions for urban planning and developing smart cities which can facilitate more human–infrastructure–technology connections. Such integrated concept models can then be further developed to allow an unparalleled degree of precision for improved urban planning, project implementation, and operations. In this way, they allow simulation and testing of plans before they are implemented, to expose problems before they become a reality, while managing urban issues in a more systematic and efficient way, from strategic planning to land-use optimisation.

Digital twin datasets could also be used to monitor and test scenarios and constraints, train personnel, and boost the performance of any number of adaptable services. Furthermore, they can monitor relationships between the real and virtual worlds. For instance, through virtually testing a design concept in production and operational scenarios, it is possible to simulate the constructability and intended functional performance of the built environment to test whether the design meets all the requirements. This opens a wealth of opportunities and potential applications which could include identifying design flaws before construction works start and testing the energy performance of certain architectural and engineering concepts. The value proposition of such applications relates to checking hypothetical 'what if' scenarios and considering and evaluating threats.

Predictive analytics and scheduling are another potential use of digital twin technologies as they can act as a validation model framework with data from the real world, creating a model that can predict virtually everything that might happen in the physical world. The Biocomplexity Institute at the University of Virginia, as an example of this application, built a digital twin simulation framework that can help state and local governments better predict the spread of any future epidemic. Such technology can also provide health support for plant and equipment, using analytics and providing real-time monitoring and tracking of physical assets, efficiency, condition, and their unique characteristics, such as malfunctions they have experienced, and a history of their maintenance and repair.

In addition to the above uses and benefits, an effective and informed support system for decision-making can be supported by digital twins as they provide more efficient and accurate asset planning, project execution, and asset operational data. This richer and more reliable information across the asset life cycle can achieve performance and productivity improvements in the short and long term for many different organisations. Furthermore, a digital twin will allow information and data flow, enhance collaboration across the supply chain, reduce silos, and increase understanding of existing built asset projects. This can improve the current performance of project teams, remove constraints, and provide much needed opportunities for collaborative improvement and partnering. In addition, readily accessible real-time information in conjunction with automated reporting can help to keep stakeholders well-informed and thus boost transparency. Furthermore, design teams can use a digital twin to improve the performance of future buildings. In this way, designers can leverage information on how facades or other building components deal with environmental stresses such as extremes in temperature, sunlight, wind, and snow. An example of such technology has been used by the University of Salford in the UK and articulated in Chapter 12. Digital twins can be configured through AI to monitor air quality and promote health and safety on sites, operational built assets, and the urban environment. In this way, individuals can get real-time monitoring and warnings, including updates of dangers and guidance for responding to emergencies.

Finally, the technology can also be conceptualised as mapping a physical asset to a digital network using sensor data, hooking up IoT endpoints on physical assets to feed, and evaluating their performance, condition, and status in real time. This has the unique benefit of generating a new value proposition where high-performance built assets enable a new north star of optimised full-life asset efficiency, not just for individual projects, but increasingly across portfolios, networks, and entire sectors.

14.2.13 Digital Twin Enablers for Collaboration and the Risks and Barriers to Adoption of Digital Twins

Digital twins can be seen as a natural evolution of BIM where persistent data is collaboratively gathered, and information is updated at key phases of a project. They are designed to monitor and improve the operational performance of a physical asset and to allow predictive maintenance. The primary function of BIM is to design and construct a building and to provide a digital record of a completed project after completion. For this reason, BIM's role is to design and construct an asset collaboratively and to create a digital record forming the Asset Information Model (AIM) of a finished project. This is useful in the operational phase of the built asset and continuous improvement of the model provides background for the digital twin. BIM is a strategic facilitator for product life cycle management (PLM) for both buildings and infrastructure assets. For this reason, a fusion of BIM into the digital twin can promote the PLM of built assets by enabling product function analysis, performance prediction, product monitoring, ergonomics analysis, layout planning, prediction of the status of equipment, process analysis, operation optimisation, and the forecast of maintenance.

The digital twin explicitly works with data fed by digital devices or sensor systems in real-time to monitor and analyse a physical asset's structural and environmental parameters, also in real time, to perform highly precise digital twin simulation and real-time data analysis. The sensors gather data on the object in real time and send it to a cloud-hosted system for processing of the data. This allows the digital twin to digitally replicate the tangible object, which offers insights into the asset and its performance, enabling users to take timely and well-informed action while promoting feedback mechanisms that lead to product and process improvements. Through linking objects to a cloud-based network that processes the collected data, the performance of entities in the physical world can be used to evaluate virtual model performance. 3D is the first step towards digital twin modelling and the method of transforming the surface of an object into the graphical model of a digital twin. The models can be built either by a 3D scan of the object or by specialised computer-aided design (CAD) or BIM software, and finally described in terms of geometries. Digital twin technology includes continually evolving AI which uses supervised and unsupervised learning algorithms on twin and sensor-based data. The transformative potential of urban digital twins lies in connecting them from a single digital twin to an ecosystem of linked digital twins, to provide more data in a broader context. Smart buildings are excellent examples of applications that benefit from digital twin machine learning capabilities including the supervised learning of operator or user preferences and involving the set-up priorities in a simulation-based, controlled test-bed.

Digital twin technology is a game-changer technology for smart cities. Urban-scale digital twins, provide a platform for smart cities where assets, buildings, and services can interact with one another, turning physical assets from static structures into connected ecosystems. Notwithstanding this premise, the built environment is yet to catch up with other sectors, in the use of digital twins, with only 5% of the built environment having started the implementation of digital twins and less than 1% of assets having one in operation. For this reason, the adoption of digital twins in the built environment globally has been covered extensively in this chapter. The narrative covered emerging markets in Asia-Pacific which are taking the lead in embracing digital twins in the design, construction, and operation of new urban set-ups and existing built environments. Case study examples were given of Shanghai and Amaravati. Despite these international examples of excellence, we are still early on in the digital twin age and the pathway from creating an urban digital twin to a national digital twin is still not explicit in the UK. However, the Digital Framework Task Group (DFTG) maps interaction and interoperability tools, to promote and develop the capabilities of a fully integrated UK digital twin by the year 2050. Furthermore, the Digital Twin Hub initiated by the Centre for Digital Built Britain (CDBB) is a platform for organisations and researchers who wish to improve governance around digital technology for the built environment.

Notwithstanding the uses and potential benefits of digital twins they are not without their challenges, barriers, and risks. For example, a digital twin needs significantly more initial investment, compared to other business ventures of a similar scale and value. In addition, there are also risks associated with dealing with such complex systems which introduce challenges including data processing and sensor data resolution. As they are representing physical assets, other challenges relate to them requiring a high degree of safety and security. Accordingly, information volume and flows also need to be structured effectively with the opportunity to make improvements, to ensure problems are addressed and that there is no potential misuse. Another challenge for the digital twin is the development of a common language with specific domain knowledge for diverse participants.

Finally, conclusions and recommendations were given in Chapter 13 and examined the future development and use of the technology. The adoption of digital twins for the urban built environment is currently being fuelled by their ability to solve significant urban-scale challenges such as net-zero carbon targets for environmental sustainability. Furthermore, improvements in technology are encouraging a new era of digital twins, resulting in better managed PLM systems over the entire asset life cycle, matched to live data. In addition, they can contribute greatly to the smart city agenda and promote many successful outcomes. These include data-driven collaborative urban modelling, planning and development for the public good, zero-carbon goals for healthy and sustainable urban built environments, automated built asset operations, real-time monitoring, and control of urban infrastructure and services. These initiatives provide value in transforming cities and towns to address urbanisation and sustainability challenges as demonstrated through the two case studies discussed in this chapter.

14.3 Implications in Practice for Digital Information Management in the Built Environment

The built environment has been, and will continue to be, information dependent. How information is generated, gathered, and managed will continue to grow as long as the industry keeps innovating with a view to improving efficiency. An aspect of such innovation encompasses how stakeholders, especially construction professionals, can better collaborate, exploiting the prowess of digital information management. The scope of digital information management varies depending on an organisation's functions, workflows, and the resources at its disposal. As part of the resources, technology is a vital aspect of digital information management. Organisations in estates deploy technologies at varying levels of sophistication depending on the nature of associated facilities management (FM) tasks involved and the job routines. The overarching vision is to comply with expected standards of liveability, sustainability, resilience, and affordability as essential pillars for future cities enabled by a value-proof business case, stakeholder engagement, regulatory framework, talent and knowledge, and digitalisation and innovation. The implication is that innovations in digitalisation must encompass the development of smart data-driven and autonomous systems that can dynamically respond to stimuli in line with users' needs. In the future, artefacts should be able to exploit the functions of innovative technologies, including the Internet of things (IoT), to improve performance efficiencies and optimise energy consumption. Emphasis therefore shifts to the digital transformation infrastructure which is useful for coping with the variety, volume, and velocity of data streaming across different mediums and drives B2C and B2B networks. While leadership remains important in establishing a sense of direction in contemporary firms, excellent digital capability is key in maintaining the competitive edge required to remain relevant. Digital infrastructure needs to be able to stand the test of time which means it requires constant improvement and updating to remain functional and relevant. Although successive levels of digital innovation remain attractive, the risks that come with digital transformation must also be adequately taken into account. Organisations must strive to keep their digital infrastructure safe from sabotage and cyber attacks. While cybersecurity may entail fortification against external intrusions, internal processes and protocols must be governed by appropriate privacy policies, within the relevant privacy law stipulations, such as GDPR.

It is clear from earlier chapters of the book that organisations which invest in digital information management can have a better chance of success in a marketplace dominated by increased competition and competing demands. The case has also been made that with the increased rate of technological change in other sectors, such as manufacturing, it is important for estates and the built environment to catch up if opportunities, efficiencies, and numerous other benefits are to be exploited. The use of digital information management systems, in terms of the various platforms, has been articulated and these platforms included building information modelling (BIM), the IoT, cloud computing and data analytics, 3D and 5D modelling and high-definition simulations, and artificial intelligence (AI). Such technologies, if used widely and correctly, can provide the medium for organisations in estates and the built environment to excel. In addition, for professional practitioners, this could enable them to serve their clients better and improve customer satisfaction beyond the levels they are currently attaining.

Notwithstanding the above potential, the built environment sector has been slow to adapt to change in the past. This could have emanated from a fragmented industry where teams frequently come together as temporary organisations to procure estates projects and then disband, with lessons learnt not being carried over to future projects. To overcome this dilemma, the short-term nature of relationships needs to be addressed in favour of longer term collaborative strategies. Such strategic reforms could include adopting procurement frameworks and partnering principles in lieu of competitively marketed short-term project team appointments predicated on lowest cost. In this sense this book has articulated the need for enhanced collaborative working built on trust and teamwork to improve successful outcomes in parallel with new 'state-of-the-art' digital information management systems. Without this, digital information management in the built environment will be severely hampered and will not attain the full scope of improvement that it is designed to facilitate. For this reason, quality, digital transformation, and collaboration are inextricably linked through a common care premise to increase efficiency, and therein generate improved cost and timescale predictability for estates projects and management practices.

Case studies have been analysed in the book and these include the use of digital twins in Singapore and Herrenberg, Germany. Analysis in these particular cases has found that such technologies have allowed the digital simulation of potential changes to assess the effects on the built environment, both positively and negatively. These simulation 'testbeds' can be trialled without the risk of harmful consequences, as could be the case in real-life scenarios where changes are made. In the case of Herrenberg, this allowed the local authority to conduct digital simulations of road infrastructure changes to assess the positive and negative effects on traffic and air quality. This reduced the risk of imposing such changes in real life without firstly understanding the effects through the digital twin.

14.4 Final Reflections, Overview, and Implications for Future Practice and Closing Remarks

The digital era has endured and will continue to metamorphise, penetrating business and society. Facilities management (FM) and estates are no different in terms of their experience with increasing levels of digital transformation diffusion. Examining the uptake of technologies in estates through the lens of the Technology Acceptance Model (TAM) reveals that perceptions of how useful a particular technology is, whether in hard or soft FM, is important. Also, the concept that pleasure derived from using the technology will lead to an intended behavioural change is vital. The extent of evident technology uptake in FM and estates requires beefing up. More case studies, more output from research and development, and credible research publications would all help to increase awareness in the estates domain. There is a need for technology diffusion to be homogenous and evident at all levels and in all areas of FM operations, including policies governing the sector. Besides policies and aspects of administration, digital information management roles in FM and estates require some level of standardisation. Professional institutions in estates can help in driving standardisation and supporting stakeholders with relevant resources and appropriate recognition.

Negative consequences associated with poor outcomes are numerous in the built environment, leading to assertions that the industry is inefficient, unsafe, wasteful, compromised on quality, and cannot deliver to time and budgetary constraints. For this reason, the book has articulated, through transformation of digital management information coupled with collaborative working in estates, a proven way to improve competitiveness, reduce costs, and increase client satisfaction. This puts more focus on creating policies and initiatives designed to implement and deliver technological reforms, and these reforms could be through professional and industry bodies, and government agencies. Notwithstanding this premise, low participation in training and education, certainly in developing countries, could possibly explain why construction and estates staff are not aware of the importance of digital enhancements within their respective organisations. Accordingly, one of the contributory factors to the slow pace for embracing digital management technologies could be a lack of education and training of those individuals entering the industry. To respond to this deficiency, organisations should promote continuing professional development (CPD) in the workplace for teaching and learning around digital information management to improve quality in construction outcomes and raise the reputation of the industry. In addition, it has been suggested that colleges and universities should tailor more academic modules and courses to the subject of smart estates and digital information management in an attempt to address this deficiency in knowledge and education. Furthermore, organisations should be encouraged to instigate CPD for their employees to counteract the deficiencies around technological advancement within their companies.

This book has discussed many of the different aspects and issues that influence collaborative working and digital information management in the context of the built environment. Notwithstanding the many benefits for the industry that can be generated through such initiatives, the pace of change is generally regarded as being too slow if tangible benefits are to be made in the short-to-medium term. Accordingly, teaching and learning initiatives, focused specifically on digital information management may prove to be the decisive factor for encouraging the required change. Such changes away from the tried-and-tested traditional models of management and a movement toward digital platforms and technologies could represent a 'turning of the tide' in favour of more modern ways of working and smart estates. In practice, as previously referred to, this could be developed and delivered through academic programmes at colleges and universities, which could be designed to encourage and motivate the pace of change in the industry.

Hopefully, this book has highlighted that a more proactive and collaborative approach is required to address some of the challenges in promoting such transformational changes. Accordingly, leaders of organisations and professional institutions should be leading the cultural change in the built environment to train, educate, and motivate construction individuals and organisations in what digital information management platforms are currently available and the benefits that they can bring for the sector. The book has identified and recommended many different platforms, practices, and measures in this regard. The various digital platforms that have been analysed include digital twins, the Internet of things (IoT), building information modelling (BIM), big data, cloud computing and data analytics, 3D and 5G modelling and high-definition simulations, and artificial intelligence (AI). Conversely, the different and improved practices and measures have mainly focused on partnering practices and collaborative working to encourage innovation, teamwork, and shared successful outcomes for contracting parties. These could be achieved through more focus on further education and higher education course modules linked to digital information management and CPD through workshops and training events in the workplace. These measures will hopefully contribute to providing a more technologically developed environment for the industry to work within. This could reap great benefits, not just for estates clients, but for all estates organisations and the future of the built environment industry at large. It is accepted, however, that to bring about these digital and cultural changes will take resources, conviction, and in some cases courage to take a 'leap of faith' in instigating different ways of working compared to what has been traditionally regarded as the norm. Notwithstanding this premise, these improvements, once ingrained within the built environment, could reap massive rewards in providing a more modern, efficient, honest, trusting, and more enjoyable working environment for all.

References

Challender, J. (2017). Trust in collaborative construction procurement strategies. *Management, Procurement and Law Proceedings of the Institution of Civil Engineers* 170 (3): 115–124.

Challender, J., Farrell, P. and Sherratt, F. (2014). Partnering in practice: An analysis of collaboration and trust. *Proceedings of the Institution of Civil Engineers: Management, Procurement and Law.* 167(6): 255–264.

Index